To Dr. & Mrs. Pierce
It was nice to
bloodred all those
wife will explain
honor to meet you both. Hope you
enjoy the book —
Bruce Kelly
'77

THE UPHILL RIVER

THE MEMOIR OF A BOY CHOSEN BY GOD
AND THE UNIVERSE TO BECOME A PHYSICIAN

BY BRUCE R. KELLY, M.D.

DORRANCE
PUBLISHING CO
EST. 1920
PITTSBURGH, PENNSYLVANIA 15238

Dorrance Publishing Co
585 Alpha Drive
Suite 103
Pittsburgh, PA 15238
Visit our website at www.dorrancebookstore.com

ISBN: 978-1-6480-4103-7
eISBN: 978-1-6480-4911-8

This book is dedicated to the love of my life, my best friend, and my wife of forty-eight years. Dolly (Caldwell) Kelly was at my side providing love, support, comfort, and encouragement from 1971 to the present. She was the major force in raising our children, of whom we are very proud.

Jason Kelly - cyber security analyst
Major Matthew Kelly M.D., Heather, Charles, Cooper, and Jackson Kelly
Dr. Diana Raub D.O., Phil, Benjamin, and Katie Raub.

ADDITIONAL THANKS TO:

Alan Director, Esq. (my brother from another mother)
Kelly Burgess, a good friend who helped edit and gave valuable counsel
Tara Sovitski who typed a lot of the early chapters
My son Jason, who set me up with the Dragon program for typing
All the Unit I nursing supervisors who taught me and kept me reined in.
All the Harmarville nursing staff who were my eyes and ears and were crucial in the care I was able to provide.
All the Harmarville therapists who continue to make it such a nurturing place.
The administration at Harmarville who tried to protect us from corporate.
The staff and administration at Punxsutawney Area Hospital

SPECIAL THANKS TO:

Carol, Marcella, and Jack for being the "source" of my river.

TABLE OF CONTENTS

1. THE RIVER BEGINS WITH A DOT

Could the source have been a tiny red dot behind the ear? How inconsequential or was it? Man has spent thousands of years looking for the source of mighty rivers. Is it the tiny stream that babbles along, then suddenly gets bigger and bigger? Is it the surface water that crackles as it cascades over the fallen leaves during a rain? Is it the underground spring that percolates to the surface? All these sources contribute to the river.

Every life is special and comprised of different events that make it unique. Life is much like a river. There are so many complex factors that determine its existence. Once created it has many twists and turns. Along its course it can sustain life or have devastating consequences such as floods. It runs its course until it culminates in the ocean where its contribution is important but indistinguishable from all the other rivers.

Creighton was a small suburban town on the Allegheny River north of Pittsburgh, PA. It was the site of the first Pittsburgh Plate Glass plant, which was the major employer for hundreds of blue-collar workers. It was as blue-collar as a town could get.

There was the Allegheny River on one side, a small strip of flat ground for houses, the two railroad tracks and the two-lane road. Next to the road were a few small retail stores and a terrace of houses that sat in the shadow of steep cliffs of clay and shale that tower about 300 feet. The walls of these cliffs were honeycombed with abandoned and a few active coal mines. In each of our hollows there were active brickyards that employed a few people. PPG Industries was the biggest employer and probably occupied one quarter of the habitable property. In addition to the multiple factory buildings was an intriguing, pink/salmon colored, two-tiered piece of property affectionately called "The Muck." It spanned an area from the PPG parking lot to the creek that flowed from Normantown hollow. Its purpose was unclear, and it was never active during the day. Through the length of the upper tier meandered a crevasse that apparently carried water at some time and emptied through a huge pipe into the lower tier where it finished its serpentine trip to the Allegheny River.

As you can imagine "The Muck" was a magnet for the children in town. They were warned by every parent that this secretive, silica-laden playground would turn into quicksand when water was added. That was no deterrent to riding bikes and playing baseball. The parents knew we were in there, even though there was a four-foot-high lip around the entire area, obstructing their view. Apparently, it was to keep water in and parents out. I remember being scolded if our secret adventure was exposed, but I don't remember ever being chased out by anybody!

The river was the lifeblood of any factory town. It provided raw material and power for the plant. It provided transportation for other raw materials and, of course, sustenance for the people. Then there was water—the nemesis. During a major flood in 1936, only the top few feet of our house remained above water. We had more minor floods every two to three years. We lived in one of a few five-room houses that were raised and had a ground-level foundation placed under it. The nuisance floods would cause my father to remove the furnace and washing machine motors, shut off the hot water tank, put everything up on shelves and put the ill-conceived pool table (for our basement) on the wagon and carry it to the front porch. Afterward, we were anxious to help our less fortunate neighbors move their furniture to the second floor.

Our house was on the river side of the train tracks, which were elevated about six feet above street level. The grade school was on the other side of the tracks, three hundred yards downstream. The junior-senior high school was a hundred yards upstream. In the 1950s through the 1970s, the trains were a constant presence. To be useful, they had to creep to a stop to deliver or receive material. When your house is on the wrong or at least the other side of the tracks, your life can be severely disrupted. One ironclad rule, very rarely broken, was that you never crawl over or under a stopped train.

Water again was the nemesis—at least to the parents. We would go to Normantown Creek, stoop over, and try to negotiate the exposed stones as you crossed under the road and railroad bridges. This would cause severe anxiety in the parents because in that thirty seconds, you could have been carried to the river by a flash flood! It didn't matter that the sun was out and normally we would be playing in "The Muck" or the "cricks." There was no acceptable argument. It was a blue-collar rule—they didn't have to make sense.

So, where does the red dot figure in this? A handsome young couple decided to start a family in Creighton. They had dated for quite a while, so their relationship was newlywed but mature. The pregnancy was routine other than an annoying bout of three-day measles early in the pregnancy. Marcella wasn't particularly sick and soon resumed the excitement of bringing a new life into the world. In the 1950s, Jack, like every other expectant father, waited impatiently to find out the sex of his first child and if Marcella and the baby were okay. All went well, and after the traditional four-day hospital stay, they went home with a beautiful, normal baby girl named Carol.

The excited young mother resumed her normal exercise routine and took care of her pleasant, low-maintenance baby. The proud papa returned to his steady job at PPG, driving a local delivery truck during the day and enjoying his new life as a dad in the evenings. Life was good and normal… until it wasn't.

Raising a baby always had its share of doubts. Is she hitting her milestones on time? Am I doing something wrong? The grandparents, aunts, uncles, and friends were reassuring that all was well and some babies were a little slower in achieving milestones. After a visit, everyone would remark "how pretty that Carol is, but did you notice she seems a little stiff? Shouldn't she be sitting up by now?" The alarms went off when she just didn't or couldn't walk.

Just like all good parents they dreaded making a pediatrician appointment only to be told they were being impatient. This visit was different. An evaluation at Pittsburgh Children's Hospital was suggested.

After a thorough exam, the neurologist explained to the anxious parents that there was a possibility that Carol had cerebral palsy. He felt there was some outside event early on that caused the damage to Carol's brain. Had there been any falls or illnesses? Marcella explained she had rubella while she was pregnant. The doctor said that there was some developing evidence that rubella could cause fetal damage when it occurred in early pregnancy.

For a fleeting moment a look of terror and dismay crossed their faces. Our baby is not normal! What did we do? Is there a cure? What can we do? The neurologist had a guarded, reassuring response: "You have a beautiful, happy little baby who will need some extra attention. Your job is to take her to therapy, be supportive and treat her like the normal child she is. The impact this will have on her life will largely be determined by how you respond. If you treat her normally, she will be normal. We will be there to help you."

The young couple went into shock and didn't hear much after "cerebral palsy". There were words that always elicited that kind of response: "cancer," "incurable," "metastatic," "Alzheimer's." Seasoned, empathetic physicians realized they were conversation enders and the topic and care plan would have to be revisited later.

Marcella tearfully looked into that beautiful, smiling little face and formed a super bond. "I will always be there for you. We will get through this. Maybe, just maybe, the doctor is wrong." Jack's strong arms were around both of them as they sat in isolated silence. If Disney were filming this there would have been a tornado of colorful rope swirling around them and forming an unbreakable bond as the music hit a crescendo. Little did they know that their moment of devastation would positively impact so many lives. That insignificant dot was turning into a small brook.

2. IT WASN'T AN EFFORT

I don't know my earliest memory. I suspect and hope it was that loud, rhythmic roar of a steam engine, thundering down the tracks with billowing black smoke. It was an unusual sight in the age of diesel engines, but I can see it as plain as day. I also remember the seemingly constant blare of train whistles because we had five crossings in town and each required the warning whistle. Our house would shake and vibrate as the train was passing, because it was only fifty feet away. Carol lived in a house next to ours. Their house was much newer and made of brick, so I imagine their family's experience was slightly less dramatic.

Growing up in such close proximity to Carol was probably a factor in our relationship. The families were friends and distantly related. There were many other kids on the block, but I suspect the early, small circle of trust started with our two houses. As Carol grew, it became apparent that she indeed had cerebral palsy. Her intellect and personality were totally normal. Her deficits were all physical. Her hands were a little clumsy, but she eventually learned to play piano. Her legs were stiff and her balance was impacted by the legs. It was difficult to know if she recognized her problem. Once the leg braces were on and the crutches were in hand, she was mobile. She bounced with each step so she could advance one leg after the other. The smallest irregularity in the pavement could trip her, but she would learn how to fall with only a scrape on the knees. She could come to a kneeling position with ease, but often needed help to get back on her feet. It required little effort from her parents (or a friend one year older) to get her back on her feet. Then she was off again with that infectious smile and her pixie haircut bouncing up and down. Nobody counted the falls, but subliminally it made an impact that she always got back up as if it never happened.

Walking the whole way to grade school would have been a challenge. There was the very steep hill to get over the railroad tracks, the major road to cross, and the very irregular sidewalks to the school. The answer was a tricycle and an able-bodied friend. I have no memory of being asked or mandated to be the designated friend. We "walked" to school together—period. I pushed her up over the tracks, then Marcella would help us cross the road as we jabbered about the day's events. Then we were on our own. The first block was easy as we passed the small grocery store, firehouse, barbershop and the print shop. There was a gas station at the end of the block, which provided a curb break. Mrs. Bruner, the crossing guard, would greet us with a huge smile and often a chorus of "Mairzy Doats." She would place the portable, yet heavy, ramp that Jack had made so we could cross the street, negotiate the eight-inch curb and finish our trip to school. Carol would get off the bike at the front steps, put on her crutches and with some assistance go up the three outside steps that had no rail. Once inside, she could handle the remaining steps while I placed the tricycle inside. At the end of the day we reversed the process and did that for years. We had no concept that our daily trek was unusual. Why was the local newspaper taking our picture going to school?

Summer vacation was a happy time for every kid. Fresh air, fun and games were the norm for most kids. It seemed almost yearly that Carol would disappear for weeks, then reappear with casts on her legs or up to her chest. They were solid white, autographed, cotton lined torture chambers, but her smile was never affected. If she had pain, you wouldn't know it. Marcella would carry her down the steps and place her on a chaise lounge on the landlord's covered patio. That was our summer world. Nobody had air conditioners. We did have fans, which would make things bearable, if you weren't wrapped in cotton and cast material. Carol rarely complained about itch, but we scratched where we could reach, when needed. We played Candy Land and made up games. We wrote and produced comedies and other plays to pass the time. There were no nearby pools, so even if Carol wasn't in a cast, we would be riding bikes at best.

As a child, I assumed each of these surgical operations was the cure for which we all prayed. Was this the summer that Carol could walk normally, after all these surgeries? We didn't discuss outcomes, but I remember a sense of disappointment when the casts came off and there was no obvious improvement. I don't know what Carol's expectations had been. Neither of us would have comprehended the importance of tendon lengthening so that she would not continue to walk on her toes. I can't say it was then, that I consciously thought about wanting to be a physician. There is no question I wanted to do something to help Carol. My experiences with her did teach me empathy, patience, and the resilience of those who conquer life's most devastating challenges.

A few years later, Carol and her family moved into their own house about five miles away. We would see each other at church, but over time our lives grew apart. Those memories and experiences were a major contribution to the person I became. There would be many other tributaries and course changes in that river of life, but there was no doubt that those years were the "source."

Carol and Me

3. SHE MADE THE WORST MEATLOAF

Every family was dysfunctional to some degree. I know there was some kind of love between my parents, but it was anything but demonstrative.

My father's family moved around a lot and his parents only owned their last house. His father was an alcoholic in his early years. He always had a job but frittered away the money on booze. His mother was always pretty out of sorts and, at best, tolerated her husband. They had a rough life. They lost their first child when she pulled a pan of boiling water off the stove and died of burn complications. Both of their sons were in the Army during World War II. The youngest son, Bob, enlisted in the Army after high school and before Pearl Harbor. He landed what was considered a cushy job in the Philippines. Once Japan invaded, he was part of the Bataan Death March and was listed as missing in action. His parents went to their graves never knowing for sure if he was dead. That was a somber environment for their surviving son, Charles, and likely made him the sullen person he became.

Charles had a gift for music and mastered the piano. In the pre-war era, he played for an independent orchestra in Pittsburgh. He completed high school, but because of his father's drinking, there was no money for further education at that time. It was never clear if he had such aspirations, but he clearly carried to the grave a grudge toward his father.

For a short time before and then continuously after the war, he worked as a laborer for PPG. Ironically, his drunken father, with only a third-grade education, became a respected electrician for the same plant.

Ruth Lord was the polar opposite of Charles Kelly. She was pretty, gregarious, smart, and very involved in church. After graduating with honors, she attended business school and worked as a bookkeeper and administrative assistant to the CEO of Braeburn Steel. She knew the Kellys who moved to Creighton and was likely interested in the fun-loving younger son, Bob. The war quashed any chance for that relationship. Charles was moody but pleasant, dependable, and his musical talents would make him an excellent organist for Janes Methodist Church.

Charles was home on leave after the war in Europe was over, and he proposed. He was to be redeployed to the Pacific, so they threw together a hasty wedding and married. The Pacific War ended while he was in Oregon, and he was soon discharged. They started and ended their life together in Creighton. They saved enough to put a down payment on the house at 922 Front Street.

My parents were married August 1 and my brother, Robert, was born August 4. That was always my preferred way of telling it—with just a hint of illegitimacy. In truth his birth was a year later. He was an only child for four and one half years. My mother would regale others about how advanced Bob was. I was the typical second child—not as memorable, fewer photos and an also-ran in the popularity department. That was just normal life to me. Growing up in a WASP family meant you had and showed little affection or reaction.

I must have been a little "Johnny Bull" at times. I do remember having a small duffel bag I would fill with socks so I could run away. Nobody followed because they knew I wouldn't cross the street at the end of the block. In that five minutes, I would forget the issue and return with the socks. At least I was "the runner."

My father always looked like a bomb about to explode. To his credit he was never physically abusive, but he made up for it verbally and with those threatening eyes. He was a perfectionist and that was to include his offspring. I would do anything to avoid interaction with him. It was just easier than potentially doing something wrong. We never wrestled or had much physical interaction. I have one memory of sitting on his lap, and he was tickling me. During the writhing I was doing, my head must have reared back and hit him in the nose. Of course, it began to bleed. I could see he was furious and I disappeared—for most of my life. I know he was proud that I became a physician and we even did some small projects together. Still, it was hard to erase his unwillingness to walk across the street for my Boy Scout banquet or chorus concert. I, to a lesser extent, became somewhat proficient on the piano and accompanied the high school chorus for six years. My father didn't come to even one of my concerts, but he never missed one of my brother's football games (even though he never played sports himself).

We had one consistent interaction when I was young. My mother would get a pound of ground meat, add no other ingredients, then pack it together as firmly as she could. Next, she would bake it for probably three hours and it turned into this foul-smelling, putrid-tasting piece of crap. They would place a slice on my plate, and I would start to retch. My father would seemingly fly over the dining room table with the flat, metal pancake turner in hand and either threaten or paddle me with it because of my reaction. I believe my mother had at most a two-week repertoire of meals so I could look forward to this twice a month! I've always resented my dad for this, but why did she keep making that damn "meatloaf?!"

In his seventies my father had to have a below the knee amputation of his one leg and spent four to six weeks at the rehab hospital where I worked. One day I was approached by his psychologist who said, "I just can't believe you became the person you are with a father like that." I took that as a great compliment.

It's strange that even though I felt closer to my mother, I have very few early memories of our interactions. She was very involved with the church and the associated women's organization. I was very self-regulating when it came to homework, studying, practicing piano and doing chores. She did support my school activities and made sure I was very involved in church. I was the adult Sunday school pianist for years and was substitute organist for my father from time to time, which I hated. I also earned a thirteen-year perfect attendance pin. Yes, that meant I was there 676 Sundays in a row!!

I don't remember ever sitting down and discussing a college education or vocation. My brother and I were on our own. We knew our parents would pay for four years of college, and it was assumed we would do well—being the "perfect" children we were.

My brother attended Allegheny College in Meadville, PA. It was a small, expensive school. My mother took a job as church janitor to help pay the bill. I assisted her for $8.00 per month. That consisted of sweeping and dusting the sanctuary, Sunday school rooms, kitchen, and social room each week. It also included stripping and waxing the social room and kitchen floors every three months. That was my first paid job, and I saved every penny I earned. I also gave piano lessons to a few of our church friend's children and that was $2.00 per week. I'd hide the money in the interior of a ceramic Nefertiti statue my great aunt gave me. When my brother graduated college, he wanted to marry his high school sweetheart. I gave him $120.00 for the engagement ring from my "bank." Sometimes I feel like I skipped childhood entirely.

In the course of the river this was early rapids, more downhill, defining, and fortunately, the beginning of a bend in the river that put the past out of sight.

4. SAVED BY THE GRANDPARENTS

It was common in the 1950s to have your entire nuclear family live close. My maternal grandfather died of a cerebral hemorrhage in his forties and left my grandmother a destitute widow at an early age. I never met him, but his absence probably had a most profound influence on my life.

My paternal grandparents were a piece of work. Individually they were great, but together they were oil and water. They married when Grandpa was sixteen and Grandma was seventeen. How they met and why they married so young was never discussed. It was obvious that Grandpa's drinking was a major source of descension. As a miner, drinking after working in that cold, dusty environment was probably pretty normal. It was a real chicken-and-egg situation as to why he drank to excess. Was it genetic? Were they ill-suited as a couple? Was my grandmother difficult to live with and that caused him to spend a lot of time in the bar? We'll never know the answers, but my suspicion is it was a multi-factorial problem.

They lived in a four-room, two-story house high on a hill overlooking Normantown hollow. I don't know why it became part of our vernacular, but anyone going to see them was "going up on the hill." It was the last house on a small dirt road that wound around one of the foothills in town. The house was damp and cold in the winter as there was no furnace, but a large gas space heater to warm the whole house. I loved going there and spent as much time as possible. It was a sanctuary from the fear and tension of my everyday life. It was close enough and safe for me to walk there even from an early age. Now the duffel bag carried socks, underwear, and maybe a few shirts!

My grandmother Kelly was a sour, needy, misunderstood person who loved her grandsons. She was about 5'9" and always overweight, but she truly was "big boned." She always had swollen, painful arthritic knees, which, sadly, I inherited. She spent most of her time in a recliner with her feet up, and I now totally understand. She took a lot of grief from everybody for being so inactive, but it was a means of relief and survival.

She didn't make meatloaf!! When she hosted Thanksgiving, she prepared a beautiful turkey and spread and made poached eggs (minus the yolks) for me, my favorite. If my dad started to complain, she gave him a look, and the conversation was over. I'm sure in my head my tongue was sticking out while I was praying there would be no later repercussions. She made fried chicken every Sunday, which we have never been able to duplicate. I totally blame her for my weight problems. She would bake a nine- or ten-inch pie, let it cool (a little), then cut it in thirds and serve it! Only years later did I discover that portion size was extraordinary.

Grandma couldn't cut her own toenails and that was before pedicures and podiatrists were in vogue. It was far from my favorite thing, but we would soak her feet, then I would get the wire cutters and begin. Those thick nails would fly in all directions. Of course, my reward would be some pastry. Thus, the river began to widen!

My grandfather Kelly was an overweight, bow-legged, balding devilish angel to me. He also loved his two grandsons. Being a drunkard was very unpopular. He adored my mother (not for her meatloaf) who sternly told him he was never welcome in her home when drinking. Upon the birth of my brother in 1946, he stopped drinking cold turkey, and to my knowledge never had another drink the rest of his life.

Gramps and I were together constantly when possible. He retired about the time I was old enough to make the trip to their house alone. My grandmother never made a store list. "Will, I need a loaf of bread," and we'd get in the car and drive past many small grocery stores to shop at the Acme—about four miles away. When we got back, "Will, I need some eggs," and back to the Acme we would go. This is how he spent his days and never complained, because it used up the awkward waking hours.

When I turned about eleven, he would stop the car at the Holy Family Catholic Church parking lot and let me drive the winding, car-lined, narrow dirt road to their house and park the car in their detached garage. The back of the cinder block garage he built was cracked due to ground settling. On one of those forays my foot slipped off the brake and the car hit the fifty-gallon drums along the back wall and pushed the back wall out! He may have had a third-grade education, but he was a genius at child raising. I was in shock, but he insisted we get back in the car, with me driving, and repeated the trip with a normal outcome. He knew, the longer I didn't drive, the more fear I would develop. I remember my father asking him what happened and he said, "the hill shifted." He never told anyone, and I couldn't have loved him more!

A lot of our history took place in cars. We would talk about everything. It was definitely a safe zone. He was a joke teller—mostly clean and oft-repeated. I didn't care. I laughed as if it was new, while enjoying the time with my substitute dad. Gramps was the second oldest of nine children who mostly lived within fifty miles of Creighton. He quit school in the third grade because his father committed suicide and, at nine years old, he had to go to work in the mines to help support the family. He was the lifelong peacekeeper in his family, and when he visited them, I was in the middle front seat (no seat belts back then) between him and my grandmother. Everyone loved Will and would put out a fancy homemade spread.

Today he would probably be arrested for child abuse, but he had a keen insight when it came to his grandson. As I hit puberty, he was right on top of it. We never did the birds and bees talk. I don't think anyone did back then. There was the strategically hidden *Playboy* magazine for his grandson to "read the articles." Let's say I had an enhanced imagination. He also noted I had some fascination for the cigarettes he smoked. One day I asked to try one. He nonchalantly removed an unfiltered Camel from his pack. After lighting it, he handed it to me and said, "You need to take a deep breath in to enjoy it." I dutifully followed directions and turned green as I coughed my lungs out. "Oh well, smoking isn't for everybody." It never occurred to me that he tricked me. It was my last cigarette. That came from a third-grade PhD! He quit cigarettes shortly thereafter. I wish I could have been so courageous with my children.

He attended church each Sunday, and I sat next to him, knowing Juicy Fruit or bubblegum would be in his suit coat pocket. I doubt church attendance was part of his routine in the drinking days. His favorite hymn was "Brightly Beams Our Father's Mercy." The chorus is:

> "Let the lower lights keep burning.
> Send a gleam across the waves.
> Some poor fainting, struggling seaman
> You may rescue, you may save."

What special meaning that must have had for him. I cry my eyes out every time I just think of it.

Gramps's health was good until late 1967. We got a late-night call. He was having chest pain and called an ambulance. It was a rather minor heart attack, but unfortunately was followed by five more within six months. He rapidly deteriorated and was continuously short of breath. Each subsequent episode, he lay in the hospital bed enclosed in an oxygen tent that was minimally effective. He was going in and out of pulmonary edema. Fluid would seep into his lungs and occupy valuable space long ago damaged by coal dust and cigarettes. He became so weak, he could no longer hold the tissue into which he spit the continuous, blood-tinged, frothy, sputum that smelled like bad Juicy Fruit gum. I would have been revulsed, but the overwhelming love I had for that man made the maneuver a minor inconvenience. I was in school during the day but spent my evenings at his side doing anything he needed. He was slipping away, and I was helpless to stop it. His breathing became so labored, I started to pray for it to mercifully end. That was a terrible way to die, and it happened on April 4, 1968. My world was changed forever. The river was broadening, picking up speed, and following a course that was becoming much clearer and more unalterable. This was about the time the river started its uphill climb.

5. HOTLINE TO HEAVEN

My grandmother Lord was another third-grade-educated genius. She fed and supported her three children through the Depression by a maneuver of buying and selling penny insurance policies— a story I don't understand to this day. She was a diminutive woman who was probably five feet at her tallest and shrunk from there. Her size and her old-fashioned braided bun of hair should have been her distinguishing characteristics—but they weren't. She had a way of making everyone feel like they were the most important person in the world. She had a genuine smile and very dark brown eyes that contained an unforgettable twinkle.

As a young widow, she sold her home to her son to maintain financial independence. She made an arrangement that we followed for many years. She stayed with my family Monday through Thursday and her son's family Thursday thru Monday. Each family wanted more of her, not less. You would never hear a comment or argument from her, but she understood everything in her environment and quietly "guided" people to do the right thing. As a child I would want to ask my mother if I could go to

Carol's or watch television or whatever. Grandma Lord would pull me aside and say, "If you ask her before she finishes the dishes, she will say 'No!.'" She gave each of us her full attention and reinforced the positive. If she heard something she didn't like, she would work a correction into the conversation, but you never felt reprimanded.

If the danger signs appeared (that my father looked mad) she would innocently gather me up to do one of my favorite things—throw rocks in Normantown Hollow creek. It was so narrow and shallow that you couldn't begin to skip a stone. She would watch me mindlessly throw stones into the creek just as my brother, cousins, and uncle did before me. The gentle ripple of a creek had a calming effect on you. I'm sure that during the two-block return trip home we discussed the behavior that was angering my father. I don't recall her being there for the "meatloaf massacres." They must have been on Mondays or Fridays. She would never have let my mother perpetuate that meal choice if she knew what transpired.

As alluded to earlier, I was a picky eater. That being said, every Tuesday at noon, she and I would eat butter and sardine sandwiches. Apparently, this was a Depression era lunch, and I looked forward to eating it with her. My mother was never there for that lunch. It was my special individual time. Later in life my dietary repertoire became relatively normal, but the thought of even opening a sardine tin turned me off. It might taste okay, but without Grandma, it wouldn't be the same.

Our house had two bedrooms and four beds. My father and brother were in twin beds in the back bedroom. My mother and I were in the double bed (as a child) in the front bedroom and my grandmother in a twin bed on the opposite side of the room. I would watch her add waves to the front of her hair with a small hot plate and a crimping device she would heat to just the right temperature. She would unravel the braid every night. She always faced the opposite wall when undressing, but I did catch sight of her oddly and severely S-shaped spine and crooked hips. She quietly suffered the ravages of severe, progressive scoliosis, which had to have caused her great pain, at times. It also made her even more popular with the grandchildren as she was the first adult we surpassed in height.

We had a black-and-white television in the house, and my father was in charge of the channel we watched. I have no recollection of my grandmother sitting in our living room. She would quietly stand in the back corner with her hand on her high hip. She had two favorite shows for which she would be in attendance. Her favorite was *Wagon Train*—a show about people who made a living guiding ill-prepared travelers from the East to their destination in the West. Indians, marauders, and the trials of nature would be coupled to the stories of people seeking a new and unsettled destination to call home. Her second favorite was *Gunsmoke*, which, in retrospect, was a surprise because there was always a fair amount of violence. Other times she would be in "her room" writing her famous letters to family, friends, and shut-ins. People would often gratefully comment how wise and comforting her words were.

She was an "ultra" pillar of the church because her whole family served as pillars. I was convinced she had a hotline to heaven. When I was in college, I would go to the pay phone with my dimes and call her once a week. By then she lived in a Methodist-sponsored retirement home, which she arranged on her own. She had her own bedroom and shared a hall bath. It was well taken care of and the halls were lined with priceless antique furniture. She, too, had to use a pay phone to answer my call. We would have a short conversation, then I would list the upcoming tests or quizzes by day and time. I don't know if she wrote them down or not. I do know she would give her friend God a call and ask him to give me the patience and organization needed to excel. I may have put in the hours to study, but I was convinced it was her hotline that achieved the *summa cum laude* graduation that would appeal to medical schools.

We were all devastated by Grandma Lord's decision to move to the retirement home. As an adult, I can now see her reasoning. She was going to a facility that had all levels of care. They would accept her Social Security as payment and give her a small amount of that money back as a monthly allowance. She knew the grandchildren were getting older and we were out-growing our houses. Again, she was taking the lead and making a sacrifice to care for her family.

Going to visit her each Sunday was no minor feat. It took an hour to get there, because you had to drive through about seven towns to get to Pittsburgh, then another two towns south of the city. My mother and her brother, Charles Lord, and their families would make the weekly trip. I would go as often as I could. Seeing her and maintaining our close connection was important to me. I also got the added benefit of spending time with my second favorite adult male in the world and my role model. Uncle Chuck and I would commonly take a little walk during the visit and catch up. He was of medium height and had a "fire plug" build. He was stocky and thick with short legs and was very solid—physically, mentally, and morally. He graduated high school, did a stint in the Navy, and then worked for Braeburn Steel where he eventually became plant manager. He was married to a prim, proper, and overly opinionated wife. They had three children. Their son Jack was a Mensa-level, underachieving student who had a fractious and bitter relationship with his mother and a limited relationship with his father—because of his mother's interference. They had two younger girls who survived the mayhem in their house and went on to lead responsible lives. Jack abandoned a National Merit Scholarship to Princeton University due to social issues. He wandered from job to job, which included electron microscopy and bank vice-president!

I think Uncle Chuck enjoyed spending time with a non-confrontational young male. He could speak intelligently on any topic. He served on the local school board for years and was treasurer of our church for life. Our interactions formed a basis for my parenting approach.

Grandma had many good years in "the home," but she gradually slipped into the dementia, which affected all of the women in her family. She "existed" for probably ten years too long. That quick wit and sparkle in her eyes faded, and she had several strokes that robbed her of her speech and the ability to swallow. Her nursing and medical care was excellent except for the nasogastric tube she endured for about five to six years. I was a physician by then and would encourage my mother to ask for a gastric tube for feeding. That tube would go straight into her stomach and she wouldn't have the constant pain and irritation of the tube that entered her nose and ran down her throat to carry nutrients. My mother finally agreed in my grandmother's ninety-third year. Two weeks later she was dead. I'm sure my mother blamed me for the eventuality that was years overdue. In her typical WASPY way, we never discussed it. My hotline to heaven was gone, but she had a profound effect on my life. The river rounded yet another blind bend.

6. SCHOOL DAYS

There was no kindergarten in 1956, nor were there pre-schools—at least not in Creighton. The school was a square, two-story, dark red brick building. It had the traditional wood floors that gave off the traditional September school smell after being cleaned and treated over the summer. There was one wall of blackboards and one wall of open closets. The outside wall had top-hung windows capped by green-tinted glass blocks to the ceiling. We didn't have a cafeteria, so you brought your lunch or went home for lunch. If you brought it, you ate at your desk then went outside to play on the asphalt playground with no equipment. Your choices were Red Rover, dodge ball or "You're It!" Can you imagine children running and using their imaginations? There was a bizarre eating event to which we would look forward. I think it was a Thursday when several moms would work at a heated, glass case with shelves from which they sold individually packaged hot dogs with soggy buns. They had a funny but not unpleasant taste. That was our once-a-week warm lunch option!

My favorite lunch was a chipped ham sandwich. Only Pittsburghers would know what that is. Isaly's was an early chain store known for ice cream (inventing the Klondike bar) and for their deli meats. They also invented the chipped ham delicacy. You start with a square ham made by Isaly's and you slice the meat paper-thin. That maneuver unleashes a heavenly flavor unlike any other. The magic is in the thinness of the slice. Any thicker and it's just sliced ham. As an adult I was listening to a local radio station and the question to callers was, "What item is most requested by displaced Pittsburghers for Christmas?" The overwhelming response was "Isaly's chipped/chopped ham!" That delicacy could be eaten with condiments but could be savored, alone, on a bun.

That foolproof lunch plan for the picky eater went well, until it suddenly backfired. In our close sleeping quarters, my mother noticed me grinding my teeth and viciously scratching my butt while sleeping. I don't remember how the diagnosis was made, but it was determined I had pinworms—probably from raw chipped ham. Our doctor prescribed something that didn't work. My usually unopinionated grandmother Lord suggested an old remedy. Mix a teaspoon of turpentine in a small amount of sugar water and drink it. It was pretty vile but later that day (or the next) a deluge of small circular worms vacated my body. Couldn't that have killed me? Apparently, it was a risk they were willing to take! We switched to fried chipped ham at which my mother excelled. This was referred to as "frizzled ham" (which I have since found on Google)! There were no other pinworm problems.

I did have one other yearly medical problem that ultimately had a bizarre treatment. I was very prone to strep throat. It happened once or twice each winter and I would be very sick with high fever, but I never missed church! Anyway, Dr. Dependable would see me or make a house call. In the early days, penicillin was only available in injection form. I would get my shot in the butt and soon would be back to normal. In the 1950s radiation was considered pretty harmless. There was a popular children's shoe maker that supplied stores with an X-ray machine to check the fit of their shoes! They also used hospital X-ray to treat acne and swollen tonsils. In 1974, I had a medical school pathology class where we learned that children who had tonsils irradiated were developing thyroid cancer as adults. I questioned my mother whether I had it and my mother's answer was, "One of you had it, but I don't remember which one." The hospital had a fire and there were no records. The question was left unanswered—for a while.

Children usually live a relatively carefree life—if they're not misbehaving. I had my first true dilemma in first grade. My mother chose this particular day to say, "We're going to the cemetery right after school. You come straight home!" Even at that age I knew that had to be a tight schedule to accomplish before the prompt 4:30 dinner hour. This was the year before I started to take Carol to school. Miss Leopold was a looming, large woman who was kind but struck fear in her pupils. She was militaristic and stern. At the end of the school day we were to line up along the wall outside class, not talk, and wait for the dismissal bell. I was obediently in line as usual and another student spoke to me. I'm sure I said, "Don't talk" and the ground began to tremble and a darkness fell around me. I looked up and saw a very angry Miss Leopold. She said, "Go sit in class and I will deal with you after dismissal." I was in shock! No teacher had ever spoken to me like that, and what should I do? My mother was anxious to get the cemetery trip done, and Miss Leopold wanted me to stay for God knows what! I don't remember any involuntary loss of bladder control, but I was terrified!

Do I incur the wrath of my mother or Miss Leopold? When Miss Leopold wasn't looking, I ran home in a panic. I must have been pale or sobbing or both, but my mother coerced me to spill my guts. In our house you were told you NEVER disobey a teacher and if you were punished in school, you would get worse punishment at home. She may have been the "meatloaf mauler," but my mother understood the dilemma. After reiterating my choice was wrong, she wrote a note to Miss Leopold, and I had a short detention the next day. Whew!

I was always a good student and most of the early subjects (reading, writing, and especially math) were easy for me. After sixth grade you went to the Junior/Senior High School, which was even closer to home. In junior high I was an A/B student. My competitive nature took root in my freshman year.

Thus, the overachiever was born and school had a new purpose. I remember that for a short time I wanted to be a lawyer. I had a unique interest in politics, and most politicians were lawyers. Late in grade school I thought I wanted to be a doctor—for no particular reason other than being helpful. The lawyer phase quickly faded. Becoming a doctor became an obsession probably about the time my grandfather became ill. My role models were my family physician, Dr. Dependable and my grandparents' physician, Dr. McQuaid. Both were well respected and loyal to their patients and vice versa. Dr. McQuaid was in the neighboring town of West Tarentum. He had no receptionist, and he had a rather strange appointment system. The first patient to arrive would go to Culligan's Pharmacy next door and get the key to his waiting room, which had chairs lined along the walls. The chair closest to his exam room was seen first, then everyone moved up a chair.

Dr. McQuaid was a portly guy with a quick wit and glasses that sat low on the end of his nose. He called my grandmother Kelly "Sadie" for what reason nobody knew. She would see him every two or three months for her knee injections. I don't know if he said something to her or if her knees felt better, but she would get a short-lived smile on her face. In retrospect I think I tucked that away in my memory bank. "Make the patients smile." It served me well in my career.

Dr. Dependable was much more serious and younger. He had more of a smirk than a smile—and piercing blue eyes. I thought, "Oh Lord, if you have to have blue eyes, I'm done!" I didn't see him as much in my teens because I was pretty healthy. He's mostly remembered for coming at my butt with those "17 inch" Penicillin needles. I knew he was well respected, lived in a nice house, and was generous in the community and church—all positives in my book.

All these impressions were forming in my school years. My brother was graduating high school and was accepted by Allegheny College—a school known for being a good stepping-stone to medical school. Yes, he too, wanted to be a doctor. What was with those Kelly boys and their dreams of escaping Blue Collarville? We never discussed what prompted my brother's interests. My career desire preceded and was independent of his. He never became a real doctor—he became a well-respected surgeon. I would often point out that the Pennsylvania license clearly separates "physician and surgeon."

I was popular in school, even though I wasn't in either of the two sports offered: football and basketball. I played a baritone horn in the marching and concert band, which in a class our size were usually the same people. I had a small group of close friends, mostly my academic competitors, but really got along with my eighty-three other classmates.

My political interests were sated by being elected to Student Council every year but one. I was elected Junior Class President by a majority of one vote and organized the Junior-Senior prom of 1968. The prom drew mixed reviews, and I was the Senior Class Vice President.

On the academic front, it was a five-horse race for valedictorian—four girls and myself. We all had the maximum 4.0 average. One girl faltered slightly, and she was out. In my junior year, I got a B in physical education, because I couldn't do enough pull-ups. The overweight football players got automatic As! I ended with a 3.989 and second to the three girls. My brother and two cousins were also salutatorians. We joked we should change our name to "Avis"—the rental car company that embraced being second.

High in the hills the river continued to take shape and now ran an uphill course with a singular destination in mind.

7. "I'LL GO TO PITT, BUT I WON'T COMMUTE."

It was a rare occasion when my father and I were in the car together. I distinctly remember we were driving across the Tarentum bridge, which was a high, long span to the New Kensington side of the river. I don't remember what the choices were, but I declared, "I will go to Pitt, but I won't commute." It was only twenty miles to the University of Pittsburgh, but there were several components to that decision. My brother had gone to a small, private college and did not get into medical school right after graduation. By this time, I began to actively calculate my approach. Perhaps by going to a large university, I could distinguish myself among a more diverse academic pool. There was no certainty in that decision, but it was attractive from many angles. I would get out of that house and make my own decisions. It was also close enough I could go home if I wanted. The cost was considerably less, and I eventually got a Pennsylvania state senator academic scholarship, which would cover one half of the tuition cost. It had to be renewed annually and you had to maintain a 3.0 average.

The other attractive part of that decision was that Pitt had its own medical school. I assumed that if I did well as an undergraduate, I might have an additional edge for admission. Nobody said that to me, but I was trying to use logic to improve my chances. I committed to Pitt.

They had four freshman orientations, each lasting a week. Mine was July 13-18, 1969. I could remember because I was there for the first moon landing on July 16, 1969. I was staying in my designated freshman-year room in Tower A, fifteenth floor, room 1501. There were three circular towers of dorm rooms in the middle of Pitt's campus. Of course, the rooms were pie-shaped with two twin beds, two built-in desks, one large dresser, and two small closets. The three towers were connected by a large common lobby on the first floor. There was a bank of three elevators in each tower. The elevators only stopped at every third floor (unless you were a housekeeper).

Using the elevators in the dorm was an *Animal House* experience. The students recognized no maximum capacity other than the physical inability to squeeze yet one more body in before the doors closed. On many occasions, the sheer weight of the elevator car would prevent it from completing its task of centering the car door and the doorframe on the given floor. That would necessitate climbing out onto the floor to exit it. As an adult, you would think of cables breaking and plummeting to your death. As a student it was a minor inconvenience. Walking down fifteen floors became a usual compromise.

Back to the moon landing—there was only one television, that I knew of, and it was in the Student Union. The event was monumental in any scenario but was heightened by being crammed into a room of academics, glued to the screen to witness history. This was a new era in that, through television, you could actually witness the triumphs and tragedies of modern science in real time. Any space launch would begin with seemingly endless hours of coverage by newscasters, repeating countdowns, interviewing experts and at times struggling to fill the void before the actual launch. That was different. Man was setting foot on another celestial body for the first time. Would the landing go as planned? Would the astronauts be killed or marooned in the process? Would all of the equipment work as planned, to gather samples? Would the astronauts get home safely? Were there people in that very room who would eventually be involved in planning or completing space exploration? The excitement was palpable. The rest was history.

The only other happening of note was the math placement exam. Coming from a small school, we didn't have honors or advanced-placement courses. Math was always my favorite subject, or so I thought. It was logical and reproducible—you just had to learn the language. We didn't have pre-calculus, but somehow, I scored high enough that I was directed to skip pre-calculus and start Calculus I in the fall. That put even more strain on the transition.

I was able to return home, leave some things in my dorm room, and work another six weeks.

8. FROM DUST MOPS TO BLOOD CLOTS

My work history was not extensive. Even though our family had limited financial means, I did not have to work during the school year (except for the janitor job). In the summer of 1968, I had a job working at John and Jerry's produce market. You did a little of everything from unloading trucks, stocking bins, waiting on customers and cleaning, cleaning, and more cleaning. John was known for keeping a clean establishment and its importance was drilled into you. The vegetables were boxed and put in the cooler each night and the bins were thoroughly washed. The floors were swept first, then mopped thoroughly. They were concrete floors, and they were very clean! In the morning the vegetables were inspected and the good ones returned to the display case. I hated the cleaning, but always gave any job my best effort.

I think I also learned about loyalty at John and Jerry's. There were certain people who felt compelled to taste the products as they shopped. It's one thing to try a grape and another to eat a whole handful of grapes, an apple, and a pear. The employees were never instructed to do this, but if you waited on an "abuser," your fingers might just linger on that scale when weighing their produce to compensate for their free food. If the owners did not make a profit, I might not be able to receive my sixty cents an hour! I'm sure we were worth seventy cents an hour, but nobody complained. It was an air-conditioned, indoor, nonskilled job, and the money was "good" for a high school student.

After graduation, I was looking for a different summer job and my father actually helped. His boss at PPG was married to the director of nursing at Harmarville Rehabilitation Center. They apparently discussed my goal of becoming a doctor, and I was offered an interview for an orderly job. An orderly is now known as a male aide. I only had the experience of caring for my grandfather and my "cleaning" history. Mrs. Nancy Smith was a large woman with a beautiful smile and a unique giggle. The interview went well, and I was offered a position at $1.00 per hour. In one year, I got a 67 percent raise! I didn't think I heard much after the pay rate. I could start as soon as school was done.

My father's supportive words were something like "Don't you dare do anything to embarrass me after I got you this job." Father-of-the-year encouragement for a kid, who always gave his best, graduated second in his class, and didn't even understand the concept of burning bridges. In spite of the "encouragement," I was looking forward to a job in the medical field.

Harmarville was an independent free-standing, 74-bed inpatient rehabilitation center for physically disabled people. It was originally built by the Federation of Girls' Schools as a home for "wayward girls." It evolved over time to address the rehab needs of people with strokes, fractures, amputations, and brain and spinal cord injuries. Rehab was a whole different world when compared to general hospitals. In the hospital, sick patients were "cared for" by dutiful nurses who provided for all their needs until they were improved enough to go home. Rehab medicine would take those whose medical problems were more chronic and try to get their lives back together. That was accomplished by taking sick hospital patients and forcing them to sit in a wheelchair and do exercises for which they had little energy. It was a slow, methodical process and gradually you saw the patient gain strength and ultimately better health.

I worked the evening shift and was paired with a mentor. Bob was a tall, thin, black Army officer who moonlighted as an orderly. He exuded confidence and charisma and was a great teacher. He taught me the proper way to transfer patients into bed and on and off the commode. He covered catheter care, measuring urine and at times testing it for glucose levels if the patient was diabetic. He taught me how to write a note and enter vital signs in the charts. That was all pretty basic. The biggest challenge was to teach me "bowel training." In rehab you soon learned that the world revolved around the bowels. Commonly, the acute care hospital would not address constipation and the patient would arrive in various stages of constipation. The head nurse or her designee, would interview each patient to see if they "voted" (had a bowel movement) that day. If not, they would get milk of magnesia that night. If they hadn't gone for two days, they would get a fleet enema. After that, they would receive milk of magnesia as an oral stimulant and a soap suds enema until results were produced. That took care of the majority of the patients but not the spinal cord patients. They needed "bowel training."

Later, as a doctor, I had insight as to why the bowels didn't move. At the time, however, I just learned that these patients had no or little movement in their legs and their bowel and bladder didn't work. The bladder was managed with a Foley catheter. The bowel needed special attention. On Sunday, Tuesday, and Thursday, they would have "bowel training."

I'm sure, I said, "I stick my finger where?" with a certain, momentary revulsion at the time. Bob demonstrated the digital exam (check with your finger) and manual removal of stool. He explained the patient could not push it out, so we had to take it out. After I regained my composure from the initial shock, he had me "try my hand." It was unpleasant work, but it had to be done. Before starting, you would prepare the bed for easier cleanup with a draw sheet (for patient turning), cloth diapers (not disposable—they did not yet exist) and a bag with lubricant, gloves, a suppository or fleet enema, and washcloths for cleanup—again not disposable. Each patient would require repeated visits, "re-stimulation," and more intervention, then ultimately cleanup. Cleanup was the worst. We had to rinse out the diapers and wash cloths in the commode and bag them to send to the laundry. Yeah, Yuck! It certainly would be a good reason to quit, but somebody had to do it, and after about the first month, it became routine.

The facility itself had its own unique charm. It was a Tudor-style building that was anything but wheelchair accessible. The patient area halls were too narrow for two wheelchairs to pass. One would pull into a room so another could pass. The women were all in one wing at ground level and the men were on the second floor of the other wing.

The therapy areas were on the first floor of the men's wing. That sounds easy enough, but the building was likely built in sections with little planning for the future. The men's wing was about a half story lower than the rest of the building. To access it, you used a very steep ramp. This obstacle was rarely overcome by patients in wheelchairs. They couldn't push up the ramp because it was too steep and all too often, they would careen down the ramp and bang into the padded wall at the bottom. I presume there was some kind of hospital inspection in the 1960s, but rehab facilities were very scarce, and they would be hesitant to interrupt the facility's work. My work was on the men's floor, and I spent a lot of time taking patients up and down that ramp.

9. LIFE IN THE PITT

Classes at the University of Pittsburgh started after Labor Day and completed each year the following mid-April. This allowed for long summer breaks during which I could save money for books and spending. In the sciences, it was not unusual to spend $400-$500 a year on books, and there were few opportunities to buy them used.

Pitt was located in the Oakland section of Pittsburgh. It was a concrete world with hospitals, universities, small shops, and old homes. I was not a city boy and was a little intimidated at first. Although home was close, I only went home about every other weekend. At Pitt, I had the freedom to make my own decisions and not have to be "Mr. Perfect."

My roommate was assigned, and we had exchanged one letter before meeting. His name was Alan—a Jewish guy from outside Philadelphia. This was almost a new social experience for me. There were no Jewish people in my high school class. A thousand questions went through my head. How religious is he? Will we get along? Will he be obnoxious? The answers came quickly. He was not very religious, we got along well for the rest of our lives and yes, he was and is obnoxious and narcissistic!

Since I moved in during orientation, the final move consisted of a suitcase and my infamous light. It was Sunday evening, and I opened the door to find three guys. The one sprawled out in the bed was Dave plus a friend of his and a guy sitting on the desk leaning on the window. I assumed the guy in the bed, with dark red hair and a wide grin was Alan.

"Good to meet you, Alan."

The bed-guy responded (while brushing the hair out of his eyes, which he would do for the next four years), "No, I'm Dave, that's Alan," pointing to the guy on the desk who looked like a better-groomed Woody Allen. We all exchanged pleasantries, then settled into a comfortable relationship. Alan was a political science major and Dave a physics major. It was clear this was a heterogeneous group, which provided many serious and stimulating discussions. Money was an issue for all of us, so we looked for cheap or free events to entertain us. Nobody was fraternity material.

Our room, 1501, was popular because we were centrally located, and the cafeteria was in our basement. We could look out our window and see "Flo's," a record shop that had four-albums-for-$10.00 sales, not infrequently. We could always muster up an extra $10.00 and usually bought albums during sales. Our sophomore and junior years were spent in Tower B, and on at least one occasion, we were awakened by a throng of horny guys who wanted our view of a buxom blonde coed who liked to blow-dry her hair, while nude, in front of her window in Tower C. That was probably my first sighting of a bare-breasted young woman, and like the Marvin Gaye and Tammi Terrell song, "Ain't Nothing Like the Real Thing, Baby."

The real distinction, between Alan and I, was the academics. We took the same English classes, but from there our paths diverged. As a political science major, he spent four years reading science fiction books, going to lectures and writing papers, which were mostly BS. That, of course, eventually led to law school!

My experience was much more intense. First semester, I had Literature I, Calculus I, Biology 80 (intro), Chemistry I (Inorganic) and German I. They just dropped the physical education requirement—thank God. With no medical connections, I was aware that I had to excel in everything. The literature course was my least worry as I was already a decent writer/reader. The Biology 80 class was my greatest stressor. I had a female instructor who seemed reasonable in class but was psychotic with her testing. It was almost impossible to anticipate her questions. I had instant fear of flunking my first Bio course! I ended up getting a B, which was a step up from flunking. "Am I going to be able to do this?" For the first time, I seriously doubted myself.

Inorganic Chemistry was also a terrifying experience. The professor was no teacher. We spent a whole class learning how to use a slide rule because calculators were in their early phase and too expensive. We each had to purchase a slide rule, and it was the only piece of equipment allowed during testing. The professor was an academic bully who would prepare tests way beyond our current level of education. On the mid-term I got a 29 percent, which was an A! That gave a whole new meaning to "grading on a curve." The freshman science classes were huge—probably 200-300 students, and they all required a four-hour lab once a week. I had two labs for each of my first four semesters. I had set a goal to never have an 8:00 A.M. class or lab and was successful, but the trade-off was to have labs from 6:00-10:00 P.M., which I did.

That was the rebirth of the overachiever. I had the tenacity to put in the time, but it was very difficult. Alan's work allowed him ample time to read science fiction, eat his three Triscuits per day, listen to the radio, or use my stereo or portable TV to pass the time, "Grrrr."

My schedule was to eat dinner at 4:30, play ping-pong at the student union until 6:00 P.M., then go to the library from 6-10 P.M., or later, to study in quiet. I tried to take Saturdays off, but that was often impossible. On the weekends, if I went home, you could see me trudging along Fifth Avenue with a bag full of books and a fluorescent lamp hanging out of the front of my travel bag, like a mine-sweeper. I was the king of the nerds. A family friend, Virginia, worked at Children's Hospital and would give me a ride home. We had great conversations, and I thoroughly enjoyed the ride to "Tensionville."

There was some fun to be had. In nice weather, we would go to the lawn surrounding the Cathedral of Learning, take off our shoes and socks and throw Frisbees. At the end, the soles of our feet would be black as coal. This was undoubtedly caused by the nearby steel mills and the car exhaust. The grass looked green and inviting but hid the toxins of our ecosystem. The familiar sulfur dioxide smell, which polluted the morning air, was just a necessary evil when you lived in a major industrial center.

10. "THEY ATE WHAT?"

Although my academic schedule was intense, I realized good grades, alone, might not make me very attractive to medical schools. I had my summer "orderly" experience, but felt I needed to show more variety. This plan was calculated intuition. I had several volunteer experiences.

I have always been fairly gregarious. I heard about doing volunteer work across the street at Children's Hospital of Pittsburgh. For probably a year, I worked as a hospital escort to transport kids to and from testing, therapies, etc. At the very least, it was an introduction to the emotional drain of helping visibly sick children. Chatting with the patients and families was a different experience from helping Carol. Again, it wasn't an effort, and further reinforced that the universe had plans for me to be a doctor.

From this, I graduated to a job that was just beginning to develop. I was asked if I could volunteer some time in the newly created "Poison Control Center." They provided a twenty-minute orientation, and I was on my own. I could study when the phone wasn't ringing. When the phone rang, there was a questionnaire to fill out on the patient. What was the name of the patient? What was ingested—time and amount? Were they having symptoms? Then you would look in the small recipe box to try to find a 3x5 card that was close to the material. Next you had to try to find an attending, or intern, who would decide what information was to be supplied. That Emergency Room was constant chaos. The best plan was to wait next to the incubator where the doctors plated their own cultures. It was difficult to get them to stop and listen.

There were times when no treatment was needed, others where a minor antidote would work. Some situations required Ipecac, to induce them to vomit. There were situations where vomiting was the absolute wrong thing to do. I was glad to be of help and thrilled I didn't have to make the decisions. There were several scary calls, e.g. an anonymous caller would ask, "What do I do if my child took some of my methadone, or cocaine?" I could tell them to urgently bring the child in to be checked. Many times, the caller would hang up, because they were afraid they would be accused of a crime. That left me with the most helpless feeling, but they had to decide to get treatment and I always hoped they did.

Occasionally, there was some humor. A guy called in and said, "What do I do if my three-year-old ate a half a tube of Brylcream, (a hair product), a half a tube of toothpaste, some of a bar soap and licked half a container of Ban roll-on deodorant?" I was desperately looking for a mute button, so the guy wouldn't hear me laughing. He heard me and figured it out as he, also, started to laugh. I was going to suggest maybe they should feed the child more, but that would not have been professional. "How awful did Ban roll-on taste?" I wondered. Fortunately, nothing had to be done. Everyone who heard the story, got a thirty-second chuckle, then resumed their work on the seriously ill and injured children. Now the Poison Control Centers are very computerized and linked to public health agencies. I felt like I was one of the pioneers in the field.

11. I'LL ACCEPT WHAT I EARN

I didn't see a lot of it in high school, but it was rampant in college—cheating. It was always my pet peeve to see people getting ahead by who they knew or a test they could obtain. There was one guy, who I would only call an acquaintance, who typified the process.

Mitt was from the Pittsburgh area and was pursuing pre-med as well. It seemed like he developed connections everywhere. He would often join us for meals, because he was rooming with one of our close friends. He wanted you to believe he was very bright, but when you got below the surface he was of limited intelligence and no common sense. He would brag about how his fraternity would supply his precious tests to assure him a good score on finals, etc. He also got to know his professors to give it that personal touch. Sadly, he did become a physician. Could I have reported him? Sure. It was a victimless crime, but for the fact he took a seat from someone more deserving. My hope was that karma got him somewhere along the way.

There was one occasion where I may have ruined another classmate's day, due to my obsession with being prepared. It was the second semester of my sophomore year and one of my courses was Organic Chemistry. Organic Chemistry made more sense to me, and I was keeping an A average. The professor mentioned he might include some questions on isomers (a three-dimensional chemistry concept). The weekend before, I carried my study lamp home and spent an entire Saturday with my molecular model. Just as I was about to give up, it clicked! It was a three-dimensional concept, and I was a very two-dimensional guy.

The test day came, and I was pretty well prepared. I was feeling good about the test, and then I turned the last page and there were four bonus questions on isomers! They were the easiest on the whole test—for anyone who figured them out. The next class, the professor was handing back the tests and explained there would be no curve because one person in the class scored 104 percent. As he handed me my test, with 104% written on it, I quietly shoved it into my folder and joined everyone else in the class looking around for the culprit. That only happened once, and it was ruined by the idea that I might have spoiled someone's grade or career.

The rest of the Pitt story is boring—including the fact we all skipped graduation. At that time, Pitt had one graduation ceremony for the all the departments in the Civic Arena—known as "the Igloo" to Pittsburghers. It was the home of the Pittsburgh Penguins. There would be thousands of graduates, and the ceremony was very impersonal. Someone did get me a copy of the commencement program where the three stars next to my name stood for "Summa Cum Laude"—an honor for which I worked very hard.

In December 1969 (my freshman year), they conducted a military draft lottery to acquire "volunteers" for the Vietnam War during 1970. This lottery was for men born 1944-1950. That was the first time they used the lottery since 1942. Everyone was in their dorm room with the door propped open. The government pulled a capsule with a date, then a capsule with a number from 1-366. When they pulled a number under 100, you could hear a wail or a moan. Those people would likely be called to service in a war that was wildly unpopular and made no sense.

They did an identical lottery in July of 1970 for those born in the year 1951 (me). I don't remember listening to the drawing, but I've always remembered my number—262. In December of 1971, they only got to 150. I declared myself 1-A and when the year ended, my ability to be drafted was over. I would always feel remorse for those killed and their families. That war was a useless cost of human life and suffering. Had I been drafted, I would probably have served. Once again, God and the universe had a plan for me to be a physician to help thousands of people.

12. NOBODY FLEW OVER THE CUCKOO'S NEST!

In April 1971, I contacted Nancy Smith at Harmarville to let her know when exams were done and I could start work. Her response was, "Administration hasn't told me I can hire you this summer, and I don't know when and if they'll give me the green light." I was speechless! I knew it wasn't my work. I loved what I did and always did extra. The staff loved me, because I would lighten their load whenever I could. During their breaks, I would put their patients in bed and collect and measure the urine volumes etc. What would I do? Mrs. Smith said "I understand you have to get a job, and I'll gladly give you a good recommendation. It breaks my heart to think you can't come back." I thanked her and asked her to let me know if she got the go-ahead.

I placed the phone in the cradle and instantly found a phone book. I looked under "nursing homes" in the Yellow Pages. (Google it!) I contacted several near my home and most of them listened to my situation, and said "We don't hire any summer help." Then I called the last place I wanted to work! "Sure, we'll hire you, come in and fill out an application." This place had a bad reputation, so of course they had a position. I could start whenever I wanted and could work 7-3. That was a plus, except I had no social life, so why would that matter. I recently broke up with the girl I was casually dating, so my calendar was clear.

I prayed to get a Harmarville call, but it didn't happen. The dreaded day arrived, and I drove to "Loserville Nursing Home." The urine smell about knocked me over as I entered the nursing unit. It was my worst nightmare. The patients had expressionless faces—some drooling. There would be no banter with the patients—they were incapable. The staff were "pleasant," but overworked, disinterested humans doing what they could to keep up with their assignments. Every patient was in a cloth diaper (no disposables yet), until their aide could get to them. I quickly learned how disheartening it was to never get ahead of the patients' needs, and the toll it took, even on a young dynamo.

Fred was the one patient who was not drooling and oh too vocal with everyone. Fred spent all his waking hours "pleasuring" himself with the hand not affected by his stroke. He had no inhibitions and would say inappropriate things constantly. We had to keep him in his room and beware of flying bodily fluids when you attended to him. "Nobody flew over the Cuckoo's Nest"—they landed right there. Daily I would ask myself, "How will I survive a whole summer?"

Ring! God, the universe and Mrs. Smith had an answer. "Bruce, I got the approval to hire you." It took a millisecond for me to say, "I'll give them my two weeks' notice today." It was like being paroled after a life sentence! I think I can, I think I can.... It was the longest two weeks of my life! I said my goodbyes and clicked my heels. I was going home!

13. WHEN YOU KNOW, YOU KNOW

On arrival, I'm sure I gave Mrs. Smith a long hug and thanked her for saving me. I was back on 3-11 shift, but that didn't matter because that was the staff and work, I truly loved.

I went to the second-floor nursing station with a pen and paper to get refreshed. I was greeted by a small room full of happy faces and a new face, provocatively sitting atop the high counter, in front of the window where we stored the ether. From her hat I could tell she was an LPN with a shy grin and a uniform that probably pushed the rules on length. She had medium blonde hair and a genuine smile, which seemed to be a permanent fixture. Once we finished, I discovered we were paired together for work. As we walked down the hall, so I could meet the patients, I noticed she was about 5'2" and had a cute little body. This was a new wrinkle. Up to that point, my colleagues were 30-60 years old and work was work—and I loved it. Dolly would add a new element.

She had an advantage. When the staff found out that I was coming back, they told the newly hired LPN that Bruce was a good worker and nice guy. Everyone was secretly pairing us romantically and later took full credit for us meeting. I had recently pulled out of a lukewarm relationship and decided to forget about dating for a while. Pitt, to me, was a place of work—not play. It never occurred to me to ask a classmate out on a date. Dolly, my coworkers told me, was in a relationship. We innocently flirted while working, but we shared the same work ethic: patients first. We were assigned A, B, and C wards. A ward had three beds, B ward had five beds, and C, four beds with a window air conditioner, the only one on the second floor. I met the patients as they returned from therapy. As usual, patients needed to go to the bathroom or get changed before dinner. We made a good team. We would share the unskilled work, and she would do the always needed dressings and procedures above my pay grade. Everyone did charting at the end of the evening, and this would afford you time to socialize. Conversation was always easy. It was nice to have someone my own age with whom I could work and talk. Don't get me wrong, I loved the other experienced women who previously would work overtime bringing up inappropriate subjects and chuckling as they made me squirm from embarrassment. It was like shooting fish in a barrel. Needless to say, I was always "learning."

Shortly after we met, Dolly told me she broke off her relationship, which was already shaky. That posed a problem. How do you date when you work 3-11? On top of that, Dolly commuted from Irwin—two exits away on the Pennsylvania Turnpike. We decided to get something to eat at the Norwin Diner. I followed her to a commercial strip, on Route 30, near her home.

We ate and talked for an hour or so, and then I made the forty-five-minute drive home.

The following day, my mother told me I was not permitted to be out until all hours of the night. She drew the line, and I stepped right over it into manhood. "I am my own boss at school. I come and go as I please. I've never been in trouble, and I am a straight-A student. I work 3-11, and if I want a social life, it will be after work. I won't accept a curfew." It likely was not verbatim, but I remember the conversation like it was yesterday. She walked away and later told me she was wrong, but she didn't like the late hours. I felt emancipated and set my own schedule.

Dolly and I became regulars at the Norwin Diner, then would go to her house for some quiet time. Rarely did that work. Her dad, who was in his late seventies, would be sitting in his chair in the kitchen. The TV was in the adjacent room as was her fourteen-year-old sister, Cindy. Dolly was one of twelve children! Having only one sibling, I couldn't fathom what that was like. She explained they ranged in age from twelve to thirty-eight, and they were never all in the same home together. At that point in time, besides Dolly, there were two brothers and two sisters and her parents living at home.

The scenario was not favorable for a developing relationship, but the mutual attraction was too strong. The scheming co-workers and Nancy Smith made sure we had the same days off. It was probably our first weekend dating, and I went to meet her mother and some visiting sisters. It was the first time I saw the house in the daylight. It had an unusual roofline and was noticeably different from the other well-manicured homes along the road. I learned her father built the house—he was a painter (not carpenter) by trade, you got the picture. I pulled into the gravel section in front of the house and had no idea what I was about to witness. Dolly's mother was a fifty-ish, salt-and-pepper-haired lady who I'm sure gave me a hug. Her "MO" was that anyone who came through the door, would feel at home and part of the family, and you did. Dolly's sister Pat (#5) was pleasant and quietly sitting at the table drinking coffee. The dynamo in the room was her gregarious sister Pauline (#2). She was making homemade donuts while smiling and chatting constantly. After about five minutes, I realized I was being grilled about my background and my plans. Pauline was and is a professional interrogator, and I was getting the works. I had nothing to hide and nothing left to tell. Everyone was enjoying the cross examination and mentally taking notes. Over the years, I, too, got the pleasure of watching Pauline work her master craft. "Painter, shmainter." Painting was Pauline's vocation, but cooking and "grilling" were her specialties.

Mr. Caldwell was an unshaven, bent over, shell of his former self. He was a World War I veteran. He shuffled to the stove and put a perfectly cooked donut in the hot grease and cooked it until the smoke was flying and the donut was black as coal. "That's the way I like it!" he said as he shuffled back to "his" chair. The donuts were great, and we settled into a pleasant conversation. Everyone involved "vividly" remembered the occasion. Most of my future visits were nocturnal (after work).

I gave Mr. Caldwell credit for putting a roof over the family. There was a large kitchen, a living room, two bedrooms, and a toilet on the first floor. The second floor had one large bunkhouse-like room at the top of a stepladder-like stairs. There was also one more bedroom on the second floor. Notice I said "toilet" and not "bathroom." There was no sink or tub. All washing/bathing was done from a basin in the kitchen. Apparently, the commode was a relatively new upgrade from the outhouse. It was made "private" by closing the curtain. The other wall was made of corrugated fiberglass.

My father, around this time, offered some more sage advice. "Don't you get that girl pregnant! Those girls from large families have loose morals. It happens, and your college days are over." From him, everything was a threat. I was twenty, and even then, he couldn't just have an adult discussion with me. It didn't matter anymore. I understood the process and my desire to reach my goal would not be derailed. We were quickly getting serious, but I could control myself. It was time to meet my family.

In mid-July 1971, I brought Dolly home to meet my parents (not for dinner!). The two of them were in the kitchen pitting sour cherries. My father had three domestic hobbies at which he was very good. He made cherry preserves, homemade root beer, and vanilla ice-cream to die for. Surprisingly he had an electric ice-cream churn. He made an ordeal out of making identical, perfect-sized, individual small ice cubes to fit the space around the turning churn bucket. He took the ice-cream maker's recipe and adapted it to use a lot of Cool Whip, which gave the ice-cream a particularly smooth consistency. Vanilla ice-cream with sour cherry preserves makes a wonderful sundae!

My parents were welcoming. My mother likely had that fairly worried face and he was "characteristically pleasant"—a demeanor he used around strangers. What a fraud he could be, or so I thought. It was a short visit, and little did they know they had just met the best thing that would ever happen to them.

We were going on our first official date. I was going to WOW her by taking her to that gourmet restaurant, Howard Johnson's, located at the top of the Chatham Center in downtown Pittsburgh. We were then going to see a movie there. We got seated and I opened the menu and instantly panicked. Those prices were way beyond what I had planned. I'm sure my clammy, shelled-shocked face told the story before I blurted out "I'm not prepared." That is one of the unforgettable quotes of our life. Dolly graciously understood, and we quietly snuck out before the waiter came. I was mortified, but she was just glad to be on a date. There were two restaurants in Chatham Center and we went to the wrong one! After we found Howard Johnson's and my dignity, we had a chicken pot pie dinner. Then we saw *The Andromeda Strain*.

The dates were starting to include future plan discussions. In an attempt to slow down one date, I blurted, "We can wait till we are married." This was about week six, and I think I just proposed! I did propose and was happy about it. Prior to this, I had done a lot of thinking. This exceptionally kind and loving woman came into my life when I least expected it, and I was ready to be "off the market." I was never really on the market— just a driven nerd. I'm sure she told somebody, but this was our secret. If Harmarville knew this, we wouldn't be able to work together. A ring and an announcement would have to wait. Nothing changed our minds.

In mid-December 1971, Harmarville was having their annual Christmas party at a venue in Oakmont, Pennsylvania. They had used nicer places the previous two years. It was free and a dress-up occasion. I went to Cogley's Jewelers in Tarentum as I had many times with my grandfather in the past. After Mr. Cogley and I caught up, I told him I had $120.00 to spend on an engagement ring. He brought out a 1/3 karat diamond, with a brushed white-gold band and matching wedding ring. It looked great to me, and I was sure I got a deal. Gramps was smiling down on me. One of my regrets was that he never met Dolly, but I know he was watching in approval.

On the night of the party, I picked her up at Strawpump, and I told her to "get "something" out of my glovebox. When she opened it, the ring box was taped to the door. We went into the house for her mother to see it. I told my parents previously, and they were concerned, but I was unstoppable. They were happy for us.

We were the center of attention at the party of hundreds of people. All our nursing colleagues were taking credit for the match. We knew each other seven months, but we were comfortable that we were right for each other. When you know, you know. Like the Allegheny and the Monongahela Rivers, joining at the point in Pittsburgh, our two lives were joining and a whole new river adventure was about to begin.

14. THE HAIR DRYER AND MORE

Dolly's family was very happy about the engagement to this kid who hoped to go to medical school. Like many families at the time, they were just glad to get all their kids through high school. Practically all the siblings were college material, but life for them was a struggle, and the older brothers quickly went into the military and the oldest sisters married and started families.

My career goal was never discussed. I don't know whether they assumed I would succeed, or it just didn't matter. I lived in the dorms during the week and went home every other weekend to get the car and go to Strawpump (that was the name of the area along First Street in which they lived). The weekends that I previously stayed at school, were now spent on the couch at the Caldwell's, whenever Dolly could pick me up. My family would have assumed the worst and her family likely assumed it was less "chaste" than it was. It worked for us.

Our birthdays are a week apart in February and we were both born in 1951. What do you get the girl who has nothing? Hand held hair dryers were not quite there, so I thought a big, clunky, tabletop olive green hair dryer would be an ideal gift. It was huge, and the weather was persistently bad. I was determined to get to Strawpump, so I started taking a series of buses with this huge package. The closest I could get was the end of First Street, and I struggled through snow to their house. She looked thrilled, but I am not sure she ever used the damned thing. After moving it several times, we gave it to Goodwill. Even they probably had to throw it away!

Dolly drove a series of $200 clunkers that her brother, Larry (#7), tried to keep running. They all burned oil, and you often had to jump them or hit the starter with a hammer or something. I was not mechanically inclined and transportation was recurrently an issue, but we made it work.

Our original plan was to marry after my graduation in December of 1972. Dolly found a winter gown on sale, probably a month after our engagement. Money had always been an issue for both of us. Shortly after she bought the dress, my mother expressed her concern about a winter wedding and guardedly suggested we could marry in the summer of 1972. She was dropping me off at Pitt after a Sunday visit with Grandma Lord. I was to give it some careful thought. I said my goodbyes, then raced up the outside steps thinking "Oh boy, I get to have sex six months sooner!" I sprinted to the phone and called Dolly with the news. We both were thrilled! Back to the sex part—yes, we actually waited until our wedding day to consummate the union. We slept together multiple times and had several opportunities, but we resisted. This "virtue" was a topic I later rejected. Sexual interaction was natural and important, but hardly the basis for lasting marriages. I even encouraged others to get all that sexual excitement out of the way and see what is left—that is marriage.

15. "WHAT DO YOU DO WITH YOUR MONEY?"

Dolly's family certainly couldn't afford to pay for a wedding, and I wouldn't ask my family who were paying for college. With my background, it was assumed we would have a church wedding. Then what? As our relationship matured, we started to discuss finances. Dolly seemed to live from paycheck to paycheck. As an LPN, it seemed like she should have some savable income. Gradually it became obvious she was buying all the household groceries, clothing the kids at home and paying some of the utilities. That was no surprise to me—it was in her DNA to be nurturing.

It was income tax time and since I worked about 4 months out of the year, I had to file to get my money back. Dolly normally did a short return and only took herself as a dependent. H&R Block was new, and we made an appointment to discuss her situation. We learned it was reasonable and only right for her to take several of the siblings as her dependents because she surely was supporting them. In the end, she got a $400.00 refund, which became our wedding money. I had no idea how much a ceremony would cost, but God and the universe had a plan and we had a wedding—which had several hitches.

Dolly returned the velvet winter wedding dress and bought a summer wedding dress at Hart's Department Store in New Kensington. Her four sisters were her attendants. It was decided they would all sew their own bridesmaid dresses. Dolly had a fondness for butterflies and found sheer butterfly material in five different pastel shades. Dolly's sister Pat, from Ohio, would make her own dress and one for her daughter Terry, the flower girl. Dolly helped her two younger sisters sew and fit their dresses. Her oldest sister, Pauline, innocently announced she was planning to alter her pattern. She was nicely asked to stick to the pattern. That was one of many disasters to be averted.

Obviously, coming up with a like number of groomsmen was an issue. My brother, Bob, was to be my best man. The three other positions were assumed by college buddies, Alan D. (my roommate), Dave, and Alan F.

Alan D. and Dave were to drive from Philadelphia on the day of the wedding (a five-hour drive). Alan D. was an amateur photographer with a fairly fancy camera. My cousin, Jack, would assist him for photos in which Alan would appear.

We needed a ring bearer from my side of the family. *Abracadabra*, nobody appeared. My brother's nephew, Larry C. Jr., was the right age and was willing to participate.

The church was free and the reception was to be in the church basement. We could only afford cake and ice cream. We couldn't begin to provide a meal. The attendees would understand. The cake was donated by a friend at work, whose sister made wedding cakes. Our church had a gift from God named Agnes Bonarett. She never married and had the time and talent to provide beautiful decorations for the church. I think we paid for some flowers, but the arrangements and the other decorations were a gift from Agnes.

Haven't heard many expenditures? Well, we were playing the loaves and the fishes game with the money we had. We had to pay for my tux, our rings, Dolly's dress and clothes for her father and youngest brother. Dolly made her mother's dress. We planned a modest honeymoon at Cook Forest (a state park in northwestern Pennsylvania), where we rented a cabin for a week. During the spring of 1972, we also bought a hide-a-bed, dinette set, and chest of drawers for our little house. Dolly's mom had recently crept her way into the twentieth century when her coal-fired kitchen stove was replaced by an electric stove from Dolly's uncle, Tom Exton. That made her three-day-a-week, mandated chore, of baking homemade bread a little easier. Dolly's father was vehemently opposed, but unable to stop progress.

Dolly and I were appalled that Mom C. had a shoebox-size freezer in a very small refrigerator that she had to defrost. On Mother's Day, 1972, we spearheaded an effort to buy her a slightly used frost-free refrigerator with good freezer space. Dolly's brothers Dave and Roy also made contributions to the $200.00 price. We had it delivered as a surprise because Dolly's father wouldn't have allowed it. He was seventy-nine and failing fast, while becoming meaner. When the refrigerators were being exchanged, he was cussing profoundly. I pulled him and his chair out of the way—dodging the cane he was banging on the floor. We lightened Mom Caldwell's mood and pissed-off Dad Caldwell... it was a good day!

The wedding invitations were bought from Kuchta's Print Shop in Creighton. It was the best we could do for the guy who kindly tolerated all the local kids bugging him for irregulars and scraps to make paper airplanes and notes, etc. We did the fancy, formal version—together. Working together was and would continue to be the centerpiece of our relationship. When you chose well, it really wasn't a problem. The rivers were approaching each other and were about to merge.

16. WE MADE LEMONADE AND MORE

With a lot of conservative planning, the day was about here. All of Dolly's siblings and families would be there. It would be the first and last time Dolly's parents would see the whole family together at one time. My brother, his first wife MaryAnn and his son, Robert Jr. were coming from Winston-Salem, North Carolina. It was coming together perfectly, or so we thought.

To play the "loaves and fishes" game, you only take one full day off before the wedding. It was Thursday, July 13, our last day of work. It might as well have been Friday the 13th. Dolly was scheduled to work "the annex." It was a small unit located in the basement of Harmarville. Only those patients independent enough for discharge stayed there. One LPN or RN could easily manage the patients. At that time, a very special patient was there, John S. He was a seventeen-year-old paraplegic from an automobile accident. He was in C ward when we both worked on the men's floor. At that time, he was angry and depressed. Transferring into bed was very painful and when we were working, he insisted we do his transfers. He was very verbally rough on his mom in particular. He was grieving the loss of his leg movement, which would never return. He had been a star athlete in high school. On one of his really bad days, he lashed out at me as I was getting his clothes out. I distinctly remember throwing them at him and I said, "You're not going to treat me the way you treat your mother." Wow, did I really do that? It was the first time I challenged a patient because of their behavior—it wasn't the last. If well timed, it could be a profound experience for the patient who needed to "reel it in" and start adapting. We later talked and have been lifelong friends.

The annex had its quirks like the rest of the building. John was in the shower and Dolly did the unthinkable—she flushed a nearby toilet. That stole the cold water from the shower hose which was pointed at John's foot. He couldn't feel it, but he got a second degree burn on his foot that blistered immediately. Dolly was devastated by her innocent mistake!

Meanwhile, on the second floor, I was approached by a patient named Art Doesnotlisten. He had partial paralysis of his legs from an auto accident. With the help of braces, from his upper thighs to his shoes, he could walk with crutches. The braces had a knee joint which would allow him to sit with them on and a lock to keep his legs straight when walking. We repeatedly asked the patients to keep the braces on the outside of their clothes. Art was a young, good-looking guy who was regaining some of his vanity. Unfortunately, he still lacked bowel function and this was a bowel retraining day. He received laxative tablets at noon. On that day he decided to put his braces under his clothes. Nature took a turn for the worse, and he had a huge incontinence of liquid feces which coated his braces from top to bottom. There was no easy way to get the braces off and clean him up. After that, I spent the next several hours cleaning crap from all the cracks and crevices of those braces and attached shoes. They were good leather shoes and the braces had leather cuffs on them. Even using a Q-tip at times, the braces and I had a distinct aroma!

Fortunately, the day before the wedding went well and we spent the evening with Dolly's siblings, who became my siblings.

The day of the wedding was more "eventful," to say the least. It started out okay, but Alan and Dave and another friend were supposed to arrive at 11:00 A.M. (Remember this was years before cell phones.) At 12:30 P.M., Alan called and said his car broke down in Breezewood, PA., which was about two-and-a-half hours away. The mechanic led him to believe they would be on the road shortly and would arrive by about 3:00 P.M., which was rehearsal time. The next call was at 2:30 P.M. and Alan said they couldn't get there for the wedding, scheduled for 6:00 P.M. Gulp! Dolly did not know about any of that. I was in hyper mode. Dolly's brother John was already at the church and I asked him and the ring bearer's father to stand in. We took off for New Kensington to get them tuxes—so much for a rehearsal. Now Dolly was aware and anxious. We got it done, but we had no photographer or camera. Jack would take the pictures, and I borrowed a Kodak Instamatic X-90 from a family friend. It would have to do.

It was July 15, 1972 and we were married in a non-air-conditioned church during a midsummer downpour with no air moving. Everyone was soaked with perspiration, and Dolly's curl strands were pretty droopy. Our minister was a young, good-looking, recent graduate of the Methodist seminary, who put Dolly (the Lutheran) through an arduous pre-nuptial course from which I was excluded (Thank you, Reverend Dean!). Actually, I was still at Pitt. Dean was married or I might have been concerned. The Methodist wedding ceremony was about twenty minutes. My father, the organist, was his usual militaristic self. The pre-wedding music started at 5:30 P.M. and "Here Comes the Bride" would start at precisely 6:00 P.M., ready or not.

The last hurdle was holding our breath to see if Dad Caldwell would respond "Her mother and I" when asked, "Who gives away the bride?" Dolly's brother Ken was in charge of him.

At the designated time, with his age-appropriate, shaky, but loud voice, he came through. We both would have fainted at that point, but we just wanted to proceed to the slightly cooler basement of the church.

We had soupy ice cream and cake, but everyone was happy for us. Just before we were about to leave, Dave and his friend burst through the door—soaking wet from hitchhiking from Breezewood. Alan stayed behind with the car. He wasn't, nor is, a hitchhiking kind of guy, preferring to stay with his father's car until it was safely towed.

Alan F. drove us in his 1971 Impala (covered in soaking wet Kleenex flowers) to Harmarville so the patients and staff could see us. Then we returned to my parent's home to open presents. We got to our little house and did the deed—several times. We had waited over a year! Dolly's family told us we missed a great after-party at the Caldwell's, but we had a pretty great time—alone.

The next day we drove to Cook Forest and stayed in cabin #4 of Riverside Cabins. This was extra special because I had spent many summer vacations in that very cabin with my grandparents. When we arrived, some day-visitors had chosen our firepit to make lunch. Dolly said, "Go ahead, we're just on our honeymoon." They quickly packed and left! Before our trip, we stopped to see my grandmother Kelly, who chose not to come to the wedding, because she wanted to be begged. I don't know why she wanted to be begged, but I refused to do it. Dolly was a little upset she wouldn't be there. For a woman who didn't like most women, she adored Dolly, who would help her shower and pretty-up. Dolly thoroughly enjoyed inheriting two grandmothers. Dolly's were deceased.

We stayed in Cook Forest for a week of hiking, canoeing, and canoodling. By Wednesday the 19th, we made a trip to Brookville Hospital because Dolly was sick with a fever. It was "honeymoon cystitis," a urinary tract infection from a lot of canoodling. It was a long year and we needed the practice. The two rivers had merged into one just like the Allegheny and the Monongahela, and a brand-new river was formed.

17. "WHY BUY THE COW...?"

In mid-1972, I took the MCAT, the admission exam for medical school. I don't remember taking it or my score. It was a better-than-average score but not remarkable. I remember applying only to Pitt, M.S. Hershey Medical Center (of Penn State) and Bowman-Gray in North Carolina. The application fees were considerable, and I budgeted our money as frugally as I could. By then we were married and living on an LPN's and male aide's salaries. Neither set of parents had the ability to bail us out. Financial planning and stability were my responsibility, and I took that very seriously for the rest of my life.

Long before applying to Pitt, I felt I might get special consideration, as I was already in their system and had an excellent GPA. It would be difficult to stay in Oakland because we would be living on Dolly's salary, which in the city, wouldn't buy much. Crime might be an issue. Dolly came with me to the interview and I really think that helped. They liked that I was married, and my spouse was in healthcare. It made me look more serious and stable. That took place in mid-September of 1972.

It always seems forever, but I got my acceptance from Pitt on November 6, 1972. The timing was perfect because the next day was election day, and I volunteered as a poll worker for then Congressman John Heinz III. I always had an interest in politics and, for me, John Heinz was a perfect moderate. I was crushed when Senator John Heinz III was killed in a plane crash in 1991. I always thought he would be President someday.

At the poll, most people knew me and asked what I was going to do. I was so fortunate and proud to tell them I was going to medical school! I rarely doubted myself, but there was a dark corner in my mind where I knew I had competed with forty-nine people for that seat.

The pressure was totally off. Getting in was the hardest part, or so I thought at that time.

Having one acceptance gave me the ability to request early consideration at the other schools. Hershey (of Penn State) scheduled my interview for late November. I had some concern about even checking it out, because I had gone with my brother to his interview in 1968. The place was still under construction with paint cans and scaffolding everywhere. It was in far better shape four years later. I was scheduled for three, one-hour interviews. As luck would have it, I had an infected wisdom tooth. The side of my face was swollen, and I was in obvious pain. I was sitting on a waiting room couch, which was backed by another couch, on which two farmers sat. They were discussing modern morality and one of them actually said, "Why buy the cow when you get the milk for free." My decision was made at that moment. I had to go to Hershey. It would be a safer and a more economic place to live, and they assured us Dolly could get a job at the Medical Center.

The first two hours went okay, but after talking so much my face and jaw were killing me. The third interview was the hardest and the questions were ambiguous and repetitious. I remember I wanted it over and later felt I might have been curt with the interviewer. Dolly and I had splurged on a room at the newly built Hershey Motor Lodge. We brought beef stew with us, because we couldn't afford both the room and a restaurant bill. I was fretting about the uncomfortable interview and that I didn't know the term "Euthanasia." Yes, I really thought he asked me how I felt about "youth in Asia"! I must have had a bewildered, uncomfortable look on my face. He explained the term and even at that time I felt the end of life should be treated with the same kind of dignity we extend to patients at non-critical times.

Several weeks later, I got an acceptance letter and I would start September 1973. Our future was set!

18. IT'S A PALACE!

After we married on July 15, 1972, we lived in a one-room house that my grandmother Lord's brother built. My uncle Chuck had bought the place, which was across the alley from his house. My aunt came up with the rent, $37.50 per month. We paid the utility bills which was more than fair. The house was shaped like an "L" with a stove and refrigerator in the leg and a hide-a-bed and lounge chair in the larger part. We did have a full bath. Unfortunately, the bathroom sink had to double as the kitchen sink, but we were young and in love and nothing else mattered. We put our mark on the bathroom. We received orange monogrammed towels for a wedding present, so we painted the bathroom bright orange. I made a stencil and painted yellow daisies all over the walls and a big flower around the shower head. It sounds gaudy, and it was.

With the house rent so reasonable, we were able to save $500.00 per month, a fortune in those days. When my last semester started, I stayed in the Tower C dorm room from Sunday night to Wednesday. Then I got my ride home and worked Thursday-Saturday.

The fall of 1972 was probably the happiest and easiest of my life. I loved my wife and my job and had a very easy Monday-Wednesday school schedule.

After I was accepted to Hershey, we made a second trip to Hershey to find housing. The on-campus housing seemed a little expensive for what you got. We drove around and didn't find much. I do not recall how we found it, but we found a trailer park in Middletown, Pennsylvania, about ten miles from the medical center. We met with a banker who happened to own a trailer sales lot. We could rent something or buy a brand-new 12X70 Schultz trailer. We did a tour and our jaws dropped. It had a kitchen in front, a dining room with built in cabinets, a sunken living room (one step) then you entered a hall which contained doors to two small bedrooms. The master bedroom was in the back with built in drawers and a closet. It would be made with our choices of carpet and kitchen appliances (the green of the '70s) and a dining room table. They assured us it would be delivered by March 1973. Dolly had been hired to start work in March at Hershey Medical Center.

It was a palace and it would be ours for a monthly payment of $106.75. We would pay for propane, but I think everything else was included in our $40.00 per month trailer park fee. If you looked out our master bedroom window, you could see the huge cooling towers of the Three Mile Island nuclear power plant on the Susquehanna River. We were literately a quarter-mile away, and down wind. Fortunately, the incident at Three Mile Island took place in 1979, two years after we left.

Trailers come furnished, but the furniture left a lot to be desired. We took a credit on the living room furniture and used our relatively new hide-a-bed and lounge chair. My parents were very helpful with the move. My father drove a rental truck with our furniture and belongings. They also paid for the optional washer and dryer which together was between $300-$500.

My father and I actually did a project together—civilly! To finish the trailer's look, you generally installed skirting around the bottom to hide the wheels etc. We could not afford professional skirting, so father and I made our own from two-by-twos and corrugated white fiberglass. It looked fine and helped insulate the floors and pipes some. As a separate project, I built a small porch, and he helped me put a roof over it. The first and last father-and-son quality time.

I needed to find a job until classes started in September of 1973. There were no research positions left, so I took a job in central sterile at the medical center. My job was to collect used OR equipment from an automatic elevator and clean the blood off the instruments, then put them on wire holders which would keep the scissors and the forceps in an open position to go through a cleaning then sterilizing process. It was a never-ending ordeal. You no sooner cleaned out one cart and three more would shoot out of the elevators. They had just started doing open heart surgery, which was a long procedure and used a lot of instruments.

We used rubber gloves, but the "instruments" would commonly tear the gloves and not infrequently the operating room nurses wouldn't remove the blades from the scalpels. It's a wonder I didn't contract a blood-borne disease like Hepatitis or AIDS. In 1973, we didn't know much about Hepatitis C, and AIDS had not yet manifested itself. Interestingly, before AIDS and its cause were known, the sick gay patients were crudely labeled as SQWIDs—Sick Queers with Immune Deficiency Syndrome. Medicine always loved an acronym—as inappropriate as it was.

This was my least favorite job, but I stuck with it until school started. Sometimes, in the evenings at school, I'd take a break and visit my friends in central sterile. I never burned a bridge—a river kid never would.

19. "DO WE HAVE A PROBLEM HERE?"

We were the sixth class to start at Hershey, and I soon learned the school was still figuring things out. At the time, most medical schools started with gross anatomy which would continue for about two semesters. We were told they weren't ready to start gross anatomy, so it would be postponed to the next term. We were on a three term/year schedule. We would get only two terms of gross anatomy? Sounded rushed to me.

We had a large amphitheater for our classes. Each row had a continuous desk with comfortable chairs. We probably only used a third of the lecture hall. We quickly developed a pattern. The front row was populated by the really eager beavers. They were all but jumping over the desk to quench their thirst for knowledge. The back was populated by the smokers (yes, we had quite a few), but I think over a lifetime they all quit smoking. Their location did not show a lack of interest—just respect. I, and the other overachievers, sat in the fringes and more toward the front, willing to do the work but didn't want to be recognized. The eager beavers would answer most of the questions.

The most conspicuous and interesting students were the two women in the middle—about six rows up. They would sit there and knit while the rest of us furiously took notes. I always thought the knitters were our version of Madame Defarge from Dicken's *A Tale of Two Cities*. Somewhere, knitted in their project, was the information they needed to retain. It was a show of confidence and their ability to assimilate crucial information quickly. Both became my friends and were two of the best students.

Hershey, being new, had a reputation for taking non-typical students. A third of our class were women, which was an unusually high percentage compared to other schools. They were, far and away, some of the brighter people in the class. Hershey also admitted "mature students," people who had already achieved advanced degrees in other subjects, for example, psychology. We had a pharmacist who was in the Air Force Reserves and would fly practice missions on the weekends. My best friend had graduated college, did a stint in the military, and then decided to pursue medical school.

There were a fair number of students who found a spouse in the class. Of course, we had our share of guys who would get in trouble for things like, nude bathing at a local quarry. Overall, we were a pretty mature bunch. Nobody committed suicide (the previous class had two, I think). A few left, a few flunked out and a couple were asked to repeat a year.

In those days, you would hear horror stories about how one third of a class would be culled from the herd in the first year. Hershey had a pass/fail system and tried to provide help for those struggling. Until that point, I had never failed anything in school.

It quickly became apparent that almost everyone there were "cream of the crop" students. I hoped, realistically, that I was at least in the middle layer. I was prepared to give it my all to succeed, I thought.

When you're an overachiever, you succeed by putting more hours and intensity into your work. I had no insight that I was suffering some college burnout. We all had the exact same schedule, including biochemistry (with lab), physiology (with lab), and medical ethics. I had taken an introduction to biochemistry course at Pitt, and I was a little cocky. I studied, but I gave it less than my best. All the courses were more intense than college, where you might cover a couple chapters a week. In med school you might cover six or seven chapters a night of much more intense material.

Physiology was an interesting experience. Our professor was a respected PhD in his field. It was much like college in that each course was very autonomous, and there was no coordination between subjects for integrated learning. This professor was the master tester. He gave what I called the "A-K" tests. The answer could be A, B, C, D, A & B, A & C, A & D, ABC, B & C, etc., all the permutations. This required an exceptional mastery of the topic. He did grade on a curve and I survived that massacre!

In Biochemistry, we had a lab and basically a midterm and final. I prepared for the midterm only to find that I had failed it by a few points. I got a message from student affairs that the Dean wanted to see me!

It was the first time I met him. He was my height but seemed much taller. He dove right into the subject, "Mr. Kelly, your

Pitt records would indicate you should perform better than this. Do we have a problem?" I'm sure I came up with an excuse, but the conversation was basically over. I was mortified! Prior to this, getting a B or C was failing to me. This was a whole new world of shame and self-loathing. I doubled down and, on the final, had the fourth highest grade in the class. There was no congratulatory meeting. I wish I could say that was my last failing experience.

I think we had two terms of biochemistry and physiology, so the pain was far from over. In addition, the second term started and again, no Gross Anatomy. It was postponed to spring. There were other courses also being postponed. So, we had an easy introduction to med school. Each ten-week term was to have ten to eleven credits. The spring term schedule arrived with Gross Anatomy to be finished in ten weeks. As if that wasn't bad enough, we were scheduled for four other courses for a total of eighteen credits! "What's the big deal?" you may ask. Gross Anatomy is the course where you dissect a real human body to learn the three-dimensional placement of bones, muscles, arteries, veins, nerves, and organs. Much like a surgeon, you must use scalpels and scissors to uncover these things. In other words, you must unbury all the secrets, try to absorb as much information as possible and it is all totally new. Had I gone to Pitt Medical School, they had pro-section, where all the dissection is done, and you need to move the structures around to study them. There were four students to a cadaver—the dead person. The thorax and the central organs were all done together. There wasn't time to do arms and legs, so you were paired off to do arms *or* legs. I was a leg man. I studied arms, but leg was my "area." There was never enough time in class to complete the task, so you would leave to get dinner then back to the lab for more work and study.

Those were the time and technical problems. That didn't begin to address that you had to wear your one lab coat when you left the lab. Everyone in our class reeked of formaldehyde and molten fat, and everyone in the building would move in the other direction when you came around. Why molten fat? Well, when you're in a confined room with intense high-wattage bulbs and dead bodies with a layer of fat, voilà, stench. That whole term is a blur to me. There was so much to do and learn and not enough hours.

We named and treated out cadavers with respect. I honestly can't remember who my partners were or the name we gave our subject. It was probably the most overwhelmed I ever felt in my life. We had four other courses of which I only remember two: Nutrition and Histology. Nutrition definitely got no attention, but Histology was important, wasn't it?

Histology is the study of the microscopic structure of tissues. The final would consist of slides on a screen, of all the different organs in the body, in cellular form. You would think they were all remarkably different, but subtle nuances made the difference. Probably two days before that final, I thought of jumping off the roof of our trailer—my only suicide thought, ever. It would have been about a fourteen-foot drop, and at most, I might break an ankle! Then I would be in pain and still have to take the test! The night before the test, we got a room full of students to study together. Someone got access to a carousel of slides and we studied them together. I think we all passed, but nobody would brag about it.

The river was stagnant. The terrain was very uphill, and it was uncharted territory for me.

20. MASTERING THE ENVELOPES

The difficulty of medical school was only one of the many challenges we faced as relative newlyweds. Once we had started school, we had Dolly's income to sustain us. There was no thought of a safety net. Dolly's family had zero ability to help. My family would have been able, in a very limited fashion, but I would never ask. Making the money work was my job, and we were budgeted to the penny. The trailer mortgage was $104 per month. We had a lot rental fee, propane charges, food, clothing, church offering, and maintenance, etc. My mother was the economic guru in my childhood home. Before Dolly and I got married, my mother and I had a conversation about the "envelope system." You got this little organized book that was made up of a series of envelopes. Each envelope would have a title and a budget: Food: $15.00/week, Clothing: $5.00/week, etc. Our food budget was exactly that. At the store, you would tally the cart value as you went along. If it was under $15.00 you were golden. If you were over, you had to remove something to make it right.

This was the big league of finance to us. I would put an equal amount into the propane envelope each month. It was our own budget plan. The envelope would bulge in October, then thin out by May of the following year. We paid for tuition with student loans at 7 percent interest. The loan covered only tuition—with a few dollars to spare! Books, of course, were extra.

The car was owned outright, and I did as much of the maintenance as possible. In those days you could open the hood and there were easily discernable parts: oil cap, oil filter, spark plugs, points, air filter, etc. I changed the oil filter, points, plugs and air filter. That saved a lot, and most people did that. We did have a special concern with the 1972 Vega. That was the first year Chevy put an aluminum block in one of their cars. We were already (in 1974 or '75) leaking oil. Chevy issued a recall notice on the aluminum block. You had to wait until you got your official recall letter to get it fixed. The car had to be under 50,000 miles and we were getting close. I can't remember all the particulars, but somebody showed me how the odometer cable was attached, and it was magic that our car arrived at the dealership with 49,989 miles on the odometer! God and a very simple pinch clip saved us a transportation fortune.

The envelope system worked well until the 1973-74 oil embargo. OPEC, the Mideast coalition of exporting countries decided to punish the countries who supported the Yom Kippur War, between Israel and the Arab countries. The embargo limited the flow of oil on which the US and most of the advanced nations were desperately dependent. Gasoline and propane are oil by-products. We lived 10 miles from the Medical Center and were making six trips a day. Dolly took me to school then returned home. She worked a steady 3-11 shift, so she would drive to work before 3:00 P.M. My classes were over around 4:30 P.M., so I would go home to study then drive back at 11:00 P.M. to pick her up and return home for the night: six trips. Something had to give. The thermostat, in the already drafty trailer, had to be set much lower. We cut our trips from six to four and some days, two. We had a neighbor who was a nurse at the Medical Center. I would bum a ride off her in the morning then stay there until Dolly finished her shift—two trips. It wasn't very comfortable to spend sixteen hours per day there, but we had no safety net for finances.

Each student was assigned a cubicle—my second home. In it was a desk, a lockable book shelf, a lockable closet and a bulletin board, I think. The cubicles were arranged in rows of six, off of a central hall. The first cubicle had the names of all the people in that row. Ours was particularly comic because of the makeup:

- Ginsberg
- Goldberg
- Goldfarb
- Goldstein
- Kelly
- Hart

Jim Hart and I affectionately thought of ourselves as the two gentiles in the law firm of Ginsberg, Goldberg, etc.

Somehow, we were always able to make the needed adjustments to come in under budget. Dolly was easy as she was raised with practically nothing. I was very familiar with living on a limited budget, but this economic downturn just added to the overall intense fog over our lives. We hit a patch of rapids where the water was running fast and negotiating all the obstacles was scarier.

21. WHY ARE WE SO TIRED?

The demands of medical school were already daunting for an overachiever. I would commonly make up for difficult and voluminous studies by adding study hours and repetition. It became obvious that there were only so many hours in the day and the nights got shorter and shorter. They were already short when you got up at 6:00 A.M. and got to bed at 11:30-12:00 midnight.

Sleep deprivation and constant school tension were a given. We had other issues at hand. Dolly getting an LPN job at the same place I went to school was a real plus, but there were minuses. She started out on a general medical floor for a while. Her ultimate goal was to work in Labor and Delivery or the Nursery. The demands of acute care nursing were much different than rehab nursing. Doing multiple procedures and having more patient responsibilities didn't leave time to do the extras, for which Dolly was known. This was frustrating and took a toll on her and our mood. Getting a transfer was almost impossible. She certainly could have gotten a job elsewhere, but then we would lose the tuition savings after two years of employment. Eventually she got a chance to transfer to the Gynecology floor. She was shown the carrot of Labor and Delivery, but little did she know she was jumping into the fire.

Hershey had attracted a superstar surgeon by the name of Dr. Newsurgery. He was doing cutting edge (no pun intended) surgeries for advanced pelvic cancer. These were known as pelvic exenterations. They were horrendous surgeries with post-op infections, gaping wounds, and tremendously sick patients. If the pelvic organs and bladder were removed, it was a "North American" procedure. If the pelvic organs and rectum were removed, is was a "South American" procedure. If everything was removed, it was an "All American." Post-op they would have colostomies, urostomies, drains, and pain management that seemed inadequate. Large numbers of these women died in the hospital, a terrible death. These were likely experimental surgeries. The previous descriptions were not to reflect negatively on Dr. Newsurgery. I'm sure that was valuable ground-breaking work. It was the environment that Dolly had to negotiate every day. I'm not sure any nurse was up to those demands day in and day out. Dolly was much too caring and personally involved to navigate those waters. To this day, we have a few plants given to her by dying patients—a gift and treasured memories of a treacherous stretch of river we navigated.

22. THEY COLLECTED THE DAMN TOLLS!

During the first couple years of medical school, we got back to Pittsburgh every month or two. Dolly had to work several weekends per month and the timing of tests had an impact on my availability. Fortunately (or not) we were able to go home for Thanksgiving in November 1974. We brought the thirty-pound turkey and the total number of people filtering in and out of the Caldwell house was seventy to eighty. Those were special occasions, because I got to meet and spend time with my new family. They all shared the bond of growing up in poverty and reacting by using their intelligence and tenacity to build a better life. One trip into the bathroom to use the curtained off toilet would refresh their memory. Having to share that experience with seventy other people was subliminally painful, but then you would re-emerge into the front of the house filled with laughter and banter. The older siblings, raised using an outhouse, were thankful there was a toilet.

Being the new kid and being in medical school would stimulate a lot of questions, but they paled in comparison to Pauline's cross-examination. The meal usually started midday and would continue to the evening. Some of the siblings would have other family to visit, but everyone wanted at least part of the day to be at "home."

The small kids would be running everywhere but would tend to collect in the back bedroom where drawing pictures and leaving messages on the wall were permitted. Over the years, it became a sacred shrine that could not be covered with paint. The kids and adults would visit the shrine each visit to see what was preserved and added. It seemed like Mom Caldwell would be standing at the sink all day. There were only so many of the Melmac and mismatched other plates, and there was no dishwasher.

Quickly, my favorite activity was "the card game." As a group, the Caldwell siblings were pretty good card players. The in-laws were the really interesting group, (and more diverse) including quiet evaluators, card counters, and the totally inept. Dolly's sister Pat (#5) was married to Miles (Jack) Benedum. He was the card counter and a Mensa-level guy who had creative ideas that rarely seemed to get off the ground. He invented the first hovercraft (flying car) and was recognized on the national quiz show "What's My Line." Across from him was Phyllis, (#3) Ken's wife. Phyllis was street-smart but was pretty bad at cards. Jack would make a rapid, calculated play, then sit for what seemed an eternity, waiting for Phyllis to ponder a really bad choice. Jack was very gregarious, but this would test his patience. You could see his face get red and the veins begin to bulge with a smile pasted on his face. We would try to pair the two of them together in some games. I could care less about my below-average play. Watching this interplay of family love and "tolerance" was priceless.

As a group, the Caldwell's were left-brained in work and right-brained at play. The other activity was the jigsaw puzzle. They would gather around the table like puppies around a food bowl. It was a sea of maneuvering, grabbing, elbowing and sibling banter. It was common that one or several of them would sequester a puzzle piece so they could "finish" the puzzle. I was rightfully considered an amateur and would be quickly culled from the herd. I was much too left-brained to be included. Everyone was cordial and respectful, but this activity had a hierarchy and I was not even on the radar.

The other Caldwell activity was crossword puzzles, which were done in solitude and had their own language. Mom Caldwell, in late life, found a lot of peace in the activity. Many of the Caldwell kids were also master puzzlers and undoubtedly used this to broaden their vocabulary and artsy skills.

After a very pleasant weekend, it was time to make the normal three-hour drive home. Strawpump was literately two minutes from the Irwin exit of the Pennsylvania Turnpike. The turnpike was the first toll road in the United States and spans the width of Pennsylvania. Our entire trip was on the turnpike. We lived about ten minutes from the Harrisburg East exit. We expected heavy traffic, but that day we got a lot more.

November in Pennsylvania can range from dry and warm to snowy and cold. We weren't watching the weather reports, because we had to get back to school/work regardless. We left around 5:00 P.M. with some leftover pumpkin pie in my rear wheel drive, orange Vega with good snow tires. Remember, in 1974 there were no cell phones. We were no sooner on the road when the traffic and snow began to hit. At first the traffic was the bigger issue, which slowed the pace. The snow, ominously, began to pick up, and we were headed straight into the Appalachian Mountains, which bisect Pennsylvania north to south. We were jabbering about family news and enduring the backup. Then we both became concerned about the weather. It was taking us hours to travel a distance normally covered in minutes. Fortunately, the gas tank had been full, and we traveled with pillows (for comfort), boots, winter apparel and a blanket. Bad weather was always a threat.

At some point, in the mountains, we came to a standstill, then would move only a short distance each hour. It was then that I learned what illusions snow and nightfall could cause. You couldn't tell if you were going uphill or downhill. The car in front of us drifted backwards, but it felt like we were drifting into it. The snow was getting pretty high and on a couple of occasions I got out to clear snow from around the tailpipe. Of course, this would drop the temperature in the car but was a necessary evil.

Dolly had to urinate, but there was no privacy and the snow kept piling up. We ate the pumpkin pie and used the pie pan for a bedpan. We were young and agile on December 1, 1974!

People were building snowmen and having snowball battles to pass the time. We repeated, multiple times, our thanks for not having kids with us.

At 11:00 P.M. we reached the Somerset exit (a total of 115 miles in six hours). The State Police were encouraging everyone to get off the turnpike. I was in the fast lane because it was moving better. I had good tires and felt we could get through—wrong!

In the next hour we moved ten feet and finally gave up, pulling to what we thought was the side of the road. We grabbed our pillows and trudged through the deep snow toward the toll booths.

I don't remember if they had a total of two or four toll booths, but it was a very small exit. It soon became clear why the traffic wasn't moving: they were collecting the damn tolls during a snow emergency while they were trying to close the road! Imbeciles! We talked to some people who told us the armory had the only working phone. We got directions and made our way to the armory. Once we got in, we had to wait an hour to use the one phone. We called my mother to report we were all right. We needed her to call the Caldwell's and call Dolly off work the next day.

The town roads were being plowed and they had a bus waiting outside the armory. We took a circuitous route to a Church of Christ in Somerset. We gratefully entered the sanctuary which was pretty full and warm. We found a section of a pew, and the floor below, and settled in to sleep. Within about five minutes, there was a loud explosion outside the church. The lights went off and the furnace stopped. It was a transformer.

We spent a short, cold night in the church. The next morning, we left the church completely disoriented about our location. We asked a gentleman, who was shoveling his walk, how to get to the turnpike. He asked, "Have you had breakfast?" We told him, "No," and he insisted we join the family for a pretty elaborate breakfast. We tried to pay them, but they refused. We thanked them and got directions to the turnpike. They warned us the news reported that it would stay closed. We got there and found they wouldn't let anybody re-enter, but if you were parked on the road, you could continue. We noticed the continued backup behind us, but the snow-covered road ahead was clear. A couple guys with shovels dug us out and we were on our way. We passed a sea of occupied cars, stranded overnight. The Allegheny Tunnel was full and the long hill, on the other side of the tunnel, was filled with cars with kids, all surrounded by drifted snow. They would have a long wait, because they would have to be removed individually and by hand.

We barely made it to the next rest stop to fill up on gas and get a piece of terrible pizza. We got back on the road, and after we crossed the mountains there was little snow and a clear trip home.

I wrote a scathing letter to the Turnpike Commission about collecting tolls during an emergency. I'm sure they are still quaking in their boots!

23. THE DREAM TRIP

Our little slice of heaven, the trailer, was located in a quaint, isolated, rural spot—with the Three Mile Island cooling towers
looming in the distance (probably a quarter-mile away.) We liked
to take a walk on the sparsely used roads. There was a covered
bridge nearby and a particularly pretty section of road with a
dense tree canopy. In the fall, it was spectacular. I really wasn't
into jogging, but tried multiple times, then gave it up. That was
a perfect area for joggers.

We had nice neighbors. An older lady on one side and a young
family on the other. Jim worked as a salesman and Dottie was a
homemaker with two small, beautiful dark-eyed girls, Jenny and
Gwen. We would visit outside but didn't do dinners or picnics—our
schedule was bad for a social life. When Dolly had a night off, we
would try to have a hot meal, a cheap date night, or go shopping.

I saw a flyer for a Harrisburg Flying Club, which chartered
trips with their own commercial-size plane. They planned a late
summer trip to Hawaii. Money was really tight, but I figured we
could afford their very reasonable price. My brother and family

were currently stationed at Tripler Army Hospital on Oahu for his five-year surgical residency. If we could get there, we would have a free place to stay.

It was to be a surprise first-anniversary present. Dolly had never seen any ocean and had never flown. It would be a great adventure! I arranged for her to be off for ten days and I was off for the summer.

I secured a job at UPS to unload trucks from 10:00 P.M. to 2:00 A.M. I had a Honda 90 I bought from a friend before college graduation. To get my motorcycle license, I had to travel about ten miles on the only route I knew, Interstate 83. With tractor trailers zooming around me, I was sure I would get sucked under them. To say I was a motorcyclist would have been more than generous. I passed the test, and now we had two sets of wheels, really one and a quarter.

I putt-putted my way to work in Steelton, PA, about five miles away. It was a pure blue-collar town, which seemed (at 10:00 P.M.) to consist of huge steel mills and bars. That was scary. At 2:00 A.M., in the rain, it was even worse. It seemed like my top speed was about 40 mph. I felt as though the hundreds of men, exiting the bars, at the mandatory closing time of 2:00 A.M., could run me down. It was the only job I quit after one day.

I couldn't find any work at the Medical Center and decided to be a kept man. I had a project I wanted to do. After my grandfather died, I did an oil painting portrait of him. I was not an artist, but I could make an almost photographic portrait from a picture. The high school art teacher gave me some tips on shading but was surprised at my ability having had no training. I had also done another small portrait, again from a picture, of my grandmother Lord, which was pretty good. Full of myself, I wanted to do a large portrait of my bride. My talent decreased with transposing to a larger canvas, but I completed it for our first anniversary. It was okay, but not the quality of my first two attempts.

On the stereo, I had a small collection of 78s that I about wore out. The one I specifically remember was "We've Only Just Begun" by the Carpenters. It was a favorite for many reasons. In June of 1973, I received notice the flying club had postponed the trip until later, and we couldn't do that. I was crushed. I told Dolly and we resolved to just get over it. We were in the Harrisburg Mall and saw a travel office. We decided to stop just to reassure us that the trip wasn't doable. A very nice lady started gathering some numbers. The cost wasn't markedly different. In fact, the price would lower if we took a side trip to another island. She suggested Kauai, and found us a reasonable package at the Coco Palms resort. The total of everything was less than just plane tickets to Oahu. We stayed in a Queen's cottage on a lagoon, which was very romantic. Elvis Presley's *Blue Hawaii* was filmed at the same resort. Our favorite place was Poipu Beach. It was quite the introduction to ocean living for both of us.

We had a great visit with Bob and MaryAnn and enjoyed the beautiful house they rented overlooking Pearl Harbor. We did a few free tours including the Arizona Memorial. My nephew, Rob, was just a toddler at the time. It was there I experienced one of my favorite things, a long walk on a beach with a baby falling asleep in my arms. The sound of the waves was very soothing.

After the trip, my parents announced that they were going to take an extended vacation to Hawaii, if we would take in my grandmother Kelly. Gulp, of course. She was living in a senior citizen high-rise but was totally dependent on my parents for shopping, meals, and laundry. Dolly was thrilled to accept the challenge since she never knew any of her grandparents. I had already had the "pleasure" of living with her and was less excited. We needed to grandmother-proof our trailer. She was a "dribbler" when she walked, so we put a plastic runner on the floor from her (my!) recliner to the first bedroom where we had a portable commode. I built a platform to raise the recliner so she could get on and off of it, independently.

When she wasn't working, Dolly would give my grandmother Kelly a shower, fix her hair and generally fuss over her. While she was there, I would go home to study in case she needed something. I would be reading in our bedroom and I'd hear, "Bruce, I'm lonely." After my red face normalized, and I was under control, I would paste a smile on my face and explain there was a tremendous amount of studying in medical school. We'd visit for ten to fifteen minutes, then repeat.

We "gerisat" two different times for six weeks each. It was novel for Dolly, and my grandmother just loved her.

24. OH NO! NOT AGAIN!

The second year of medical school is seemingly more relevant. You study Pathophysiology, which is how the various diseases affect the body and how you diagnose them. We also had Pharmacology, which was extremely interesting. We had some good professors, but Dr. Arthur Hayes was exceptional: young, articulate, and passionate about hypertension. He kept everyone's attention. He went on to be an FDA Commissioner from 1981 to 1983. We also had Genetics and various other courses.

This was all new to me, so I did my normal super study and seemed to be in the third layer of the five layers of cream. The goal was always on the horizon: just get through the first two years. The third and fourth years were all clinical, working with patients in the hospital or doctors' offices.

We had a course on death and dying. We learned the stages of grief, but never in my training did you get any practical advice about how to discuss terminal or catastrophic illness, or how to manage family dynamics, etc.

Everyone was thrown into that abyss without a parachute. Your first time leading those discussions or informing a family of a death was a horror show. You struggle for words and watch your audience's reaction. That told you whether you needed to expand on your topic or take a different approach. You also had to learn to put the key words (the show stoppers) at the end, because they disconnected further brain function. "Cancer," "metastatic," "Alzheimer's," "AIDS," and "incurable" are the bullets that will kill any ongoing conversation.

Near the end of the second year, you had to take part one of the National Medical Board exams. It would concentrate on the first-year topics, in particular. There was no study book, internet, or any organized way to prepare. I went through course books and tried to reinforce what I could. It was a one-day test, and we got the results in a few weeks. I had failed by four points! Not again. This was even worse because in six weeks, I had to take it again, or I couldn't continue school.

There had been a lot of questions on the Krebs cycle, which is the molecular system that generates energy for the body and the organs. There are various points in the cycle, and specific reactions, that create ATP—the "gasoline" of life. There was no doubt that this was crucial to every living being. That being said, I don't recall ever standing at a patient's bedside and using my knowledge of the Krebs's cycle to diagnose or treat.

I had learned the Krebs's cycle in great detail, but burnout and depression were setting in. I would try to make myself study, but spent many days avoiding it. If I had failed by a lot, I would almost have felt better! Board part one was infamous for being the hardest. The repeat test was also given at the Medical Center. I was not alone. Probably one-fourth of the class had failed. We trudged into the room and spent the day reliving our potentially career-ending nightmare. Fortunately, I passed the second time.

25. THERE IS NOTHING LIKE A HEART ATTACK WITH RAGING DIARRHEA

On July 1, 1975, I started my first hospital rotation. I was assigned to General Medicine, three months of hell! It had a bad reputation for being brutal. I was eager to learn from a body instead of a book. At the end of our second year, we had practiced normal physical exams, taking a history and filling out the appropriate forms. We practiced starting IVs on each other, but that was no preparation for what was to come.

Medical students wore short white jackets with pockets filled with medical diagnosis books, stethoscopes, reflex hammers, otoscopes and many loose, unorganized papers. Hershey did not employ phlebotomists, the people who specialize in drawing blood. That task was left to the students. There is an unwritten rule in medicine concerning procedures, "See one, do one, teach one." In training hospitals, everyone is busy. On the first clinical day you had to find an "experienced" doctor to show you where supplies were and how to do the procedure needed. After seeing it once, you were to muster the confidence to do it yourself. After successfully completing a procedure, you were expected to be able to teach a colleague. "See one, do one, teach one."

When drawing blood, we had to learn which tests required specific tubes of blood, and to organize them. Then you had to gather your other supplies: prep, gauze, tape, and a vacutainer (which is used to enter the vein and hold the tube to be filled). If you were smart, you also brought a butterfly (a small needle with handles that looks like it has little wings attached). You would hold the wings and insert the needle while praying that some blood would appear in the attached tube. That was like finding gold to us. It was rare you got to draw blood on a normal patient. Our patients were elderly, frail remnants of a body ravaged by cancer or other diseases. They would be covered with gauze patches to indicate previous "digs." You had to develop a talent to choose your vein wisely: relatively straight and no immediate branch that became more prominent when the tourniquet was applied. In the very ill you were attempting finger veins not much bigger than the needle. It was imperative you master this, because you had other work to do. This was called "scut" work, and it was a necessary nuisance.

If you were in an ICU, you might have to draw "blood gases." This required a sample of blood from the artery, hopefully rich in oxygen. You would get a glass syringe then draw Heparin into it to coat the needle and the syringe chamber to keep the blood from clotting. Then you would discard the Heparin and isolate a pulsating artery in the wrist where you commonly felt for a pulse. You used two fingers to try to feel the strongest pulse. Then you inserted the needle until the syringe started to fill with bright red blood. You removed the needle then capped the syringe and rushed it to the lab, yourself. There was a fifteen-minute window for accuracy. This test could measure the amount of oxygen, carbon dioxide, and other factors for analysis.

The patients would see you coming (all private rooms) and meet you with dread and disdain in their eyes. "I'm tired of being a pin cushion; you're gonna get one try and you're done." That was the kiss of death, a jinx. You almost always had to stick them two or three more times, while they winced in silence.

That was an opportunity to start multitasking. It helped if you had empathetic chitchat about their illness, while sticking them for blood. You could also discuss why that particular blood was needed. If they concentrated on your voice, the needle symptoms were less painful. I could always find something to talk about. You might get a useful update on symptoms or a therapeutic update on their family. Often, it was very early, and they weren't awake to talk. You hated the process, but the precision I developed doing it would later serve me well. Medical school education was more of an introductory exposure. You were low man on the totem pole.

The students reported to an intern (first year out of med school) who reported to a second- or third-year resident, who reported to a fellow (subspecialty training after residency), who reported to the attending physician. It's sort of like the "begats" of the bible. It would also "begat" misinformation as it carried up the chain. The wise attending would ask his own questions, do his own exam then chide you for missing details. I remember an occasion where I asked the patient, "Have you been in a car accident?" The answer would be "nope." The attending asked, "Have you ever been in an accident?" The patient answered "Yes, these symptoms started after the train accident." The attending glared at me. Even though you would think a "car accident" question might naturally segue into the train mishap, it didn't. Lesson learned. I did my own share of glaring in the future.

That rotation had a very memorable experience of which I was not the star. We were rotating with Cardiology and making rounds with the "Fellow," Dr. Rod. One student, of the three of us, was relating a history of a man with a heart attack. His pain was controlled with Demerol (an IV narcotic) and his heart rhythm was stable. Back then, most patients would receive some Valium (a sedative) to keep them calm and an antacid to prevent stress ulcers of the stomach. The student's presentation went well until he announced he had done some research and discovered that magnesium hydroxide (milk of magnesia) was an excellent antacid. The patient was getting a tablespoon every two hours. Dr. Rod looked at the student and said, "You thought it was a good idea to give an acute heart attack patient raging diarrhea?" There was no Prilosec or Nexium back then. There were "balanced" antacids like Maalox and Mylanta, which had magnesium (a stimulant) and aluminum (a constipating agent) to prevent diarrhea. I was stifling a laugh and rejoicing that I hadn't done it. My Harmarville experience would have prevented me from making that mistake. The student was likely obnoxious or the nurses would have persuaded him that it was a bad idea.

The Hippocratic Oath has a section "Primum non nocere." "First do no harm." Mistakes are made when training to be a physician, you prayed they were minor. This also reinforced the premise that all medical students should have some prior nursing-level experience to give them empathy for those who actually deliver the care.

The river was now flowing thru heavily populated areas and seeing how people depend on it.

26. "I DON'T WANT TO DO THAT, OR THAT..."

Once we started our third and fourth year, we rotated through all the various departments. In addition to the overwhelming amount of medical information you were to absorb, you needed to see if any specialty put a fire in your soul. About halfway through your fourth year, you would need to apply for residency positions to continue your education. Thus, there wasn't a lot of time to decide.

Medicine and Surgery both had three-month rotations. I think the remainder were one-month rotations, like pediatrics, obstetrics, urology, etc. I had to believe that everyone hated their first rotation. It was then that you had to learn the "scut" work, the paperwork, the geography of the hospital, how to interact with your superiors and the nurses. Then there was competition with the other students for good cases, the better teachers, and a better spot to visualize any important sightings. We must have looked like puppies competing for a place to feed! The three-month rotations had many students assigned—maybe ten to twelve. The one-month rotation would only have one-to-three students.

All physicians are expected to be teachers. A good doctor will educate the patient about their disease process, inform their colleagues of developments, etc. As in life in general, there are good teachers and bad ones. It seemed to me that the overachievers were better teachers, because they already struggled and knew the uncertainty of learning. The whiz kids were the worst. They felt they knew it all and didn't want to take the time to bring everyone along. I would learn that medicine had many of both. You learned to seek "the teachers." Every issue was new to you. You prayed your condensed "help" books would have some answers, because there was no time to run to the library. Remember, no smartphones, Google, or computers back then. How did we survive, let alone prosper?

I don't remember any specific cases from that first rotation. It was a blur of diabetes, heart disease, kidney disease, hypertension, etc. Hershey was an odd hospital at that time. It was certainly a tertiary-care hospital for that area. That means it would collect the most difficult cases, but likely had less of the more mundane problems like mild heart attack, mild stroke, pneumonia, etc. People were used to going to their local community hospital for those issues. From a medical student's standpoint, it was like attending college before high school. It was assumed you could figure out the treatment for lesser illnesses.

Hershey served a special geographical location. There was a good, diverse, mix of patients that came out of the Harrisburg corridor. Hershey and Palmyra provided a stable, middle class, blue- and white-collar clientele. Lancaster and the area between Hershey and Lancaster were populated by farms, many of which were Amish and Mennonite. The Amish provided more than their share of unique challenges. Because they live in defined communities, and usually married within the community, there were a certain amount of unique genetic manifestations and unique disease problems. It presented a challenge to learn normal from "unique." In large cities, the teaching hospitals also act as community hospitals and the experience would be different.

I had a pediatric case which I will never forget. It was an eleven-year-old Amish boy who presented unresponsive. Cardiac and vital signs were normal, CT scans were first developed in 1972, but it took years for them to be mass produced. We had plain skull x-rays and the physical exam. The illness progressed rapidly, and the history was not very helpful. He did have some papilledema (swelling of the optic nerve) which you see by looking in the eyes. If there is pressure behind the eye, it will cause recognizable changes. He demonstrated Babinski reflexes in his toes, which indicates damage in the brain or spinal cord. When you stroke or scrape the bottom of the feet, the large toe will extend upward. It wasn't much to go on. We knew there was mild fever and signs of pressure in the skull. We had to do a spinal tap. I was too low on the chain to perform it, but did watch them interpret the results. He had meningitis, but it didn't look or act like typical bacterial meningitis.

This kid would have had considerable interactions with farm animals, particularly cows. He would have been exposed to blood (at slaughter time), inhaled infected air, drank unpasteurized milk, etc. Regular bacteria could be seen on a microscopic slide and grew in three to four days on a culture plate. Those tests were negative. The most likely diagnosis was TB meningitis. The tuberculosis mycobacterium took six weeks to grow in a lab. That youngster didn't have six weeks.

He continued to worsen and eventually passed away. He had been started on anti-TB drugs, but they were of little help. His death was a tragic loss, but it raised some ethical questions. TB was usually a respiratory disease and was opportunistic. Only two percent of TB patients will get TB meningitis. An opportunistic infection is one that most people's immune systems could prevent. Did he get it because his immune system was deficient genetically? In 1975 we had not yet mapped the human genome. The doctor who spoke to his parents, could not give genetic counseling. The patient likely had a higher than usual exposure to TB on a farm and was drinking unpasteurized milk.

Before he died, I had to give a presentation to the attending, who happened to be the Dean of Student Affairs. He had a reputation for being a "tough audience." The resident helped me prepare a short, concise history, physical exam results, lab findings, and a differential diagnosis (a list of possible causes). He listened intently, asked a few pertinent questions then walked away. This was a good sign?! He gave no negative feedback (great!) and had few questions. If you're a person who needs positive feedback, you should avoid medicine. The absence of negative feedback would be good enough. It didn't have to be that way, but it was. You can see all the lessons learned from this one case. No wonder it was etched in my brain.

The death of the patient and how to deal with it was probably the hardest lesson of all. You adopt your patient and try to make sure you do your best to treat them. At the same time, you have to maintain some emotional detachment, so you can make rational decisions and can move on to the next patient. That sounds cold, but to survive in medicine you have to find a balance between compassion and detachment.

27. "TAKE A DEEP BREATH." "NOOOOO!"

I had a few months before the next big rotation—surgery. I knew from the beginning I did not want to do surgery. I'm not sure why, but it was a fact. I practiced tying a surgical knot, which is basically a square knot, on the rung of a chair. Obviously, there was much more to surgery than that. Knowing what to remove, how to do a repair and how to follow up are the things a future surgeon would want to learn. I was concentrating on the bare minimum to pass the course.

Because Hershey was a relatively small hospital, we had to do some of our rotations at community hospitals. Hershey had an affiliation with Geisinger Medical Center in Danville, PA. It was far enough away that if you did a rotation there, you had to stay in their dorm. I wasn't interested in boarding away, so I would always choose the closer site, Harrisburg Hospital.

Harrisburg Hospital was a dated, somewhat dilapidated, medium-sized, community hospital located in a low-income neighborhood of Harrisburg. That was always a chicken-and-egg question for me. Was the hospital location chosen because the land was cheap and the population underserved, or was the hospital built in a nicer area which evolved into a low-income area because of the medicine needs, lack of transportation, etc.? I had no problem with the locale of any hospital at which I worked. Excluding the personal safety concerns, the patients came from the entire social spectrum. The meaning of that would become clearer.

At that time, if you were having surgery, you were admitted to the hospital the day before. This meant that every afternoon you became a History and Physical machine—quickly cranking out limited histories and physicals, ordering and evaluating labs and EKGs and clearing the patient for surgery. This was exhausting work because you did it after standing all morning in surgery.

I'm sure I saw an appendectomy and cholecystectomy (gall bladder removal). Two surgeries stick in my mind. The first was a leg amputation. That was the first surgery in which I participated. The surgeon was young, but already had a good reputation. The patient was prepped, and everyone scrubbed in. The surgeon picked up a scalpel and did a deep slice of the posterior calf from the knee to the ankle. There was minimal bleeding and the surgeon said, "We will have to do an above-the-knee amputation." Elective amputations were always done because of circulation issues. This method of determining where the amputation was to occur seemed rash and reckless. In retrospect, that was probably the most accurate method. The above knee amputation would heal well and there would be one surgery. Later in my career, I would see surgeons using their hearts instead of their heads and do minimal amputations, only having to revise them higher when the wounds wouldn't heal.

The most memorable surgery was a gastric bypass surgery done by a seventy-plus-year-old surgeon known for this expertise. On a previous day, I was walking past his OR and couldn't believe my eyes. There was a pannus (the excessive abdominal fat fold/folds in the super obese) suspended from the ceiling by meat hooks one might find in a slaughter house. In addition to rearranging the digestive organs to make them less absorptive, he was attempting to reduce this fat flap for the patient's comfort and convenience.

I entered the OR and thankfully saw a very obese patient on the table but fortunately no meat hooks. The surgeon was a good instructor and demonstrated the anatomy and the procedure. Present were the surgeon, a nurse anesthetist, several OR nurses and myself. He completed the bypass and closed the abdomen by suturing various layers. Only the skin was left, and he smiled and said, "I have to go to the bathroom. You go ahead and close." I was in shock and the OR nurses were chuckling. Did he know that I had never put a single suture in a living being? Gulp!! I picked up the suture, dreading the task at hand. This will sound like a fish story, but the incision was about three-feet long. I was concerned about the sutures holding. Would the edges match on the other end? Sweat was pouring off my forehead and stinging my eyes. I wasn't even half done, and the anesthetist said, "Open your eyes." It took a couple seconds before I screamed "Don't wake him up, I have a lot of sutures to do!" An awake patient would feel me putting in each suture. I don't know how they responded, but the patient was still and I completed my task, which took well in excess of one hundred sutures. I left the OR, and the surgeon was dressed in his suit, sitting on a gurney swinging his legs and laughing.

"What took you so long?"

I replied, "Thanks, those were the first sutures I ever did."

He said, "See you later," and promptly left.

Surgery at Hershey was a different world. In the OR was the surgeon, a resident or two, several students, and the essential OR nurses. It would look like hyenas attacking their kill. The one surgery I remember, was a Whipple procedure for pancreatic cancer. Dr. Hot Stuff was known for his expertise and temper in the OR. This was an unusual and lengthy surgery. There was more than the usual horde of people because this was a real learning experience for the surgical residents. The students would hold the retractors to expose the surgical site. There were so many people, I could only see the back of the person next to me and only my arm was a participant. About hour four of the procedure, Dr. Hot Stuff said, "You learning a lot, Kelly?" I was tired and cranky, bored and sore from standing the extended time in that position. Without thinking I said, "I'm not learning anything, because I can't see anything." You could have heard a pin drop. People didn't speak to Dr. Hot Stuff that way. Everyone was waiting for the explosion! Dr. Hot Stuff stopped the surgery and had people move, so I could see the surgical field. He calmly explained what he had been doing and the exposed anatomy. I thanked him and he resumed, with me holding a retractor but now able to see the surgery. I'm sure that story circulated for a while. It was nice of him to do that, but I already knew, "I don't want to do that."

28. "I WANT TO HAVE A BABY"

Some rotations were easier than others. None of them gave you a written test, but you had to impress them to pass.

We were struggling in many ways. Every day was a challenge for both Dolly and me. She was still in gynecology and it was testing her limits. I was looking for something to give us both some relief from the continuous financial stress. I found out about the National Health Service Corps. Much like the military programs, the government had a scholarship program which provided tuition reimbursement and a monthly living stipend worth more than Dolly could generate. We would need it to cover my last two years. The program required a three-year commitment after residency. The minimum scholarship was three years. They accepted me, but I would have to accept a year's tuition and living stipend retroactively, in cash! That was a no-brainer! Dolly could eventually quit working and we could start a family.

During the first two to three years, Dolly had an IUD, and we had several "scares" when her period would be late. An early pregnancy, i.e. before we were ready, would have been a major financial disaster. We were literally living check-to-check. We had $15 per week for food, which didn't buy a lot. Thank goodness that was about the time Hamburger Helper came out and it was a help. In addition to the oil embargo, there was a coffee shortage/embargo and coffee became very expensive. It got to the point we made a pot of coffee on Monday and drank from it the rest of the week. I don't remember how long it lasted, but after that I couldn't tolerate "stale" coffee ever again.

The checks started to come in and this was non-taxed money. We had money in the bank! Out came the IUD and the pressure was on. If there was ever a woman born to be a mother, it was Dolly. She wanted a baby and that was that. Except for the rigors and stress of medical school, this would be a rather pleasant project, but at the time it felt more like additional work. Every month she got her period was a disaster. To her it seemed like forever, but soon she was pregnant, and all was well. She had typical morning sickness, but otherwise did well, except for the "dreams."

In our trailer park, our trailers were thirty to forty feet apart. You really didn't hear much from the neighbor's trailer. Throughout the pregnancy, Dolly would have these disturbing cat dreams where a cat would be attacking her. Awakening from a sound sleep, it would take me a couple seconds to figure out what was going on. At the beginning, I would try to shake her awake. But when I touched her, she perceived that as the cat biting or getting ahold of her and she would scream louder. She was always in a deep sleep and it was very difficult to awaken her. After trying everything else, I resorted to a crisp slap on the face and she would awaken. It never left a mark but seemed the only thing that worked.

The worst part of these events was the intensity of the screams. We're talking blood curdling, full-volume screams you might hear in a life-threatening situation. How did the neighbors not hear that? Why aren't the police coming? The trailer had to have been more soundproof than I thought possible, thank goodness. The screams did not last long, but it seemed like an eternity at the time.

The rest of the pregnancy was pretty routine. We were preparing the smallest bedroom for a nursery. Every trailer wall had medium brown paneling which was okay, but not for the baby's room. My mother was a wall-paperer and she had taught me the basics on an occasion when I was sick in high school. To make paneling look "realistic" there were shallow vertical groves to resemble the joints between planks. I had to use joint compound to make the walls smooth. We chose a bright yellow Raggedy Ann and Andy wallpaper. In 1976, you didn't learn the sex of the baby until it was born. With that wallpaper, we were ready for any outcome. We went to a remnant store to find some carpet. I think the room was six feet by eight feet. They had a perfect kaleidoscope-colored piece of shag carpet that I installed. This baby was going to be stimulated! The room was ready and now we needed furniture.

We found a "deal" that included a bassinette on removable rockers that could convert into a swanky baby carriage with four large wheels. The same wheels could hold the high chair seat and be used as a fancy stroller. The high chair seat attached on top of a table that could later be used as a desk and chair. If you bought the whole set for $800.00 (I think) you got a good quality wooden crib "for free." The scholarship money was a godsend and we were ready to buy.

By that time my Vega was high in mileage and burning oil. We bought a new car, for which we paid cash. We ordered a persimmon color with a brown vinyl top, 1975 Oldsmobile Cutlass S that came with a ridiculously powerful V-8 engine. I remember shaking as I wrote the check for $4,700.00. Dolly wanted air-conditioning, and I relented, if she agreed to work another month before delivery. By then, Dolly had gotten her dream job in the nursery and an extra month of that would be tolerable. It worked out well because she ended up being three weeks late! We had to wait six weeks, but the car was beautiful and best of all it had that new-car smell I so dearly loved for the rest of my life. About the same time, we added a second vehicle for about $300.00. It was a Dodge Rambler that had been a state car. It was big and light gray with a poor paint job covering the bureau information that had appeared on the front doors. It ended up being pretty reliable for a few years.

I tried to schedule rotations without on-call obligations for the time around delivery. My mother offered to come stay with us starting about two weeks before the due date. She was there for six weeks, but without my Dad, she was a pleasure. I demanded a "meatloaf" moratorium, but I'm sure we ate our share of overcooked meat that six weeks.

What do you do when you are in the last trimester of pregnancy in January-March of a Pennsylvania winter? Our answer was to bake every dessert for which we had a recipe. Cookies, cakes, pies—we could have started our own bakery. Of course, we all gained weight, but it was relatively minor.

Around late-1975, I had my obstetrics rotation at Harrisburg Hospital. You generally only got to observe, but you had to take call and do history and physicals. We had a thirtyish black female who was in to deliver her fourth baby. She had deep vein thrombosis (DVT-blood clots) of one leg for which she was being treated. We didn't even think she was in labor, but she started to feel some pressure. The nurse called me to check her. The patient was in no distress, and as I turned to get some gloves she yelled, "Whoa" and a baby shot out of her vagina, lying facedown in a small lake of bloody liquid. Surprisingly, I calmly turned the baby over and cleared its mouth as it began to cry. I always counted that as my first delivery. I only had one delivery in med school, but did pick up some early experience, checking for dilation which would come in handy.

Dolly had the usual Braxton-Hicks contractions of late pregnancy, but as we got closer to her due date, they became rather severe. We knew the first baby would likely be a long delivery, but we had ten miles to drive and didn't want to tempt fate. Her mother had twelve full-term deliveries at home and quietly accomplished the feat without waking the other children.

When Dolly had contractions, we would time them. If they were regular and eight to ten minutes apart, we would go to the hospital. On two occasions, we made the trip, but she was checked and sent home with a diagnosis of Braxton-Hicks. I'm sure that happened to a lot of young couples, but it was embarrassing for a third-year medical student and an OB/GYN nurse. I picked up several pairs of gloves and more chux pads (disposable absorbent pads). She had to sit on a chux pad in the car. I didn't want her water breaking on my new car seats! From then on, if she had contractions, I checked her myself and made sure she was dilating before we made the final trip to the hospital.

We were admitted on March 23, 1976 but our bundle of joy didn't arrive until March 24, 1976. We had taken Lamaze classes, which were becoming pretty popular. We went to the hospital with my mother in tow. Dolly was three centimeters dilated, as I predicted, and she was admitted. We think the whole process was about twenty-three hours. "He" was pretty traumatized with low Apgar scores (scoring the health of the baby) and a head like the "Coneheads" on *Saturday Night Live*—except his was bruised. Otherwise it was a difficult but not atypical first delivery.

Jason was a spoiler. Comfortable in his psychedelic bedroom, he nursed well and started sleeping through the night within about two weeks. He drenched his homemade diapers. Disposable diapers had not been readily available, or we couldn't afford them. From a bolt of flannel, we cut and sewed twelve dozen reusable hour glass shaped diapers. He had a stool in the nursery then nothing for a week. A lay person might think "Yea, my baby doesn't poop." To a third-year medical student it's, "Oh no! He has Hirschsprung's disease." That is a baby born without all the nerves needed in the rectum to push stool out. We used the family practice clinic for our pediatric care and made an urgent appointment. His exam was normal, and we were told to watch a few more days. *Abracadabra*—a nine-day poop. He settled into a predictable seven-day schedule—"Yea, our baby poops once a week!"

29. A NEW NORMAL

Just like any new family, we had to adjust to our new normal. The baby care was a mild learning curve, and Jason was pretty easy. He religiously took two naps a day and slept through the night. I was a hands-on dad—still fairly rare in the 1970s.

School was going well, and I continued my pattern of "I don't want to do that." My path finally became clear: family medicine. It fit my overall personality as a jack of all trades and a master of none. In your early senior year, you had to decide on a residency to pursue and submit an application for multiple sites (you had to find the time to visit the designated hospitals and decide if each was a good fit.) Simultaneously, the hospital was deciding if the student was a good choice for its program.

The students and hospitals each developed a ranking list and then on a given day, the lists were reconciled, and they announced the "match." You may get one of your requests or you may be un-matched, the worst of all.

Fortunately, I got my first request, which was Conemaugh Valley Memorial Hospital in Johnston, Pennsylvania. It was a medium-sized program with six slots and had two rural satellite offices. I thought I wanted to do rural family medicine, I'm not sure why.

Conemaugh Valley had about 600 beds, and its family medicine residency was well established. The hospital had been well funded in the past by the then-thriving steel companies. It had a well-organized student relations office that arranged and paid for the student's move, local housing, furniture (if needed) and utility bills. The take-home pay was maybe a little less, but the pre-tax perks were great! Residency would start July 1, 1977.

I had the fourth year to finish, and there was a required research project. I had no interest in research. Some students got positions with ongoing laboratory experiments and did their thesis on that. I chose the clinical option and decided to do a paper on paraplegic rehabilitation and maintenance of achieved goals. During my Harmarville days, once the patients were discharged, I never saw them again. I developed a follow-up questionnaire about independence with ADLS (activities of daily living), time ambulating (if possible) etc. Instinctively I thought they might get lazy, and many did.

I submitted my thesis proposal, and it was accepted and sponsored by the Family Practice Department. Next, I had to find a set of patients. Rehab was done locally at the Polyclinic Hospital in Harrisburg. I got permission to collect cases from their files and then made a plan to visit each patient at home. The paper was no masterpiece but gave me a chance to see how these people adapted to a life-changing incident. Dolly would go with me before Jason was born. Just like everyone else, the patient would take the path of least resistance. Quicker is better and the laborious braces and crutches/walkers soon were cast aside. Later I would learn this was part of the healing process. My rotations were relatively easy, and we were cruising toward graduation. The government would do the moving and we were assigned to a two-bedroom townhouse in the Richland section of Johnstown. It was called the Birch of Wallace. We were "moving on up."

We got a buyer for our trailer and ended up with $1000.00 profit. Not bad for a four-year-old trailer. A single guy lived there for probably the next thirty years. Just before the trailer was dismantled, our youngest child got to tour the "palace" and the wallpaper and shag carpet were still there!

Jason was doing well and hit his milestones on time. In fact, he walked at ten months. The trailer had a step-up dining room and kitchen. which posed a considerable problem when he began to crawl and walk. He would get up just fine but took many tumbles down that four-inch step. Fortunately, it was carpeted and he didn't really get hurt. To lessen the trauma, we would make a fuss and clap when he recovered without crying. It might not have been our greatest parental moment, but we thought we were doing him a favor.

30. THE DARK NIGHT TURNED BLACK

The move went pretty smoothly. The mover packed and delivered us to Birch of Wallace. There were some toddlers in the complex and a very nice sixty-year-old lady next door, relieved to have dull, quiet, non-partying neighbors. There was a swimming pool and the apartment was comfortable for three.

We had a couple weeks to exhale, but money was still tight and with a one-year-old, we couldn't be involved in much. Richland occupies high ground above the city of Johnstown. It had a relatively new mall and most of the retail area was in Richland.

The hospital was a ten- to fifteen-minute ride down the hill to Franklin Street. Conemaugh was one of three hospitals in Johnstown and was the largest. Mercy Hospital was right next door, and we had no involvement there. Lee Hospital was located on the flats of Johnstown. There was a power struggle between the hospitals to which we were oblivious.

When CT scanners first came into existence, they were distributed regionally. I don't know how the competition was conducted or its rules. Lee Hospital (the smallest) was awarded the CT scanner and it was just coming on line around July 1, 1977.

Conemaugh, like many hospitals, was a maze of interconnected buildings, built in different years. The complex spanned two blocks along steep Franklin Street. There was a parking building in the center. The hospital acquired a nursing facility on the other side of the parking garage and connected it to the main hospital with an enclosed walkway—only on the fourth floor. This large and somewhat inconvenient structure would add physical stress to the mental stress awaiting.

Learning medicine in a residency was challenging, rewarding, terrifying, and exhausting, at least for the overachiever. You felt like you mastered all of medicine in medical school. In truth, you spent the last four years learning some basics, deduction, and organization. You really didn't know much of anything before residency. *Poof!* One day you are a student gliding along, then *Poof*, the next day you are the person who does the admission, formulates a diagnosis, writes the orders, and manages the care, with a responsible attending.

On July 1,1977 I was assigned to general medicine with Dr. Clyde Harriger and a second-year family practice resident—Rob Martsoff. Dr. Harriger always had a large hospital practice and was very well respected. He had the ability to remember tons of facts about patients, their relatives, and their family dynamics. He always had a serious face and a dry sense of humor. Each new resident would hear the same talk, "You only order what you need, don't kill the patient, and don't order them Percocet." He explained that even then, Percocet was the most addicting opioid and people on it would call him any time of the day or night to get it. It was all sage advice.

We (Rob and I) would admit patients and present them to Dr. Harriger as we rounded on all of his twenty-plus patients in the hospital. He would make only necessary suggestions as he gauged our level of competence. He became more comfortable with us and all was going well.

On July 19, 1977, I was home and a very strong breeze began to blow. It was about 10:00 P.M. and was already dark. As I went to close the front door, I noticed an almost perfect line of intense darkness overtaking the normal night sky. I remember thinking, "That's weird." I had early rounds the next day, so I was going to bed. All of a sudden, it began to pour, and the most intense thunder and lightning began, which was relentless. It looked like midday, and the lightning was the sun. We couldn't sleep. I got up and went down to the living room. The power went out but seeing outside was easy. Between our building and the next was a yard, which had a huge storm drain in the middle. Water was backing up and was about one to two inches below the threshold of our patio door. I went around getting things off the floor. I thought one of our other buildings had power, so I decided to call and report our power out. The operator said, "Get off the phone. Don't you know we're having a major disaster?" We had no idea what was happening around us.

Johnstown sits in the bottom of a of bowl surrounded by some of the highest peaks of the Appalachian Mountains. This storm settled into the "bowl" and dumped twelve inches of rain in twenty-four hours. Many of the local dams and flood control measures overflowed and the Laurel Run Dam failed, releasing a tidal wave that swept over Tanneryville and killed forty-one out of the total eighty-four deaths. Downtown Johnstown had six feet of water. People described manhole covers shooting from the ground due to the overwhelmed drainage pipes.

I wasn't sure what to do but eventually ended up at the local fire station with Dr. Harriger and his black bag. There was no route open to the hospital and there wouldn't be for several days. All of a sudden, the ambulances began to arrive with these muddy, tree-like objects. "We need these people pronounced." I hadn't had to do that yet, and I'm sure I looked scared and per-plexed. "Just check their pupils and feel for a pulse—they're dead." It was really a formality, but it had to be done before tak-ing them to the makeshift morgue at another site. Dr. Harriger just happened to be the emergency response medical director for Cambria County and would be tied up at this site and others for the next two weeks.

The dead patients turned out to be the easiest. People started arriving with lacerations and fractures and we had very little supplies. Dr. Harriger had some xylocaine, sutures, and alcohol in his bag, but it was no ER. I had to try to clean wounds with soap and water, anesthetize the area with needles that were too large, and close with sutures of inappropriate sizes. A visible frac-ture would get a homemade splint and a prescription for an x-ray to be done later.

Most people were in shock, but stable. Some were so trauma-tized we had to try to sedate them and we did what we could with a small supply of Phenobarbital. Everyone wanted to tell their story, but we had to keep things moving. I would get sent home late in the evening, after an emotionally and physically exhausting day. There was a large strip mall near us, and its parking lot was converted to a helicopter landing pad. The noise generated seemed to be continuous. I remember thinking, "In a small way, this must be what it's like in Vietnam." You just couldn't rest at night. Miraculously, our second child was conceived during this time. Dolly must have taken advantage of me during a nap or something. I just couldn't conceive that we conceived!

On day three, we found a circuitous route to the hospital, which took about forty-five minutes. Rob and I met at the hospital and proceeded to diagnose, admit, treat, and discharge patients ourselves for two weeks. Nobody died, I was learning fast, and Rob was an excellent working supervisor. The learning process was accelerated and was truly invaluable. Without the disaster, it would have taken me much longer to sharpen my history and physical, diagnostic and treatment skills.

The remnants and scars from that night would last a lifetime for those who suffered the most. In our residency program we had to do an increasing amount of outpatient work. First-year residents had one half day in outpatient. Mine was Friday afternoon and was truly a blessing. We had an excellent female pediatrician who worked to precept with residents and that gave us better than average pediatric skills. We also had a young male psychiatrist there on Friday afternoons. We opened our normally structured office to serve as a walk-in clinic. There were people needing primary care, and it was a great learning experience. We used the hospital's social service department to try to arrange psychosocial follow-up and help for the patients. Each had a more harrowing story than the previous patient, and it was important to give each the time to tell his or her story.

Dr. Harriger returned, assessed our work and commended us for a good job in his absence. We resumed a more normal schedule by August of 1977. I was doing my individual morning rounds in D-Wing (previously a nursing home) when this eighty-plus, petite, pleasant patient reached under her bed and pulled out a six-pack of beer, "See what my grandson brought his grammy?" she proudly announced. I was about to launch into a lecture about hospital rules, and consumption of alcohol when I suddenly saw the bigger picture. Everyone was trying to adapt to a new normal. She was medically improving and happy—I could let this slide. You picked your battles every day and this was not battle-worthy. If the nurse found and confiscated the beer, I would support the nurse. It was the patient's lucky day.

31. SHARPENING SKILLS AND EXPANDING THE FAMILY

When you look back on it, your medical learning really started in residency. It was scary, overwhelming, and inspiring. Every disease you encountered was one you would remember for the nuances of presentation, its severity, the treatment course, and the progression to recovery. Each case was a new chapter in your own private text book. "How did the story develop? How sick did the patient look? How were the vital signs at presentation? What did the labs show? How do you pick the right medication? Does this need to be hospitalized or treated as an outpatient?" While you were learning all of this, you needed to develop some confidence in proceeding alone, a method to interact with the attending (in a timely fashion) and an ability to interact with patients to develop their confidence in you.

At the age of twenty-six, you appear too young to be knowledgeable. Many patients wanted to use my first name to converse. I respectfully would ask them to address me as Dr. Kelly. We needed to establish a hierarchy so they would be more inclined to accept my suggestions. You don't want these people to be your friends, but your patients. I maintained the "Dr. Kelly" rule through to retirement. Much of what we had to ask of the patients was unpleasant. As a doctor, your authority would give the issues weight. As a friend, it would make treatment harder. Some of the patients would ask, "What's your first name?" And I would answer, "Doctor!"

Being a good first-year resident is like being a high-wire artist. You need to be independent, aggressive, and a quick study. To keep your balance, you must be cautious, practical about your ability, and willing to learn from anybody. The wise resident knew the nurses had a wealth of knowledge and liked to teach. The more receptive you were, the more they would guide you and have your back. Having worked in the nursing world, I had respect for what they had to offer. After all, they are the front line and know more about any given patient than the doctor. Conversely, if the nurse is new and eager to learn, it was well worth your time to educate them. That always paid dividends. As their mentor, you earned respect, referrals, and excellent care for your patient. The nurses had their own cast of characters who were quite entertaining.

After my three months with Dr. Harriger, I had a month of ER work. Conemaugh's ER was usually not as busy as a large city ER, but there were plenty of cases. There were usually only two or three physicians on any shift. It was unique in that an attending was there all the time. You would approach them with questions, but mostly with a diagnosed patient and a plan of care, be it hospitalization or prescriptions and discharge. Most of the ER work belonged in the doctor's office, but due to convenience, would end up in the ER. It quickly became clear that the most important qualities were organization, decision-making, and thoroughness. I was pretty good in all of those areas, and the nurses again would respond favorably. If you quickly saw and evaluated the sore ankle, ordered the studies needed and moved on—the nurses would organize the studies, anticipate your needs, prepare the procedures and keep you moving and productive.

One problem universally hated in the ERs was the nosebleed. The most common was the anterior nosebleed, which occurred on the septum and was stopped by applying pressure. Sometimes they required prolonged pressure, which was accomplished by packing the nose, which was painful, time-consuming, and variably successful. In 1977, we still had liquid cocaine, which was an excellent anesthetic and vasoconstrictor (to stop the bleeding).

It was a slow afternoon and a product detail person brought in a new catheter that could be inserted in the nose and blown up to stop the bleeding. There was a longer, larger balloon to cover the anterior bleed and a smaller posterior balloon to put pressure on the even more dreaded posterior nose bleed, which commonly couldn't be seen. You could use a balloon on each side for particularly difficult cases.

As luck would have it, a bad nosebleed came in that evening. The nurses and I were anxious to try the new treatment. I put a catheter on one side and blew it up. Momentarily the bleeding stopped then started from the other side of the nostril. We put a second catheter in and things went well for a few minutes. The patient said he could feel blood going down his throat and indeed it was—indicating a posterior bleed component. I blew up the posterior balloons and the bleeding stopped. We were preparing to discharge the patient with an appointment to see the ENT doctor the next day. I went into the cubicle with discharge papers and prescriptions. There sat the patient, when suddenly blood started to trickle out of each eye and down his cheeks! I was transfixed. Surely this was a religious moment. I stood there, silently staring and feeling a mixture of religious wonderment and helplessness. One of the seasoned, middle-aged nurses stood behind me and quickly, but "sanctimoniously" questioned, "Remember the nasolacrimal duct?—DOCTOR." The "Doctor" part was a little snide, with a chuckle. Each eye has a small duct which connects with the nose for drainage of tears. It's the reason your nose may run if you're crying. If all other routes are blocked, the blood can back up through the duct and flow down the cheeks. The nurse already called the ENT doctor, and I explained the situation. The surgeon came in to surgically manage my "religious" situation. The nurse was in stitches, yet I was able to give a coherent explanation to the patient. I thanked the nurse for the anatomy reminder and we all had a good laugh.

I later did a lot of moonlighting in Conemaugh's ER, and that particular nurse and I became friends. We were both working one evening when an ambulance arrived with a girl who had been assaulted by her boyfriend. I went into the cubicle to evaluate her. A few minutes later, out of the corner of my eye, I saw a tangle of bodies fly by me. Apparently, the boyfriend snuck in the ambulance door and was about to clobber me from behind. My good buddy saw him and picked him up and pinned him against the back wall. I can still see his legs kicking and hear the expletives flying until our security arrived. Not only was she smart, but strong—and once again she "had my back." I'm sure she no longer survives. I hope God had a special place for her, she deserved it.

We didn't get a lot of violent trauma, but we got our share. The third-year resident and I heard there was an ambulance in route with a sexual assault victim. He told me to take it for the educational purpose. The ambulance arrived with a white female in her fifties who was a little messed up but overall in minor discomfort. She explained she was returning home from work. She was walking over a small dark bridge, when she could sense she was being followed. She turned around, was attacked, and knocked to the ground. Her assailant told her not to scream, but the pain was horrifying. He finished and left.

I was doing her abdominal exam and she seemed pretty uncomfortable. There was no rape kit but a list of things to obtain. Next, I had to do a pelvic exam with the speculum. She was in the stirrups and we began. I expected this would be quick and simple as she had a vaginal hysterectomy and should have a blind pouch remaining. I started the visual exam and couldn't immediately interpret what I was seeing. This pink and blue hose-like structure kept appearing. "OMG that's small bowel!" I thought to myself. I left to retrieve the resident who was sure I was overreacting. He looked, turned pale, and said, "Call the gynecologist!" The man had thrust so forcefully, he tore open the five-year-old incision at the end of her vagina. She required emergency surgery and multiple antibiotics to protect her from infection. She did okay. I don't know if her rapist was ever caught.

On the other end of the spectrum was the ridiculous. One afternoon an ambulance pulled in with a fifteen-year-old young lady who was dramatically in some distress. I went to get a history and found her complaint to be "I get such bad cramps with my period and I want it all to stop." Incredulously, I turned to her mother who told me she was so hysterical at home she didn't know what to do, so she called the ambulance. After satisfying myself and the attending that she had no emergency needs, she was discharged home with instructions to see her PCP. This was likely a weekend day, but clearly an emergency room and ambulance abuse.

As a first-year resident, every case was a learning experience. We had a unique situation in Johnstown, in that a large part of the community was supported by mining. We had a large contingent of end-stage COPD patients who would arrive in bad respiratory distress. We had a set of rooms in the back corridor just for them. They would have to be evaluated for infection, but once cleared of that, they would go to the holding room while they got their "cocktail" of aminophylline (rarely used now) and a steroid—like solumedrol. Usually one or two bags would stabilize them, but they had to be administered at a controlled rate, which might take eight to ten hours. We could loosely monitor them in the back while continuing to see more acute patients out front. The objective was to avoid putting them on a ventilator because commonly they would not survive weaning from the ventilator.

Working there was a learning experience about danger in the emergency room. When really busy, we would use the COPD rooms for stable acute patients. We had a white male, in his forties, who was found collapsed on the sidewalk. I did an assessment and could only find that he passed out from being drunk. We started an IV for hydration and put him in the back. Later I went to check on him and found him dressed and removing his IV. He wasn't sober enough to leave, and I was trying to convince him to stay. Somehow, we became positioned with him between me and the door. He wasn't a happy camper, and the next thing I saw was him removing a switch blade from his boot and flicking it open. Great! I'm about to get stabbed and I'm back here alone. Then he put the blade under his arm band and cut it off. Danger averted, but lesson learned: don't let crazed patients get between you and the door.

Having been a male aide, I was exposed to all the indignities of care. I had cleaned up urine, fecal, and vomiting messes and wasn't fazed by much of anything. There was one case that almost made me vomit and pass out. A fifty-year-old white male presented with a chief complaint of pain in the roof of his mouth and trouble breathing. On exam, his tonsils were so swollen, they touched each other. I had seen that in myself and other patients but there was more. He had a lot of swelling in his soft palate which is near the tonsils and behind the roof of the mouth. I reported my findings to the attending and he agreed we had to call the ENT doctor. Dr. ENT came in, and asked me to assist with a procedure. I was to manage the suction and hold a retractor. Dr. ENT had a headlamp and proceeded to use a scalpel to slice open the swollen soft palate. Immediately there was a "tsunami" of extremely foul-smelling pus pouring into the mouth and down the throat. My large suction couldn't begin to keep it cleaned up.

The patient felt pain, then immediate relief because the pressure was released and he could breathe easier. I was able to stay for the whole procedure, but it left an indelible memory for life.

On the home front, Dolly was busy taking care of an active toddler and becoming very pregnant with our second child. She had a lot of nausea with that pregnancy and she was prescribed Bendectin, which she used sparingly. We moved from Birch of Wallace in January of 1978. Dolly had found a cute three-bedroom house about a quarter mile away, and the hospital was willing to rent it for us. It was a small ranch in very good shape. It had been home to our landlord's parents. Dolly's brother and sister-in law were bringing a rental truck and the weather was awful. I had been on call and hardly made it home in all the snow. I figured we would have to reschedule when all of a sudden, the truck appeared. We loaded it up and made the short trip to the new house. Rob and Donna (my resident buddy and his wife) helped with Jason and the move.

There's not much to do in Johnstown in winter, so we got settled in pretty quickly. Before we knew it, the second pregnancy was about to end. Dolly was two weeks late with this one and again, we didn't know the gender of the baby. We had a much more subtle nursery for this one. I was working when Dolly called and said she needed to come to the hospital. We got her settled in, and the nurses decided they would give her an enema, since it would be awhile. I went to the snack bar to get a quick burger. I no sooner started to eat and I heard "Dr. Kelly stat to OB." I ran up to the delivery floor, and she was starting to push. My least favorite obstetrician was manning the floor and didn't believe the nurses when they told him she was ready to deliver. We both got there in time and Matthew Charles Kelly was born April 27, 1978. I called my father to tell him, and before I could tell him he said, "I suppose it's another boy." He never disappointed. I'll give him this: he was a good grandfather to all the grandchildren. He saved his patience for the next generation. Lucky them.

Matthew was the polar opposite of Jason. He was a poor sleeper, crapped liquid poop several times a day, and was very territorial concerning his mother. At about six to seven months, Dolly had to isolate herself when she nursed him. If I walked by, he would stop nursing and glare at me. That was his "mommy time," and it wasn't to be interrupted. Had he been the first child, we might have waited longer to have a second. He liked to scream at 3:00 A.M. and would only settle down if you faced him toward the television and rocked him. On the nights I was home, I would take my turn so Dolly could sleep. I was usually so sleep-deprived from the previous on-call night, I was afraid I would drop him or fall on top of him. When you're young, you are more resilient.

That was the busiest time of my life and unfortunately, I was absent for much of his childhood. Dolly picked up the slack, and he turned out to be the most devilish of the children. I didn't feel my absence was the cause!

Through all these experiences, the river was developing its own unique course and continued its uphill climb.

32. I GOT MY LICENSE!

At the end of your internship (now known as the first year of residency) you had to pass part three of the national medical boards. This test covers any topics in medicine and those who maximized their exposure would usually pass. We had to go to a testing center and the closest was the University of Pittsburgh. One of my best friends in medical school was doing her pediatrics residency at Children's Hospital of Pittsburgh. She was taking her test in Oregon and offered her apartment for me and the other residents to use while in Pittsburgh. After the boards part one debacle, I reasonably had concerns.

I never felt confident about passing, but I did well. Technically, I could have started to practice when the license arrived, but the two additional years of residency would prove invaluable.

We had a small crisis at this point. We should have had six residents from the beginning, but we only had five. One of the residents decided to switch to an OB/GYNE residency. Another one of the residents left to enter private practice. Now we had three second-year residents left. Second year is very busy. The six new first-year residents had to be monitored and a second-year resident had to be in the hospital every night for backup. Third-year residents traditionally would take call from home. We had three residents to cover the work of six—being on call every third night! I took it upon myself to create an on-call schedule that would have a third-year resident take one night of call every fourth night. Doesn't sound like much, but having to stay over-night every fourth instead of every third night would help prevent burnout. I composed a witty, guilt laden poem about the third-year residents and their lack of empathy. Surprisingly and happily, they agreed with the on-call compromise. They were a pretty good bunch of guys, and we were eternally grateful.

There were six incoming first-year residents. Our residency used a team approach. Two first-year, one second-year, and two third-year residents were a team. We would cover each other for vacations. This was particularly important for our "private" out-patients. When you saw a new outpatient, you would be their doctor until you graduated. If you were away, one of your team-mates would see them, if needed. The first-year residents had one half day in the office. The second-year residents had three half days and the third-year residents had five half days. It not only broadened the learning experience, it provided continuity, and it gave you the opportunity to learn to practice with others who had their own individual styles.

I lucked out and got two of the brightest and mature first-years. We got along great and would continue to be friends long after—for the rest of our careers. Their group of six contained some real characters who needed shepherding.

I was the second-year backup on a pediatrics rotation with a first-year resident whose confidence was not in line with his ability. We had a sick baby who needed a spinal tap. The key to success was having a nurse secure the baby in a ball formation, carefully marking your target and putting the needle into the proper level of the spine. The first-year set up the procedure, but we were missing some items. I told him to prep the patient, but wait for me to return before inserting the needle. His confidence told him to proceed without me. I returned with the additional supplies in time to witness bright red blood shooting out of the needle. I pushed him aside and saw he wasn't in the center of the back. He likely hit the aorta or some other artery. We removed the needle and applied pressure and monitored the baby until it seemed stable. Then he had to start from scratch, mark his spot (with my guidance) and this time successfully entered the spinal canal and collected the spinal fluid.

When we were done, we had a very necessary talk about following instructions, his inflated ego, and how he would personally monitor this baby for the next twelve hours. He was scared (and so was I), but the baby did well and that day marked a correction in the resident's pathway to doom. He had to talk to and confess to the parents what had happened. He had to own his mistake. There were no repercussions. I learned that the "hotshots" could be corralled, and in the future, I worried less about them and more about the ones who hadn't made their mistake—yet. We all made mistakes, but you prayed they were minor and you had to learn from them. "First, do no harm."

33. DELIVERING BAD NEWS

During medical school, we had a class on Death and Dying. We learned about the stages a dying patient may go through. That was valuable information. We never discussed how you approach families with news of a tragedy.

I was working the ER at Conemaugh when I was faced with delivering bad news. The ambulance arrived with a middle-aged, very thin black woman who had been in a motor vehicle accident. There was no CPR being done, and it soon became apparent why. The unfortunate lady had a long thin neck with an obvious fracture/dislocation. The neck was horribly flexed to the side and death would have been instantaneous. Her car was T-boned and the force caused a whiplash type injury. The head would have whipped from side to side and the long thin neck was not able to stabilize the force of the head movement. The family was on the way.

It probably was a fifteen to twenty-minute wait, but it seemed a lot longer. I had witnessed a couple of events where the attending or resident delivered death news to a family. In both instances, the patients had been in the hospital and profoundly ill. In that scenario, families began to prepare themselves for bad news, but it was always a shock. I was not prepared for this particular scenario.

The victim's husband arrived at a most inappropriate time. The ER was full, every room, and I needed to deliver the news. I tried to find a secluded corner and told him she was dead on arrival. I was about to explain that the actual event would have been instantaneous, when he ran away, screaming and crying, going from room to room trying to find her. I had to physically grab him with the help of a nurse, and usher him to where the body was located. We had her covered, out of respect and because the appearance of the neck dislocation was quite gruesome. Against our counsel, he demanded to see her and the sight set off another episode of wailing. He attempted to run through the ER, but the nurse and I had ahold of his arms and we guided him to a chair. What can you say to ease their pain? He was in shock and likely not able to focus on my words. It is somewhat comforting to know they didn't suffer, but that is only a part of the big picture. The husband suddenly and unexpectedly lost a wife, lover, mother of his children, and maybe wage earner for the household. He needed some support and we wanted the name of another family member. He gave us the victim's sister's name. The nurse called and asked her to come to the hospital for an emergency. We moved the victim and patient to a room with a door. You desperately try not to deliver a death notice over the phone. The sister arrived and the previous scenario repeated. It was the ultimate trauma for the family, but it took a toll on those delivering the news. You question if you chose the best way to deliver the news. How could you have made it easier for the family? Some people react drastically. Others will cry and sob and want to sit down.

There are times the family is too far away or has no transportation, and you have to tell them over the phone. You can try to request another number of a loved one who can tell them. If all else fails, you can ask the police to check on them, and find someone to be with them. Then there's the need to ask for a funeral home, etc., so the body can be removed. It was a complicated process.

34. AM I IN BRIGADOON?

Having my medical license opened up additional financial opportunities outside of residency. At about that time, a central Pennsylvania hospital decided they had to expand to a 24-hour/day emergency room. We'll call it "Brigadoon General." Previously, the ER was open, but no physician was on site. There was an on-call doctor who would be contacted to arrive and handle the situation. Life in rural hospitals was very different. A management company was hired to find 24-hour/day physician coverage. They contacted the residency for volunteers to work 12-hour shifts for $25/hr. That was a fortune for those carrying student loans and receiving minimal salaries for residency.

Dolly and I sat down and discussed if we could handle this. We had a two-year-old and a newborn at home. If Dolly went back to work, she couldn't begin to match that income and we would have major child care expenses. Because we had furnished housing, we were unprepared for our next move—to our own home. At this point, I was on in-hospital call every four days and the available shifts were 7:00 P.M.-7:00 A.M. If I did the extra work, it would all be profit—no child-care expenses or juggling two people's schedules. One person, two schedules and $300 a pop. We gave it a name—moonlighting units or MUs. I wanted/needed a piano which, new, cost $800.00 or 3 MUs. I could buy a new piano! It was a no-brainer. I figured we would need about $6,000-$8,000 to buy furniture for a house. The downside was being away from the family, working on less sleep and more child care responsibilities for Dolly. This was a bridge to economic stability.

I signed up and was approved to start. My first shift was "epic" to say the least. During the first two to three hours, we saw some colds and other minor issues. Then we got a call there was a car accident, and several ambulances were in route. "Trauma Centers" were just being established, and there weren't any nearby.

I was working with one RN—period. She had to do the intake (including insurance information), and provide nursing care for the patients. The x-ray and lab techs were on call from home. It was literally the two of us.

The ambulances arrived carrying six black patients from South Carolina. They were very poor and undereducated. The two adults literally did not know how old they were. The four children ranged from six to thirteen years old. The thirteen-year-old had been driving. Seat belts were just beginning to appear, and their old car had none.

The adrenaline was high, and we quickly got organized. Post-it notes had just arrived and with pad in hand, each patient was assessed. On the Post-it, I wrote the labs and x-rays needed. The Post-its were pinned to their pillow. The nurse had already called lab and x-ray, and they were on their way. Everyone seemed stable, but they had broken arms and legs and lacerations but no obvious abdominal trauma. The thirteen-year-old girl had a minor head laceration, but she also had unequal pupils—a finding which can be ominous. The patient's parents could not tell me if it had been present previously. We did a skull x-ray on her and collected all the other patients' labs and x-rays. This took several hours. Next, I called the surgeon on-call to re-evaluate, treat, and admit the patients.

I called Dr. R. U. Forreal and awakened him from sleep. I began to give him a synopsis of the patients and almost immediately heard snoring on the other end of the phone. This was a landline, and the only phone in the home! I looked at the nurse and she said, "I'll call the police." The police had to drive to his house and awaken him to come to the hospital. Apparently, this "wake-up" had been needed on many previous occasions.

I had done my own triage and decided the thirteen-year old's unequal pupils were problem #1. This small hospital had one X-ray view box in the ER, and her first skull film was ready to read. Everyone had to read their own X-rays until the radiologist did the official reading in the morning.

Dr. Forreal showed up, had no interest in my concerns, and picked up other leg and arm X-rays. Every time he took a film down, I put the thirteen-year old's skull X-ray back up. He would set it aside with total disinterest! I needed to know if she required transport to Pittsburgh for care not attainable at Brigadoon General.

After several cycles of the above, I said "Please look at these skull X-rays so I can arrange transport to Pittsburgh if you think it's necessary."

As God is my witness, he turned to me with obvious disdain and said, "Don't you know black people can't fracture their skulls?"

OMG! Did he just say that to me?! My jaw dropped, and I was speechless. What is an appropriate comeback line? He ignored my question and continued his evaluation of the other X-rays. The girl was alert and stable, and all of them were at the mercy of Dr. Forreal. They disappeared into the hospital, and I never got any follow-up.

"What had I gotten myself into?" I followed protocol and they became his responsibility. The rest of the night was quiet and that was the worst night I ever had there. Sometimes you would see three to four patients and sometimes none at all thanks to nurse No Nonsense. She was a middle-aged, obese woman who knew everyone in town. Before she started the paper intake, she did a verbal assessment. You could hear her through the door. "Those are cold symptoms, not an emergency! Call your doctor in the morning." One of the town drunks would wander in, and she would be screaming, "You're just drunk. Go home and sleep it off."

The pace at Brigadoon was very variable. You might see twenty patients in a 12-hour shift, or you might see none. That wasn't common, but it would happen. I preferred to be busy. As was true of any ER, you would see the comical patients as well. A young father ran into the ER screaming, "I think my daughter swallowed a bracelet!" A pretty and scared three-year old was sobbing but was in no distress. I ordered a one film X-ray and saw the evidence.

"Did the necklace have a small heart on it?" I asked.

The father said, "Yes," as if I were psychic. It was a pretty tiny necklace and could easily take the "natural" route out of the body. I reassured the father and sent him home to "screen" for the evidence over the next several days.

Even in 1978 small-town America, there was a representative of just about any human variable you could find in a big city. A man walked in one evening and said, "I think I have a problem. There's something stuck in my ass." He didn't want to elaborate, as if not being precise would make the problem go away. After an x-ray, it was obvious what he had done. Welch's grape jelly came in a distinctively shaped jar. There it was, with a metal lid on it—out of "reach." I was glad to pass that "urgency" not "emergency" off to the surgeon on call. I did hear they used suction forceps to retrieve the evidence. Suction forceps had not been used, obstetrically, for years in most hospitals. Of course, Brigadoon General had one.

One evening, an eleven-year-old boy came in, and said he was molested. I can't remember who he accused or where it happened. There were no obvious external injuries. We took a rectal swab. It would have to be processed in Johnstown, and there was no mechanism for transport. There was a chain of possession for potential criminal evidence, so I carried it with me the rest of the shift and took it to the lab at Conemaugh Valley and signed it in. I have no follow-up of that case.

On TV, hospital sex is the norm. That was never my experience. An ER, which could be inactive for hours at a time, created an atmosphere for entertainment. There was one particular LPN who was quite proud of her exploits with one of the day doctors.

Said doctor, interestingly, had a handsome, fit "valet" to take care of his "needs." Wow, was my life with a wife and two babies dull.

Some people might consider their physician a "Guiding Light." I had the experience of being such a light. One snowy evening, I was on my way to Brigadoon General and was cautiously driving over a small stretch of straight road. I had been the only car on the road for miles when all of a sudden, a single light came from nowhere behind me, and disappeared. I really didn't think much of it until returning to Johnstown the following morning. There was a small plane parked in the median strip between the four lanes. I presumed they couldn't land at the airport, due to snowy conditions, and used my lights to guide them to a safe landing.

The river hit a section where it wound back and forth so that you could never see what lay beyond the bend.

Note: Brigadoon was a Lerner and Lowe musical about two Americans discovering a Scottish village named "Brigadoon," which rises out of the mist for one day every one hundred years.

35. "SHE'S RUNNING AROUND TOWN AND I CAN'T MAKE HER STOP!"

The residency was blessed with an excellent pediatrician and psychiatrist, who were there to teach and help with difficult cases. The pediatrician was willing to provide child care for the residents' children, and she was an excellent example of proper, compassionate care, great teaching, and patience. The psychiatrist was a young male, a little more reserved, but an excellent clinician.

My first-year office hours were Friday afternoon. I was seeing my last scheduled patient, when the receptionist got a frantic phone call from a local hair salon, that she had a lady claiming "hair pain." We were always open for new business, and this particular afternoon the psychiatrist was in the office. He heard the patient complaint and said, "I better stick around for this one."

The late middle-aged, dyed blonde white female arrived very agitated and wild eyed. We tried to get a better handle on her symptoms, but basically it was top of her head pain—just in the hair.

Her sister arrived and filled in the details. They lived together, and she had known schizophrenia since her early twenties. She was inconsistent taking her meds and would have visual and auditory hallucinations, when off the meds. Dr. Head Shrinker pulled me out of the room and gave me a tutorial on long acting, injectable antipsychotics. Prolixen came in an injection good for thirty days and we made arrangements for her to come, monthly, to the clinic for the injection. We saw her a month later and she was happy and calm and her sister was so thankful we found a medicine that handled her symptoms. Her compliance was not an issue.

Months later, I was paged for an outside call, and it was her sister calling from a pay phone. She was huffing and puffing as she said, "She's running around town, and I can't make her stop!!"

I called Dr. Head Shrinker, and he related she was having extra-pyramidal side effects. Those were a known set of symptoms, including motor restlessness (the inability to stop moving). She was otherwise doing well with the monthly injection, so he decided we should try adding Cogentin to control the side effects. It worked great.

Six months later, the patient was refusing to be seen but wanted her injection. I told them there would be no refill unless she was seen. They made an appointment, and we made several discoveries. First, the sister brought in several photos from Bell Telephone, where the patient had been a professional model. She also showed us a news clipping of her dating a former celebrity. The patient had told us these stories, and we had assumed they were delusions.

Next, the sister described that life couldn't be better. If she wanted the patient to cut the grass or clean the house, she would withhold the Cogentin, and the patient could complete these tasks in record time. If she wanted the patient to relax and watch a movie or go to church, she would give her the Cogentin.

Dr. Head Shrinker and I looked at each other and convened a "sidebar" in the hall. At first blush, this had an ominous ring to it, but on evaluating a little deeper, the sister took good care of the patient, and essentially gave up her life to help someone with a difficult illness. If she found the perfect balance for them—good for her. The patient couldn't function on her own, so the plan continued unchanged, and they both did well.

During my one medicine rotation, I was introduced to "Bob" a large, gregarious guy recently diagnosed with lymphoma. I spent a good bit of time with him and his wife explaining the disease, prognosis, and treatment. We just clicked and he asked me to be his PCP. I was thrilled. Most of my patients had no insurance and I had a good patient with good insurance.

Bob did well with his chemo and the lymphoma came under control. Unfortunately, the chemo was cardio-toxic (damaging to the heart), and he developed heart failure from an enlarged heart! His exercise tolerance was limited, but he made the best of his time. He had some background in construction and accompanied me to Punxsutawney to check out a house we would eventually buy. He pointed out good and bad findings, and was very helpful.

We loosely kept in touch because my schedule, in Punxsutawney, quickly became hectic. I got word he passed away, and Dolly and I made a trip to Johnstown to visit his wife. By then, we had our last child—a daughter who accompanied us. Bob's wife went out and bought her four of the prettiest and most expensive dresses. We were thrilled, and she told me Bob would have done the same. I learned so much from him and was always open to a father figure.

The river "matured" and settled into a steady flow. The uphill river was leveling out and we were catching a glimpse of our future.

36. FINISHING UP TRAINING AND MOVING ON

Third year residency is more about teaching, finding a practice, and studying for the Family Practice Boards. One person served as chief resident for the year and was elected by the residents, with the blessing of the director. I held that position from July 1979-June 1980. I had to assign the rotations to be sure everybody had the opportunity to graduate. I had to make, or assign someone to make the on-call schedules. I had the responsibility to assign punishment if someone was goofing up, and they did.

During the second and third year, we were assigned to a satellite clinic. The larger clinic was in Nanty Glo, which was a coal mining town about thirty minutes away. The second site was in Colver, PA—about forty-five minutes away. It was housed in an abandoned hospital called the "Miner's Clinic." The Miner's Hospital was built in 1914 by the Eastern Coal Co. It was run by Dr. Alexander Martin from 1924-1974. Conemaugh Valley arranged to use it as a teaching clinic and a feeder site for Conemaugh Valley. The "Hospital" was condemned, but they made a couple of exam rooms and a waiting area for the clinic. The associate program director, who was to be the onsite mentor, took a job elsewhere. The clinic would close unless someone would work there unsupervised, except for phone-supervision. I volunteered, and the community was ever so grateful. I saw patients, did minor ER work (like lacerations) and referred to other doctors as needed.

It was a small practice, but I treated it as my own. My most exciting patient had hemochromatosis (he made too much blood). Once a month he went to the hospital and gave a unit of blood, which they couldn't use. It was a hardship for him to take a half day off work each month. I offered to remove the blood at our clinic. He took the blood home and sprinkled it around his garden to keep the deer out.

This was when I was bargaining with the National Health Service Corps about where we would be sent to work off my commitment. Practically all the sites were just office-based clinics in rural towns. I really wanted a practice with a hospital component. I found one in Punxsutawney, PA—yes home of THE groundhog! They had just placed one physician there and felt the practice was too small for two doctors.

I visited some other clinics, but aggressively lobbied to go to Punxsutawney. What the government and I did not know, was that during that year, five local physicians died, and the doctor with the largest practice had a severe heart attack. He was never able to return to his practice. The physician already working in our clinic was inundated with new patients and needed help. Once again, the universe and God were plotting the course of the river and it aligned with my wishes. The letter finally arrived that I was assigned to Punxsutawney. Dolly and I had visited, but I don't remember meeting Dr. Bill. I found out he completed one year of internship after med school, then went to Punxsutawney thru the National Health Services Corps.

Shortly thereafter, I got an introductory call from a very young Mr. Dan. He was the director of the clinic, which had its own board of directors. He found out I was moonlighting to make extra money. He posed a scenario where I would spend the weekend in Punxsutawney, and cover the practice so Dr. Bill could get a weekend off. It was a great opportunity to explore the area, the hospital, and the patients in the practice. Dr. Bill didn't have a doctor to sign out to, so he was a medical island. We made arrangements to meet in Punxsutawney and figure out the particulars. The clinic arranged for me to have temporary privileges at the hospital.

The first words out of my mouth were, "I don't want to do deliveries," and Dr. Bill said, "Neither do I." We instantly became friends. He told me about the practice, and the clinic made me a generous offer to cover a weekend. Bill and his wife offered us their house for the weekend. They had two children and told us to bring the kids. The house was ours. We set a date and I did my first Locum Tenens (covering for another doctor).

37. CAN YOU GIVE ME A WAKE-UP CALL AT 7:00 A.M. ON SATURDAY?

The appointed weekend arrived and Dolly and I, and the two boys left for Punxsutawney after my Friday office hours. This was late winter/early spring of 1980. It was getting dark when we arrived. The house was empty, and we found the key and entered. For a short time, everything was fine. We toured the house and settled in when BANG—a transformer blew.

This was an all-electric house at the end of a lane with no other neighbors or street lights. Suddenly we were in a pitch-black house and had no idea where there were candles, matches, flashlights, etc. We fumbled around, got the kids to bed and were getting ready to sleep ourselves. Remember, no cell phones or clocks with backup batteries. You literately couldn't see your hand in front of your face. I found a land phone next to the bed and learned that phone lines had their own electric supply. I called the telephone operator to connect us to the Punxsutawney Area Hospital. I explained who I was and our electric predicament. I asked if the hospital operator could give me a wake-up call at 7:00

A.M. I wanted to be prompt on my first day of work. That seemed innocent enough.

Dolly and I both grew up in small towns, but Punxsutawney was a "rural" small town, which is a whole different animal. I arrived at the hospital with a stethoscope around my neck, ready to work. By then, I was used to walking into rural hospitals and "owning" my duties. What I wasn't ready for, was everybody knowing about my call to the operator the previous night—and I mean everyone. They only knew the new doctor used the hospital operator for a wake-up call. The power being out in a pitch-black, strange house, never entered the conversation. I'm sure the majority interpreted this as an entitled doctor, abusing hospital personnel for his own needs. After the surprise of how infamous I was, I just went to work doing patient care. They soon learned I was as far from "entitled" as you could get. The staff were very welcoming and helpful. Several patients asked, "Why are you here on a Saturday?" Apparently, the local doctors would skip weekend rounds to preserve their sanity. Dr. Bill made weekend rounds, but these were new patients. I assured them "our" patients would be seen seven days a week. Nobody was really sick, but I did admit a couple new patients. Nurses, lab techs, x-ray techs, transcriptionists, and patients got a taste of the new doctor's style. It went over well. It was predicted that Dr. Bill and I would make a good duo. I was shocked I didn't receive an alarm clock as a welcoming present.

We did several more of these weekends in the next few months. Bill and I met, and worked out a schedule we used for the next three years. One of us would be on hospital call for a whole week then end the week with a 24-hour shift in the ER. It sounded brutal and could be at times. Overall, Punxsutawney's ER was quiet, and it gave us ample time to get our sign-off ready and dictate the discharge summaries, while we were in the ER. Our regular salaries came from the federal government and were pretty small. The ER money was extra and helped.

The non-hospital person would work four and a half days in the office, finishing at noon on Friday. It allowed for a little more relaxed weekend before the week on call. We decided to incorporate the twenty-four hours in the ER for another reason. Punxsutawney is geographically in the middle of nowhere. We were closer to Erie and Altoona than Pittsburgh. It was hard to recruit doctors to work the ER, and often the hospital would get foreign-born residents with poor English and medical skills. I saw a patient who had been in the ER the previous day, with a weak arm and leg. He had drunk one beer earlier that day. The resident in the ER was from a "dry" Middle Eastern country and wrote on the chart, "The patient was drunk" and sent him home. I took one look at the patient and told him he had a stroke. I wanted to put him in the hospital. I was furious, and that resident was denied further privileges. You haven't done the work unless you addressed the patient's chief complaint.

Within the first year, Bill and I were forced to make a pact that, whoever was on call, would physically go to the ER and see all the pediatric cases. The ER doctors often had no pediatric training and did a terrible job managing pediatric cases. Our "special" care was being recognized in the community and surrounding areas. We were seeing 150-200 new patients every month and we would have 10-15 patients in the hospital all the time.

The new docs were soon getting some special attention. The hospital's women's auxiliary approached us with $20,000 (to fund a project of our choice), to improve patient care.

We were instantly on the same page. The hospital had an eight bed CCU/ICU that was well equipped. What the hospital needed was a telemetry unit, where the cardiac patients could have 24-hour heart monitoring, but were free to walk around and get stronger. I think we purchased six monitors and the hospital worked on getting more nurses trained to use them. Bill and I insisted on writing the rules for use of the telemetry unit. Both of us had seen how these beds were abused in other hospitals, and we wanted a better system. We did not have a cardiologist, pulmonologist, or nephrologist on staff.

We had to do everything ourselves, unless it was too complicated, then you prayed they were stable, and the weather was good enough to transfer them. Dubois and Indiana, Pennsylvania both had larger hospitals and more subspecialists. Punxsutawney had another unique option, which we tried and were glad to use. Two cardiologists from Shadyside Hospital in Pittsburgh had local family ties, and they each had a weekend house in the area. These gentlemen were well known and respected. One of our clinic board members was a son of the one cardiologist.

A person would present with a possible heart attack and be admitted. If they were very stable, we treated them for several days and sent them home. There was a segment of the population who wanted to go to Pittsburgh. Invariably, they would be too unstable for transport, and we would have to "stabilize" them for several days so they could go to Pittsburgh to be "saved." It was a little frustrating, but I think the cardiologists appreciated our hard work and judgment. It was a nice safety net for us.

This was the time when Allegheny General Hospital in Pittsburgh was developing a level 1 trauma center, including Life Flight—helicopter transport. The first winter in Punxsutawney, I was working in the ER, and the ambulance brought in an eleven-year-old girl from a sledding accident. I met the ambulance at the door and saw clear fluid coming from one ear of the unconscious patient. She was leaking cerebrospinal fluid. I immediately called Life Flight who was in the air before I finished the report. They arrived, picked up the patient and were in route to Pittsburgh within thirty to forty minutes of her arrival. The family were visiting relatives and were fearfully aware that Punxsutawney couldn't handle this. The girl was taken to Children's Hospital and did well. The family was so grateful, I got a huge fruit basket at Christmas for several years.

38. WE NEED A HOUSE

Making arrangements to work in Punxsutawney was infinitely easier than finding a house. The country was in the midst of a mortgage crisis, and there were very few houses on the market. Most were too small or too tacky—like shag rug on the walls. The mortgage rate was climbing daily, and we would be on a tight budget with my government salary. We finally found a four-bedroom house very close to the hospital, which a contractor had built for his family. We agreed on a price, but the closing was still a month or two away. The bank kept calling and increasing the mortgage rate. When it hit 13 percent interest, I called the bank president and told him if he didn't lock us in at 13 percent, we wouldn't make the move. He was on the hospital board and knew how badly my services were needed. He locked us in at 13 percent, while the rest of the world was at 18-19 percent. The federal government was to provide movers and working with them was the next nightmare. I had trouble getting them to commit to a date. I was to start working July 1, 1983 and wanted the move completed before that.

The date was set, but I had committed to an ER shift at Brigadoon General. We had a station wagon in which I placed our grandmother's clock, because I didn't want it damaged. Dolly had to oversee the packing and the kids.

Loading the large truck wasn't an issue and the road trip was okay. Delivery would be another issue. To get to our new house, you had to turn onto an alley-like street, then turn to descend a very steep, single lane, dirt road and then you had a choice. You could bear left and ascend a steep dirt driveway to a flat area in front of the garage. If you chose to go straight, you had to make a very, very sharp left turn and a steeper yet, incline to the garage. It was a poor man's circular driveway. For some unknown reason, the driver chose the latter and could not make it up the hill. In fact, he got hung up so bad, they had to summon a tractor trailer-sized tow truck to get it out. This was early evening and had become the town spectacle, with a sizeable crowd watching.

Dolly was furious they chose the obvious worst choice. She was afraid the van would topple over and she was trying to corral the four- and two-year-old. I was at Brigadoon General, with no idea this was occurring. The house phone had not yet been connected. After the situation was "stabilized," the movers parked the truck and didn't block the wheels. The men were walking toward the house, and the truck began to drift. Dolly told them, and fortunately they got it stopped and blocked.

Now it's pretty late, and Dolly was trying to get the boys to bed. The van driver asked if the men could sleep in the house. Dolly wisely and angrily told them "No!" She was there, alone, with two children and three men we didn't know.

After my night in the ER, I cheerfully drove to our first house in good spirits. Needless to say, I was welcomed by a sleep-deprived, angry, exhausted spouse, who had lived through the previous day's ordeal. The delivery was completed and the event was chapter two of the new doctor's noteworthy arrival.

I did a quick tour of the house and found the wood-burning stove in the basement was missing. It had a large hood above it, to send the heat into the cold air return and make the furnace more efficient. I called the realtor about the situation, and the seller took it because it had been his father's. That was not satisfactory, because it was never listed to be removed. It was used as a perk to buy that particular house. The seller offered no compromise and the realtor was useless. A new wood burner would cost me about $600.00.

I was upset, but wasn't going to add litigation to our arrival. In early 1981, the realtor contacted me about a mistake they made. The seller paid the taxes for all of 1980, and six months should have been our responsibility—about $600.00. My answer was "Good, we're even!" Karma—you gotta love it!

39. MAKING IT OURS

The house was only a few years old, but needed some finish work. The day-one project was to remove the tacky mirror tiles from the one living room wall. The seller was hurrying to finish the project before closing. He had three-quarters of it done when we toured, and we felt it would be rude to request he stop. The wall was easily repaired and I gradually repainted the entire house.

Of greater concern was the kitchen. There was an eat-in area, which was about eight inches higher than the adjacent, sunken family room. There was no railing to prevent you from falling off the edge. I went to the local lumber yard to purchase spindles, newel posts and top rail for the project. I had previously worked on some wood projects, but this was the first of many "finish" projects. It always seemed that I would fall just a little short of perfection, and the term "90 percent job" was coined. I would always share my critique with Dolly and vice versa. We decided 90 percent fit our image. LOL

While we tackled the inside, the outside needed to be maintained. It sat on an acre of very steep slopes. The slope between the driveway and the house was so steep, you literately had to crisscross that section while holding the lawn mower against the hill. I usually did all the grass cutting, but that section always had to be done by me. We bought a used Sears lawn tractor from the owner. It worked for a while, but then started to be undependable. It would always stop at the bottom of the yard and it became a common sight to see Dolly and I pushing it up the hill with Jason (the four-year-old) driving. I was forced to buy a new one. Finding the time (and dry grass to cut) was very challenging.

That "circular" driveway would obviously be a problem in the winter. Punxsutawney was close enough to the Appalachian Mountains that it got a lot of snow. I traded my car for a used Jeep Cherokee with 4-wheel drive. You had to rotate the four hubs into position before it would convert to 4-wheel drive. After all that, there were several occasions where I almost flipped it over, trying to get up the driveway. We hired someone to plow, but nothing drove well on ice.

It, too, needed service, often, and fortunately I found a local mechanic who didn't inflate the costs. It had some lap seatbelts which saved the day when Dolly was rounding a corner, and the door next to Jason flew open. Those Kellys were pretty dramatic.

40. ALWAYS "LOOK" CONFIDENT

I think I received a solid education in Johnstown, but medicine can challenge you with a seemingly infinite number of symptoms. As an overachiever, with little to no specialty backup in town, it was important to know the limits of your personal expertise and not get in over your head. Most of the serious problems occurred in the evening or night. Probably within the first month, during my on-call, a patient was admitted with a heart attack. It was my routine to go and evaluate patients admitted to the ICU/CCU, immediately. That allowed me firsthand information, because the EKG and labs were already done. Second, it reassured the family that the diagnosis was correct, and we could discuss the treatment plan.

I arrived and evaluated the EKG. Indeed, it showed signs of an MI in progress. It also showed some cardiac irritability called second-degree block. It was a sporadic finding, and I proudly shared with the nurses that this was a Wenckebach, Mobitz Type 1 rhythm. Everyone was impressed, including me. They researched my face for further guidance, and if they read it right, there was none. I was able to make the diagnosis, but had no idea about its severity or treatment. I was trying desperately to maintain the "confident" look, but inside I felt incompetent and frazzled. I made some lame excuse to be absent for a few moments, then literately ran to the medical library to research the unanswered questions. Fortunately, they were easy to find. I returned and eloquently told the family and nurses that this rhythm variation was common and required no treatment. In residency, this type of event would be normal and expected. As an attending, this was a little lacking. It's expected that you know everything (which is impossible), and it was a lesson learned. Don't discuss the problem until you know the answer and the plan. Navigating the demands of medicine would be based on evaluation and planning, to get all the steps in the proper order.

In the office, patients would present their symptoms and you were expected to have an instant answer. A lot of the problems were common and easily handled. There was one problem for which I felt ill prepared, and at times, shocked.

There are a lot of farmers in the Punxsutawney area. One would expect they would present with various and sundry orthopedic complaints like back and joint pain, muscle weakness or maybe depression. That's not what happened. They all wanted to talk about sex! I had no class on sexuality, had been married for eight years, and was still learning with my one sexual partner. I can imagine sitting there with my jaw on the floor and my eyes bulging from their sockets. Were the patients reluctant to discuss intimate details? Nooooo! They seemed to relish jumping into the topic and being very graphic. Fortunately, we did have a good part-time urologist on whom I could depend for backup. That didn't answer all the questions. Farmers and sexuality knocked me for a loop.

I had a young female on my list. Good, at least it wouldn't be a sexual question. She was seated and I was poised, pen in hand. The next thing I know, she launched into a tearful account of how her husband demanded sexual encounters five to seven times per day. Really? More sex? She was discussing how this was wrecking her life, and I'm thinking "How does that work? Where does he get the energy? What's he eating and how can I get some of that food or supplement?" Get your head on straight, Bruce! The poor patient was a teacher, and she went to school exhausted after repeatedly being awakened for sexual encounters. From my vast and knowledgeable experience, I reassured her that this was a "little" excessive, and she needed to convince her husband to come in for an evaluation. Perhaps he had excessive hormones or some other medical condition. We determined he was caring, but relentless. It really didn't fit the rules of rape or abuse. Her complaint was of exhaustion. I know we did see him and did some tests. I don't remember any extraordinary answers, and they never returned for follow-up.

That was an example of another learning experience. If you either make the right diagnosis or if you can't diagnose, you get no answers or follow-up. That was a difficult predicament but very common.

In our case, we were so busy seeing new patients that you did not have time to reflect on those that got away. We were seeing 150-200 new patients a month, which was rare for a startup practice. In fact, at that point in time, we were the first National

Health Service Corps (NHSC) site to make money. All their other sites lost money. We were making so much money, that the equation (to handle losses) was forcing the clinic to send the surplus money (far in excess of our costs) to the federal government. Our manager, Mr. Dan, requested our situation be evaluated. The result was the formation of the "private practice option." The clinic would use the money to pay off our obligations. In return, we could receive a more reasonable salary from the clinic, but still had to work off the years owed.

It was a win-win. Our salary about doubled and we were no longer government employees. The clinic would manage us as independent doctors. That really relieved our financial pressures and gave the clinic local control.

41. NAVIGATING NORMALCY

After our arrival, with a flourish, things finally started to settle into a pattern. In my immediate world, there were two distinct hemispheres: the inpatient and the outpatient. I much preferred the inpatient, because the patients were more complex, you could see their improvement or deterioration each day, you got feedback as to what did and didn't work and the time it would take to see results. When you're fresh out of residency, you really learn your craft. Once again, you were much smarter if you learned from everyone around you.

I had done a fair amount of ICU work in residency, but this was a brand-new game. All of a sudden, I had to manage patients on ventilators. There are many parts to ventilator management, and I knew none of them. Fortunately, we had an excellent respiratory therapy team who knew what to do and how to manage inexperienced doctors. When calling me for orders, they had their plan in mind and guided me through the necessary orders and their rationale. When possible, I would try to find time to do some additional research, but that required having to go and spend time in the library (no internet yet) and often that time wasn't available. In a bigger hospital, you would have a pulmonologist and a cardiologist to manage these issues. Working in a small hospital is like a bad version of the children's game—you are always "it."

I had a patient, Mrs. Fiesty, who was a sweet old soul. I made some house calls and she would be hospitalized off and on with heart failure. At the end of each encounter, she would say, "I'm 99 and want to reach 100. That's your job, Kelly." We got her to within about two weeks of her birthday when she passed away. It was an unreasonable request. We just couldn't get her there. Morbidity (dying) was an ongoing problem for us. We had 10-15 people in the hospital all the time. Their average age was probably in the eighties. It seemed like we had 1-2 deaths every week. People wear out, and we had a very elderly clientele. It didn't take long for Dr. Bill and I to decide we were practicing in the Elephant's Graveyard of Pennsylvania. People would be born and raised in the Punxsutawney area. Many would move away for the productive years of their life. When they became elderly and frail, they would migrate back to Punxsutawney—to die.

Mortality medicine was depressing, but it helped me hone my skills to manage the patient and provide support for the family through this natural and unavoidable cycle of life. "Are their affairs in order? Are they and their nearest loved ones talking about this?" Nobody would want to talk about death, because it would upset the patient. More often than not, the patients would have worse anxiety from the silence, because they wanted to talk about it. The three most common concerns were, "How long do I have?" "Will my family be okay?" "Will I suffer?" I always told the patient I was a poor prognosticator but would give my best guess, on the low side. If they lived longer, it was a miracle. If they died much earlier, you endured the accusatory "I thought we'd have more time?"

Often, the family would need prodding to open a meaningful dialogue with the patient. If they wouldn't, I would ask them to be present for my rounds and I would start the discussion, then give some guidance as to what should be discussed. Sometimes the family would request that the patient be kept in the dark about their situation. With the exception of those so confused they wouldn't understand, I would refuse to cooperate. It wasn't fair to the patient and almost uniformly they already knew and could sense what was happening. The easiest of all the issues was comfort. I could assure them I would be relentless in controlling their pain and anxiety. There might be a time when their wakefulness would have to be sacrificed, but I would try to avoid that.

Although many years have passed, there are some memories that remain vivid. In rural communities, of the 1980s, not every town had an ambulance. To transport patients, you needed a long, roomy vehicle which could accommodate a stretcher and some additional people—like a hearse! Yes, in many small communities, the funeral director was their "grab and run" EMS system. They always wore their uniform: black hat, black trench coat, and black pants. Sometimes they would want to stand at the foot of the bed and "wait." If I was working the ER, that would freak me out, and I would ask them to leave or go home. I'm sure it wasn't intentional, but it was very "vulturish."

Every hospital had their regulars, as did the doctors. One of mine was a neighbor who lived at the bottom of our hill. He and his wife, in their seventies, had no children. He was a smoker and his life's work was grass management at the local country club course. Now retired, he cut his grass several times per week. His yard looked like a putting green. I was rapidly learning that my grass was my enemy. Somehow, I had to simultaneously find some daylight hours where the grass was dry and it wasn't raining.

Anyway, "Elroy" had COPD and would appear in the ER about once a month in respiratory distress. He would have to be put on a ventilator, from which you were never sure you could wean him. He always improved, and as soon as the tube came out, he was cussing and complaining about his care. I would discharge him, he would smoke, then repeat the cycle. I happened to be working in the ER when he arrived in less than his usual severe distress. He needed to be hospitalized but not on the vent. After I told him that, I asked, "Who do you want for your doctor?" He was shocked and said, "You." After about eight of the above de-scribed cycles, I decided to lighten my load. I said, "I've decided to refuse you as a patient, because you're abusive and noncompli-ant." He was in a tailspin. He likely wore out his welcome with every other physician in town, and he literately begged me to take care of him. I told him he had to stop the foul language and had to stop smoking. He cleaned up his act, but of course continued to smoke.

There was a hospital incident that gave me a reputation I didn't deserve. In the 1980s, one could smoke in their hospital room and it was quite common. I had a female patient, admitted with respiratory problems because she was a smoker. My habit was to take the patients chart to their room when I made rounds. The patient had her ashtray on the bedside table. I misjudged and hit the edge of the ashtray with the chart when I set it down. The ashtray, very dramatically, flew across the room and crashed into the wall and floor. Of course, I would always encourage the smokers with COPD to stop. It was done in a calm and civilized manner. The rumor mill version was that I flung the ashtray across the room in a fit of rage over her smoking. I guess the takeaway was, "You better quit smoking if you're seeing Dr. Kelly." That was a reputation worth keeping. The river was gaining a history. Like most history, some was true, some fictional.

42. "I WAS WRONG"

It was more a romantic idea than a researched desire. I had no background in rural living except for the short period of time when my grandparents had a little cottage in Harrisville, PA. I loved that place. It was a musty, small house that sat on a big lot with a huge weeping willow to shade the house and hold the tire swing. The house had a water well, and a hand pump in the kitchen was the only access to water—what fun! I don't remember an outhouse, but it's hard to fathom that there was an inside toilet. They likely had a Porta Potty or something. I don't know the story of the cabin's purchase, but I can surmise that it had to do with the fact that my grandfather's youngest sister, and her large family, owned a sizeable farm across the road.

My great aunt's family was much older than me but they were open to letting me help collect eggs and go on small trips around the farm. That, and the two farmers in Hershey, completed my rural experience. All my exposures were pleasant. They occurred where the spaces were wide open, the air was cleaner, and the people seemed a little less complex. That would be a great place to practice medicine.

In Punxsutawney, there was room to spread out. We already owned a home that was far beyond those in which we were raised. The air was cleaner, but the people were complex, in a rural way. They had an unhealthy trust that what the doctor said was gospel. If you were a narcissistic doctor, that was a good fit. We had some local doctors who did not deserve their trust. Medicine, in general, was and is an inexact science and was no place for those who lacked that insight. I never minded being questioned and usually could explain a situation in laymen's terms. It was easy to lapse into a conversation, using the medical jargon that you labored long and hard to learn. It was a different story to translate those issues into simple terms. I remember a case where I fell victim to my own, personal, chronic disease. I liked to keep things light, and I had/have a quick wit. My mouth was often miles ahead of my brain.

I had a late middle-aged male with severe hypertension and an excessively dutiful wife. Our choice of blood pressure medicines was pretty limited, and if you had bad hypertension, the side effects of those meds were as deadly as the disease. His wife had learned how to take his blood pressure and did so about four to five times per day. She recorded them in a log, which she brought each visit. I wasn't sure "he" could speak. She did all the talking. Curiously, his BP in the office was somewhat elevated, but not near the blood pressures she was recording. I asked her to bring in her blood pressure equipment so we could check it for accuracy.

His next visit (probably in a week), the whole scenario repeated. I had our nurse check his pressure with our cuff and then theirs. The readings were identical. I told the wife I was going to keep her blood pressure cuff and see them back in two weeks. She began to protest, and I said, "You know there are two kinds of people in this world. There are those who have high blood pressure, and those who give it." The dynamics in the room were complex. The nurse ran for the door with her hand over her mouth. The wife had a look of shock on her face. The patient had a subtle smirk on his face, and his eyes were saying, "Thank you." After a dramatic pause, I explained her attentiveness was making him anxious and increasing his blood pressure. His blood pressure increased her anxiety, and they were in a vicious cycle. Together, they were to find things to do other than worry about his blood pressure. I had no doubt he would be back.

The patients were challenging and that was good. The social situation was more challenging. We were in the middle of nowhere. The town's people were inviting and charming but not very inclusive. In the moments where we had some downtime, we were in a rut and isolated.

People knew I was busy, and they may not have wanted to interfere with our free time. There were a lot of social activities organized within the clans, but we had only a few invitations. I didn't hunt or fish, and free time, if not consumed with house projects, became a problem. We spent my free weekends in Pittsburgh with the families. My vigilant wife got creative.

I was not an artist, but I had considerable talent as a copier. The portraits I had done of my grandparents were eight by ten. I learned that doing a larger scale painting had a negative impact on the quality of my work. Those efforts were good for someone with no art training.

Dolly knew I was struggling to adapt, socially, to our new environment. She had the insight that the time was right for me to receive some formal art training.

There was a very talented elderly lady in town, who gave classes in her home. We'll call her Miss Artist. Her hundreds of paintings were an inspiration. Her teaching ability was more "osmotic." She really didn't demonstrate techniques, but she did talk some about concepts. There were about ten students in the evening class, and she would walk around and critique. Everyone there had some innate talent, and the results were pretty good. She liked you to start a new picture at least every two weeks. Between classes, I would sit in our family room, after the kids were in bed, and work on my project. Miss Artist did spend some time on mixing colors and conversely, looking at a color and figuring out its components. Between the pressure of producing product and developing a talent I enjoyed, I was pretty productive. Christmas of 1982, I presented three, sixteen-by-twenty floral pictures as presents. My inspirations came from Christmas cards, vacation pictures, and on occasion, magazines.

My largest painting was inspired by an unusual occurrence. I was on call and had to go to the hospital at 3:00 A.M. to check on an evolving heart attack. After I got the patient stabilized, I had to talk to the family in the waiting room. They decided to go home, and I doubled back to the waiting room. While there, I had caught a glimpse of a fall picture of a New England village, in a magazine. Deciding it was doable, it became a twenty-four-by-thirty picture that still hangs above our mantel.

Dolly was busy with two children and sought solace with our neighbors, Nancy and Ralph. Besides being some of the most pleasant and welcoming people we ever met, Nancy made a killer pot of coffee and Dolly's favorite—German Chocolate cake. Ralph worked for the post office but was a competitive farmer, with his neighbors. He would share some of his bounty with us, when he wasn't trying to fool his neighbors with early plantings or early harvesting.

In total, our time in Punxsutawney was rewarding, memorable, educational, and eye-opening. Just as the terrain can make a river radically change course, the Punxsutawney experience made us re-evaluate our rural medicine experience and desires.

43. "WHY ARE YOU LEAVING?"

We kept in touch with several of the Harmarville employees and one in particular knew my commitment to Punxsutawney was soon to end. One of the Harmarville "hospitalists" was going to leave, and they would need to replace him. We hadn't been closely in touch, so Darlene RN wasn't sure if we were staying or not. She mentioned to two of the internists that I might be interested.

Rrring. The house phone rang (no cell phones yet) and Dr. Phil introduced himself and explained that Harmarville was in need of a doctor. This was in 1982. He asked if I would have dinner with several of the doctors to discuss the situation. We were in Pittsburgh every other weekend, so we arranged to meet. Drs. Phil and Milas were about my age and had worked at Harmarville for about two years. They were three years out of their internal medicine residency, tried to start a private practice, but it was slow to grow. They found part-time work at Harmarville that rapidly grew into full-time positions. Harmarville moved from their quaint small facility of about seventy-six beds to a huge 120- (eventually 202-) bed facility with large spaces, large rooms, no ramp (lol) and a mission to expand. This required tremendous courage, faith, and planning. The facility was practically full all the time, and there was one internal medicine doctor on each of the five, forty-bed units. We had dinner and discussed my current situation, which wouldn't officially end until June 30, 1983. Their immediate need was going to be for July 1, 1982. That wouldn't work, but they felt another opening might occur in 1983.

Obviously, that dinner wasn't the start of my employment, but the seed was planted. Our Punxsutawney practice had grown so large, it would soon be too large for the two of us. The clinic would need time to find a replacement. Even though there wasn't a specific job lined up, we were committed to move back to Pittsburgh. I let Dr. Bill and the clinic board know our plan. There was no such thing as a secret, more about that later.

Life was continuing to evolve, and the work needed to be done. Our personal life was also evolving. We decided to have a third child, and Dolly became pregnant in mid-1981. On October 9, 1981, Dolly, in her first trimester, began spotting and bleeding. Our friend and gynecologist, Dr. George , checked her, and she was having a miscarriage. It was a sad day, and I canceled my patients. It was Jason's open house for kindergarten, and Dr. George felt the process would take a while. We went to the open house and did some other errands. We returned to the hospital, and she had a D&E (dilation and evacuation of the dead fetus).

We had no idea miscarriages were so common. Nobody talked about those experiences until it occurred, then you got support from friends and relatives. We had two healthy children and the demands of life prevented us from becoming too depressed.

We both realized that an aborted fetus was commonly not healthy. We discussed whether to try again. I felt we shouldn't close our reproductive life on that note. I wasn't around much for Matthew's infancy and wanted to take advantage of the fact that this child would have a more full-time dad.

Dolly became pregnant in the spring of 1982. Her first trimester symptoms were different than the first two pregnancies and suggested the possibility of having a girl! We had a backup plan. Dr. George was a dark-skinned Indian who married a very white American. They had two beautiful daughters. His wife was pregnant with a similar due date. We made a pact to swap kids if they had another girl and we had a boy. Nobody would notice, LOL!

My practice was maturing, and I was learning more each day. When you're newly out of residency, you don't feel confident to take firm stands or trust your intuition. We had a fifty-year-old male come into the hospital with a heart attack. His course was a little rocky, but we got him stabilized and he went home. He remained pretty weak and was unable to return to his job as a landscaper. At that time, they were doing CABGs (coronary artery bypass grafts), but they were only doing them on patients who had ongoing chest pain. I sent him to Johnstown to be evaluated. They decided to do a catheterization and suggested he have surgery. He wanted my opinion, and I told him I would defer to the cardiologist. My gut told me to suggest he refuse, but I didn't go that route. He was applying for disability, and we were hitting roadblocks. He had the surgery and unfortunately died on the table. He had two pre-teenagers and a wife at home. I felt guilt for a long time. I could have prevented the surgery and justified my stand. He may have lived, or died suddenly, there was no way to know.

The hospital administrator was removed from his position and a board member resigned. I was asked to serve on the hospital board, much to my surprise. I accepted and got to see the other side of healthcare. Getting to know the board members was a pleasure. They were very committed to providing the best care they could, and the hospital was a testimony to their efforts. After one of the meetings, a board member approached me and said, "Would you be willing to see my wife for a thorough physical? I mean everything. She is an Amway disciple and hasn't seen a doctor in over thirty years." I assured him I would.

Some time went by, and there she was on my list for a physical and a PAP test. She was a very pleasant (and healthy), late-middle-age female. Everything went fine until we did the PAP test. I got the speculum positioned and suddenly there was a large, slightly raised, serpiginous (irregular-shaped) mass on the vaginal wall and extending onto the cervix. I didn't know for sure what it was, but it wasn't good. Knowing her doctor avoidance problems, I asked her permission to bring the gynecologist down to take a look at it. His office was above ours, and he was available to see it. He explained that after the biopsy (which he did right there), they would talk about the treatment. It was a vaginal cancer, and she had a curative surgery done. Once again, the stars and planets aligned and through a quirk of fate, I played a part in saving her life.

I quickly learned the downside of giving a one-year notice of my intent to leave. All the patients would ask why I was leaving, and

I developed an oft repeated answer. "Our parents are all in Pittsburgh and are needing more help. We need to be closer to take care of them." That was part of the decision and the least arguable. That scenario played out daily, and I had some guilt about abandoning my practice. Dolly was pregnant with our third child and the boys always needed attention. Working at Harmarville would free up a lot of time for family and to really enjoy a new baby.

The river took a sharp change in course, and we couldn't begin to anticipate what would lie ahead.

44. THE BLIND INTERVIEW

Nothing is simple when you uproot a physician. There are loose ends to tie up, a job to secure, and a new place to live. I spent considerable time, fastidiously planning to make the change seamless. The prolonged goodbyes were painful. I needed to re-connect with Harmarville about a job, and we needed to find housing and sell our house.

My initial Harmarville dinner must have gone well, because they were willing to continue talks. They still didn't know if there would be a position for July 1, 1983. The medical director invited me to interview. Between his initial contact and that interview, he got word a position would become available. It was their most difficult job to fill. Nobody told me that last part.

On the appointed day, I showed up in my best suit and made small talk with the medical staff secretary, Peggy, who would be-come a lifelong friend. Finally, the medical director was free and I entered his office. I was greeted by a white haired, stocky, pleas-ant gentleman who had a smooth, sing-song voice. He asked me to sit, and I tried to hide my obsession with his face. He was wearing the darkest, wraparound sunglasses I had seen in my life. He was relatively new in his position and was interested in my previous Harmarville experiences and my practice in Punxsutawney. The interaction was pleasant enough, but I was freaked out by those glasses. He said he had a corneal abrasion. I never realized how much I depended on eye contact during an interview!

He then explained that the position available would be on the spinal cord unit. I would be working with two physiatrists and my responsibilities would be the medical management of forty patients. I would be salaried, so there would be no pressure to see each patient daily. I would be on-call about every fifteenth weekend and one weekday twice a month. I hoped I wasn't drooling. Every physician rotated through the on-call schedule and would take call for the entire building. They had a cadre of retired nurses who dictated the complex rehabilitation discharge summaries. Forget the blind interview, sign me up!!!

I was contacted and given a "provisional" hiring. One of their current internists thought he would be leaving in June, and I could have that spot—if available. The guy was actually a med school classmate of mine who was waiting on his wife to finish her surgical residency in Pittsburgh. That all took place in late 1982.

Life had to go on as normal, even when you were juggling many situations. Dolly's due date was at the end of January, 1983. She had been three weeks late with Jason and about two weeks late with Matthew. The obstetrician was a friend, and I needed some certainly for patient scheduling. It was decided Dolly would be induced 1/31/1983, unless she delivered earlier. Early that day, she was admitted and started on Pitocin (to initiate contractions). Around 5:00 P.M., the obstetrician completed his office hours. He checked Dolly, and she had a few more centimeters to dilate. He cranked up the Pitocin and before long she was pushing. As with the first two births, I was in the delivery room with her. Ultrasound had not advanced to be able to discern gender.

The whole hospital knew we were delivering. The moment came, and Dr. George swung the baby up as he yelled, "It's a girl!" Dolly and I let out a scream of delight heard all over the hospital. We finally got our girl, and we were thrilled. (Dr. George got his boy.)

Dolly was rooming-in and nursing the baby as she had done the previous two. The next day I took the two boys to see their mom and the new baby. Her name was Diana Michelle, and they were discharged after a couple of days. I pulled the car into our garage, and seven-year-old Jason ran out to meet us. As soon as we got Diana out of her seat, Jason said "Give her to me." Uh, that wasn't happening. "Go and sit on the couch and you can hold her." Matthew showed up, but even at five years old, he could see the writing on the wall. He was no longer the baby. The emerging theme carried through their life, until they were college age. Jason would be Diana's protector and Matthew the nemesis, of sorts.

We had the nursery set up and we settled into a rhythm. Our unused living room was the perfect place to rock a baby to sleep. Setting a schedule, and keeping to it, worked well for us. Bedtime wasn't a hassle. If they had a bad dream, they could crawl in bed with us, but would always wake up in their own bed.

I remember really enjoying Diana as an infant, not because she was a girl, but because I was a seasoned father and there was less professional pressure, because I had more confidence and could relax on my downtime.

That was a slow moving, relatively calm part of the river.

45. FINDING A PLACE TO LIVE

After getting the July job offer, we had to find housing. We chose a realtor who was a little mature but very invested in our housing needs. We needed four bedrooms and a dining room big enough for our furniture!

I don't remember seeing many existing homes before we were approached about building a new home. We made an appointment to meet the builder. He had several lots available in Cedar Ridge, in West Deer Township. After hearing our needs, he took us to a home he built. It had four large bedrooms on the second floor with two full baths. The first floor had a large living room, large dining room (our furniture would fit!), family room and a spacious kitchen. We instantly fell in love with the house. Could it be done by July 11, 1983? He assured us it could. The cost was $87,000. It would be a construction loan, so we didn't start paying until after it was completed.

We saw the lot in Cedar Ridge. It was in the back of the plan with woods in the back, so there would be no houses behind us. It seemed like the houses were so close to each other, but they were probably forty feet apart. This move was for the kids. No more arranging play dates. This place was almost all families with small children. It was to end up being six hundred plus homes. We signed a contract.

Of course, we, nor anyone else in the family, had built a house. We came back to Pittsburgh every other weekend, and we had to use a fair amount of time to pick out colors, siding, brick, carpet, linoleum and light fixtures. We had to move quickly, because the whole process had a four-month window!

We would go to the site every other week. I knew the builder didn't want me going through the house, but I caught many mistakes that were easier to correct at that point. I would leave messages on the mistake and call the contractor on Monday. His patience started to wear thin. I didn't care. This only helped move the project toward the finish. The costliest mistake was completed just prior to move in. They installed the wrong carpet in the living room and dining room. He wanted to move back our move-in date, but I couldn't reschedule the movers. Ready or not, here we come.

In spite of the fact that I gave them a year's notice, they did not have a new doctor to replace me. Dr. Bill was going to stay and get a new partner sometime during the next year. Dr. Bill left in 1984 to do ER medicine in the south. We had built the practice to about eight to nine thousand patients, and it could easily use three doctors. Indeed, by 1985, there were three doctors inheriting the practice we built.

On top of building the practice and formulating the charts with up-to-date forms and flow sheets, we had a lot of local bad habits to break, not of our making. A vast majority of the patients believed that once you got your blood pressure under control, you were cured! We had to do a lot of re-education. We also had many patients showing up to get long-acting steroid shots for their seasonal allergies. That was effective, but *not* usual practice and had many possible serious side effects. Bill and I were fortunately on the same page and did the harder job of re-educating them. As difficult as that practice was, I learned a lot and learned to take charge of the patient's health care whether there were specialists involved or not. I seriously accepted the family practice model of not only providing but coordinating each patient's care. That would serve me well in my next job. I bought several books on neuroanatomy but rarely used them. My education would be completed on a daily basis. The river took a major change in course, and I was up for the challenge.

46. SO MANY DIVING ACCIDENTS!

There were many emotional hurdles when returning to a former place of employment with a new title and much more responsibility. Doctors that I revered, insisted I call them by their first name. They surely wondered how well I learned my craft, but were welcoming and ready to let me assume my new role, independently.

Nurses, to whom I reported in the past, were ready to call me Dr. Kelly, and it was a necessary change. The title helped define the power structure, which had done a one-eighty since I worked last. I was now thirty-two and looking a little more mature. The patients, many my age, needed to call me Doctor so that my orders would be taken seriously. Unfortunately, in spinal cord dysfunction, there are a lot of unpleasant things the nurses must do to the patients or teach them to do to themselves.

From a medical management standpoint, I knew nothing about giving the orders. Unit I was the spinal cord unit, and it was manned by Dr. Gil who created and fostered the spinal cord team. It had already, in seven years, become quite a tight-knit group and could be dismissive of outsiders who didn't know the topic well. Dr. Gil was pleasant, but had little time for me in the first five years. He would often change my orders after I left for the day. I had to learn to assess if it was an improvement of my order or yet another instance of him marking his territory. He especially made a routine of this after he was off for vacation. His English was pretty good, but he still had some difficulties as an immigrant from Costa Rica. I believe his mother was French, and he fashioned himself to be more French than anything, more on him later.

My other partner was Dr. Andy. He was my age, blond (with the start of a comb-over) gregarious, and excellent with the patients. He was boarded in Spinal Cord rehab and was the designated spinal cord mentor for all the University of Pittsburgh rehabilitation residents, who would rotate through our unit. That gave me an easy path to learn the rehabilitation side as well as the medical management of the patients. Gil and Andy would each have twenty patients, and I was responsible for all forty.

I remember a few of the names, but distinctly remember we had thirteen patients from diving accidents. Some from four-foot pools, some from diving boards, one from a motel diving board, and one from bodysurfing. The most memorable was a young man who, on his brother's wedding day, re-created what they had done as kids a hundred times. He climbed onto the garage roof and dove into the four-foot pool, during the reception. There were two major differences. He was fifty pounds heavier, and he was drinking. In fact, that was the common thread in all these accidents, alcohol. People didn't realize that alcohol could impair their depth perception. An act, that was relatively easy when you're sober, could turn into a catastrophe when drinking. The dive angle became too straight down, and the arms couldn't prevent the weight of the body from driving the head into the bottom of the pool, causing a neck fracture. All thirteen were quadriplegic, meaning all four of their limbs were paralyzed. Commonly, their breathing would be affected by paralysis of the diaphragm. Many had tracheotomies, allowing air to directly flow into and out of the lungs. Most had supplemental oxygen, which required a lot of attention. A quadriplegic, at that time, would be in rehabilitation for four months.

You might wonder why such a long rehab. They would arrive pretty sick and just getting them up in a wheelchair and to therapy, might take the best part of a week. They were often hypotensive (low BP) and the nurses would have to recline them, put on abdominal binders and support hose to try to keep their BP up. The low BP might make them nauseous, then you had to deal with that. They really wanted to stay in bed, but the nurses would work with them and encourage them. Some needed blood pressure elevating meds, from me, before they could get up. It was a process, and there was no way to speed it up.

With the respiratory problems, they would have a lot of lung secretions, which were continuously disruptive. If they could cough it loose themselves, the nurses or therapists (or doctor), had to be there to collect it in a tissue for disposal. Some were too weak and needed assisted cough. When the patient tried to cough, someone would push in on their stomach, much like a Heimlich maneuver, to get the secretions out. The patients and families had to be encouraged that this was a better method than using suction. The only help they would get in the hospital was suction, but it only cleared the oropharynx (mouth). Sometimes, the RN had to suction through the tracheotomy tube, which had its problems also.

The other twenty-seven patients would be made up of quadriplegic and paraplegic patients from other sources: car accidents, ATV accidents, falls down stairs, etc. There were always a few Multiple Sclerosis patients, whose problems more closely mimicked spinal cord patients. The bottom line was that each bed was filled, and as soon as one emptied, a new admission would come in.

We always had a rehabilitation resident with us. The first was James, a very athletic, Ryan O'Neil look-alike who graduated from Georgetown Medical School. He was a local young man with good medical knowledge and stiches in his head from a game of lacrosse. He asked me to remove his sutures, which I did. His main focus was to learn spinal cord rehab, but he was also supposed to learn the medical management from me. He was already pretty proficient, and I had one rule, "Don't order a test unless you know what to do with the result." It cut down on unnecessary testing, and made them go to the library to research their new find. Jim was one of the best residents. The rest were all individuals with a mixture of good knowledge and management skills.

On Thursdays, Dr. Andy, the resident and I all made rounds together on his patients. We would review their strength, rehab progress, medical problems and labs. It took three to four hours, but was educational for me and kept all of us up-to-date on those patients.

Dr. Gil would do his own thing at random times of the day, and I would try to evaluate and keep his patients healthy. That was the other unusual aspect of that job. If the patient became too sick to attend programs, we lost valuable time. That forced us to treat empirically, before all the lab tests were back. It was a talent you had to learn, and some doctors were better than others.

Andy and I had an easy relationship. We would constantly make jokes and interact. It was an instant friendship. We had each other's back. He was much more meticulous and thorough, but he also had half the number of patients.

I would arrive at 7:00 A.M. and would leave when everything was addressed. Sometimes it was 5:00 P.M., or it might be 8:00 P.M. Multiple admission days were the worst. We hardly ever got a summary from the referring hospital, so we all competed for the hospital records, which might be six-inches thick, to summarize their story and formulate a problem list, on which we would work.

The mornings were spent seeing the patients, doing an exam including checking for swelling in one leg. In the young population, DVT (blood clots in the legs) and PEs (blood clots which travel to the lungs) were our nemeses. Often, the referring hospital did not recognize the two most important post-trauma facts. When limbs became inactive, the DVT rate would go up. The other unrecognized factor was that, in the post-trauma period, the blood thickened in a way we couldn't measure, and that, too, increased the chances of DVT and PE. The local trauma center sent everyone on Heparin, a low dose blood thinner, and those patients usually did well. Heparin had to be given by injection into the stomach or thighs where there was a fatty layer. It would take me about two seconds to belittle the tattooed patients, when they began to complain. I would keep it humorous, but they soon learned to keep it real.

Nemesis was too mild a word, when you helped transfer a new patient from an ambulance litter onto the bed, and they instantly got gray and short of breath. If the clot was big, you could give them oxygen, bag them, or anything else, and they would die before your eyes. This happened too many times, and it would break your heart. They were often in their twenties or thirties, with a life ahead that would be unfulfilled. "There, but for the grace of God, go I." How often that thought went through my head. Many of the patients were my age. They had tremendous physical obstacles and emotional hurdles to overcome. They needed compassion, not sympathy. I soon learned they also needed a kick in the pants, but that was best done by their colleagues.

47. "QUIT BEING SUCH A WIMP"

The Harmarville, to which I returned, was the Taj Mahal compared to the previous building. It was one eighth of a mile long, with an extra-wide center hallway. The first section built consisted of three semicircular pods, each with forty beds. Each pod had its own designated PT and OT facilities. There were plenty of offices for the doctors, a nurse manager, unit manager, nutritionist, and two psychologists for each unit.

The main hall had skylights, and the outside walls were made of huge windows allowing plenty of light in and a perfect view of the spacious, beautifully landscaped patios between each pod. No cost was spared in making this a very pleasant environment for those admitted for weeks-to-months of care. In addition to the regular staff, Harmarville became a renowned teaching center for those going into physiatry (rehab medicine), OT, PT, and nursing. There was a commitment, not only to serve our patients, but to properly educate the caregivers of the future.

With that kind of description, you would expect the patients to have all the current amenities, not so. I didn't know the history of some of the decisions, but I certainly supported them as I became more knowledgeable about how rehab worked.

There were no phones or TVs in the rooms. That seems barbaric, but it was so helpful. Besides their time in therapy, we wanted the patients out of their rooms, visiting and bonding with each other and their families. Weather permitting, we wanted them outside, getting fresh air. There was a lounge with a TV and a pay phone at the back of each unit.

The rooms, too, were unique. There were four 2-bed rooms and eight 4-bed rooms on each unit. Rooms 1, 2, 4, 17, 19, and 20 had oxygen and suction units in the walls. The more critical patients were in those beds. Men and women were kept separate and we tried to put patients with similar injuries together. The nurses could be more efficient working with four patients at a time. One nurse could feed two patients at once. The rooms were huge, and you could get stuck in a ward (four-bed room) for a long time.

The patients talked to one another. They shared their triumphs and defeats. Most of all, they shared their fears and feelings. It was more therapeutic than any professional intervention. They would talk the talk and "ride the ride." The biggest problem was making them understand that each injury was unique in its problems and prognosis. An improvement in one did not translate into an improvement for all. Some were recent admissions, and some had been there for months. The "newbies" might cry and be terribly depressed. The roommates would cut them some slack for a while, but there was a limit. The non-educated "therapists" would work their magic. "Quit being such a wimp! At least you can feed yourself!" You would think this would cause a lot of anger and hostility, but it didn't. It was the kick in the pants from their peers that often got them going. They could be ruthless and funny. The sociopaths—the drug dealers, jailbirds, etc. were some of my favorite patients. There was an unwritten code that you showed respect for those providing you care. It was a rare occasion that we had to redirect a patient's anger. We had a middle-aged, female, holocaust survivor who was a professor at one of the local universities. She was admitted with a spinal condition that was undiagnosed, and she was angry. I can't imagine the life she lived, but I also couldn't continue to let her disrupt the whole unit with her seemingly continuous, screaming complaints at everyone around her. She belittled the nurses and therapists alike.

One afternoon, she was in rare form, and I felt I had to intervene. I grabbed her wheelchair and pulled her into my office. Suddenly she was quiet, and I remember the exact words I said, "There is a minimum amount of decorum we expect from all the patients, and you are not meeting it. If you are that unhappy about your care, we will arrange to transfer you to another facility." She began to cry and had no insight as to how disruptive she was being. She apologized and did a 180-degree change. She actually returned several times and finally had a diagnosis of A-V malformation in the spinal canal. This condition caused abnormally high pressure in the vein, which would swell in size and cause space-occupying problems. Sometimes they would rupture. She eventually had surgery and did fairly well.

The facility, and all the physicians, had a strict policy about alcohol and marijuana. Most of the patients had jaded backgrounds to say the least. They were all warned, on admission, that they would instantly be discharged without meds or equipment if caught. We really couldn't do that, but a few were discharged with minimal medication and an off-the-shelf wheelchair. They could request readmission, but that required an apologetic letter and some convincing.

If all that sounds a bit militaristic, it was. We had a limited amount of time to organize their medical issues and address their physical needs, which could be permanent or a moving target. Performance altering substances could not be part of the picture. We had enough balls to juggle.

There was a potentially dangerous element to our work. Pittsburgh, like most cities, had its share of gang warfare. It was not unusual to have a "Blood" and a "Cryp" gang member in the building simultaneously. We made sure they were on different units. We also had a secret weapon.

"Bunny" was a large black man who was caught in the wrong bed and body slammed onto his head by an even bigger and angry husband. He had a permanent, fairly severe, quadriplegia. He couldn't feed himself and was dependent for all his care. He did eventually learn to drive a power wheelchair. He was very pleasant, respectful, and gregarious. Everyone loved this guy, even though his size and weight (about 280) made his care more difficult. He seemed to know about a gang member's admission before we did. He would go pay a "visit" and there would be no trouble. We don't know what he said, but it was effective. I began to refer to him as the black "Godfather" of Pittsburgh. Even after discharge, we would call him to make a "visit" and work his magic.

He was a gift from God, who protected us. He also went back to and got caught selling drugs, which were stuffed in the sleeve of his parka. The jail couldn't physically handle his needs, so he got a lot of parole.

The point of all this was that I had to learn to use all the tools around me, and let nature, in its infinite wisdom, do its thing. It was a process.

48. I ALWAYS HAD TWO TO THREE JOBS

Before we left Punxsutawney, I started to do some moonlighting in the Kittanning ER and continued to do some weekend shifts after the move to Pittsburgh. None of these were big city hospital ERs. The majority of the work was more urgent care work, with some moments of true trauma. Kittanning had a real homey feel to it, and the staff were very cordial. It was bigger than the other hospitals, and the departments had 24-hour staffing. The medical staff was supportive and there was decent representation in the subspecialties. There weren't a lot of shifts available, so I did some work at another local hospital.

That hospital had a whole different feel. I worked every Thursday evening for six hours and a 12-hour shift every other weekend. My first day orientation was conducted by an unhappy nurse, showing me where to find Betadine, suture material, and sterile trays. She let me know that was a one-time orientation. That was the first hospital I worked with unionized nurses, and I was not impressed. They were competent, but there was always an air of aggravation. They had a large number of poverty cases, which also contributed to the mix. There were always two doctors on, and we were kept busy.

Each ER had a most-memorable case. At Kittanning, a very elderly man was brought in covered in rat bites. He was accompanied by his son. The patient was not senile and was very pleasant. We were updating his immunizations and we were very concerned about rabies. At that time, it was more of a presumptive diagnosis. The rabies shot regime was very painful and prolonged. The son asked, "How often would this regime have to be repeated?" His intent was to take the old man back to his shack and let him continue to be a rat feast. I'm sure there was smoke coming out of my ears. I replied, "Never, because a decent human being would never let him live like that again. Get him out of there tonight." The son looked shocked and acted like that was a novel idea. I don't think it was purposeful elder abuse, but ignorance. Some people just can't see the obvious and need more "guidance." It's one thing to live in poverty and make due with very little, but it's another world to think that rat bites would ever be acceptable.

On the downtime, at Kittanning, we would have pleasant interactions. One of the EMTs had grown up in the Amish community. She brought in the best Amish sugar cookies and gave me the recipe. We used that recipe for the rest of our lives.

Back in the "Union" hospital the atmosphere was quite different. There was one nurse who never adopted the union attitude. She was often there when I worked, and we worked together well. She eventually came to work at Harmarville, where we continued to be friends.

There was a lot of venereal disease that came through that ER a fair number of alcoholic regulars, and repeat psychiatric cases. We had a young girl come in with abdominal pain and vaginal discharge. That always required a pelvic exam, but this one was different. My friend, Pro, was assisting me and we both thought we would pass out. After inserting the speculum, and getting some lab specimens, I could see a foreign object. I removed 9 tampons that her overly zealous boyfriend kept pounding into her. The stench was awful and the girl was febrile. We had to admit her with PID (Pelvic Inflammatory Disease). The boyfriend would also have to be treated. I left a script for his meds, knowing the nurses would likely make his injections as painful as possible. This episode ranked right up there with the previously described peritonsillar abscess.

I juggled the three jobs until 1987. I was thankful my health and energy allowed me to do that. I learned from all those experiences, and the river continued a slower uphill climb.

49. HARDLY EVER A DULL DAY

Some days were more challenging than others. Catching problems early and keeping the patient in therapy were the goals. The ever-vigilant nurses and aides would notice an area of skin, on the patient's buttocks, that was red and firm to the touch. As much as we tried to prevent skin sores, with special mattresses and wheelchair cushions, it was an imprecise trial and error method. Once discovered, the patient would not be able to sit until the redness and the firmness resolved. We always had rehab residents, or therapists in training. Anytime one of these situations would arise, I tried to be sure that we had them see the problem firsthand, feel the relative firmness of the skin and learn the appropriate treatment. Most important was training the family or caregiver to evaluate these situations, so they could intervene at home. If ignored, the superficial skin area could turn into a deep ulcer, which was a much bigger problem to treat.

We had a patient who was moderately obese and a quadriplegic from a freak accident. He sat in his chair too long and developed one of those skin areas. In addition to telling him he couldn't sit in his wheelchair, I had to explain the positive, that the problem was caught early and would resolve with the proper care. "It is what it is" was a favorite motto. We would monitor and take care of it. The patients would try to bargain, but getting an open skin sore would be no "bargain."

From the other side of the unit, I heard a scream and ran to find the source. A thirty-year-old patient, from a motor vehicle accident, was in a "halo" apparatus, for a neck fracture. They looked barbaric but were the best way to stabilize a neck, much like using a cast to stabilize an arm fracture. A round ring was attached to the head by a series of four screws that would penetrate the skull about a fourth of an inch deep. Next, a series of four rods would attach to the "halo" and a rigid vest, that would remain on the patient for twelve weeks. The neurosurgeons would tell the patients eight to ten weeks, but they hardly ever removed them before twelve weeks. I firmly believed you had to be honest. I tried to prepare the patient, before their post-op visit, that the surgeon, in the end, would decide on a twelve-week time period. When they returned with the halo still in place, they would thank me for my honesty and vent their anger at the surgeon for being less than candid.

Back to the scream. The "Halo" patient was being transferred to his wheelchair when the front two halo pins dislodged from his skull and tore the skin on his forehead above the eyes. That was another "religious experience," watching the blood run down over his eyes and cheeks. I was likely transfixed. Dr. Andy was nearby, held the patient's head steady from behind, and ordered the nurses to get a hard collar from the in-house orthotics department and call an ambulance. Once the collar stabilized his neck, he was cleaned up and transferred back to the hospital for evaluation and replacement of the halo. That was the first time that had happened. We had the orthotics department get us a torque wrench, and we began checking halo patients once a week. The pins in the skull could loosen over time, and this way, we could check that it wasn't coming loose and prevent another occurrence. We also began taking x-rays, on admission, to see how deep in the bone the pin went and how thick that patient's skull bone was. We ended up with a wooden toolbox, made by one of our paraplegic patients, to carry the necessary wrenches and other halo equipment. One of the patients called me Dr. Goodwrench, and that was my title on the days we checked halos.

In addition to my normal work, every once in a while, I would be asked to take a new assignment. As a family practice doctor, you're trained to be open to new challenges. A patient in Pittsburgh was diagnosed with a chordoma—an expanding tumor of spinal cord tissue which was extremely painful. A company named Medtronic, developed an implantable pump (in the abdomen) with an internal catheter that ended in the spinal canal. It had the potential to pump medicine right into the problem area. The medicine chosen was Morphine. Those earliest pumps had no computer. It contained a bellows mechanism that would push the medicine in at a constant rate. The pump was built for a specific city, according to its atmospheric pressure. To change the dose delivered, you had to change the concentration of the medicine. The patient would call and report his pain level. We would decide on a change in the concentration, then a compounding pharmacy would mix it and send it to us.

This poor guy was always in pain, but the pump helped some, and his willingness to participate was groundbreaking. The pump had an access port into which you placed a needle to remove the old medicine, and put in new medicine. He would lay on his back, and with all the force I could muster, I would force the medicine into the pump which would push back on the bellows. It was uncomfortable for me, because it required so much force.

Toward the end of his life, he came in and couldn't lay on his back, because the pain was too intense. With him on his side, I had to prep the injection site and get the needle into the pump. After removing the old medicine, I prepared to give it the tremendous heave ho, and surprisingly the medicine went in easily. My first reaction was that I must have missed the pump and pushed the medicine into his belly! I drew back on the syringe and the medicine reappeared, so it had to have been in the pump. From then on, we did the side-lying method. It wasn't the last involvement I had with Medtronic.

We lived in an area that very rarely has tornadoes. In 1985, there was an F3 tornado near Butler, PA. Shortly thereafter, we had an admission with a mid-back fracture. This sixty-year-old man, and his wife, were headed to the basement of their home when the tornado was approaching. His wife made it down the steps, but before he could follow, the wind picked him up and tossed him against a tree. Yet another unique cause for a spinal cord injury. He was able to return home in a wheelchair months later.

One day, Dolly and I got a call from Shirley, Dolly's oldest brother's wife. She told us that our nephew, Scott, was admitted to a hospital in the Washington DC area with paralysis.

I called and talked to Scott. His story was awful, but believable. He had gradual onset of leg weakness. He went to the ER, was checked and sent home. The weakness worsened, and he called an ambulance to take him to the ER. Again, they couldn't find a reason and called a cab to take him home and get him up a flight of stairs! The taxi driver tried to drag him into his apartment, but wisely decided to take him back to the ER. Apparently, the cab driver had a heated exchange with the staff, and Scott was admitted. On spinal tap, they found an odd oral bacterium in his spinal fluid. He eventually had surgery, but the paralysis of the legs didn't improve. He was on antibiotics for the next six to eight weeks.

I tried to investigate the hospital's reputation, but I couldn't find much information. I knew I wasn't impressed with the emergency room. His mother wanted him to come to Harmarville. I wasn't comfortable with a direct transfer, so I contacted the trauma team at Allegheny General in Pittsburgh, and they went into action. The next thing I knew, all the arrangements were made. He was coming by air ambulance to Allegheny General to be evaluated, then transferred to us when he was stable.

When you're a physician in a large family (that uniformly doesn't go to physicians), you get a lot of calls. The Caldwell's were my family, and I was always happy to help. Scott's father (Dolly's oldest brother, George-#1) had recently died. He developed adenocarcinoma of the kidney which had metastasized. We found out he was sick when his wife called and said he was in the hospital.

I got permission to review his chart and see his X-rays. He was very sick. His lungs looked like they were filled with popcorn. His chemotherapy was making him very sick, and he was scheduled for more the next day. I asked if I could speak to him alone. I asked him what he wanted to do. He asked about the chest X-ray and I told him it looked pretty bad. He was dreading the next chemo. I told him he had the right to refuse it, and when the oncologist showed up, he told him, "No more chemo." The oncologist started to protest, and I took him into the hall. I said, "We both know he's dying. The chemo will make him sick for the few hours he has left." The oncologist agreed. George died the next day.

George's family lived about forty-five minutes away, but we were all busy with our children, and we saw them maybe twice a year. George's wife was overwhelmed. I offered to go with her to the funeral home. Their oldest son came with us. I had no insight as to their financial situation. The funeral director was a little pushy and wanted to sell them an expensive coffin. They made a more modest purchase. Then he started describing the vault options. The most expensive had a rubber seal to keep the water out. I started to speak to Shirley, and the oldest son began to sob and said, "I don't want my dad to get wet." That ended that discussion, but I was angry with the funeral director's handling of the situation. Shirley, and the family, were still adjusting to life without George when Scott was transferred to us.

Scott arrived and put his full effort into his rehab. He began to recover leg strength and was up and walking. Fortunately, he responded well to the antibiotics and had no other setbacks. He eventually could walk, unaided, but had a wide based, flat-footed gait. That was very typical of the "incomplete" injuries. They could recover significantly, but there was always something a little off. I told them it was like a scar on the skin—a small reminder of the time when things were worse.

More often than not, the work-related accidents that caused the injury involved work situations they could never resume. We had a fifty-year-old male who was a barn roofer, who fell off a roof and never regained leg movement. That guy loved his work and unbelievably could climb the ladder using just his arms and resumed barn roofing. We were continuously impressed by the resiliency of our patients.

50. "NEVER GET SURGERY ON JULY 5TH IN A TEACHING HOSPITAL."

When I was in my second year of medical school, we had a patho-physiology course which was very demanding. In two ten-week terms we had to learn the function of all the organs and what diseases they could get. I could never absorb everything and it was easier to learn when you were working on a patient. I did remember they told us they were starting to see thyroid cancer in adults who had radiation to the head and neck as a child.

X-ray technology was vastly misunderstood in its infancy. Children's shoe stores had X-ray machines that you stood on, and you could see the bones in your feet. It was supposed to help select the proper size of shoe. Kids also got radiation for chronic tonsillitis and bad acne and there was no cause for alarm, or so they thought.

Knowing I had huge and frequently infected tonsils as a child, my doctor asked (during my pre-drivers physical), "When did you get your tonsils out?" My reply was, "I didn't." I remember thinking it strange he asked me that, since he provided all of our care.

In 1985, while shaving, I noticed that I had a lump on my throat. I called my mother to ask if I had radiation to my tonsils. Already in the early phase of Alzheimer's, she replied, "One of you did, but I don't remember who." I contacted our local hospital and they informed me they had had a fire which destroyed many of their records.

I saw my PCP, who confirmed the lump. He suggested Dr. Thyroid at Presbyterian Hospital in Pittsburgh. He was the local expert on thyroid surgery. Since talking was very important in my job, I needed a competent surgeon. I had an initial appointment with Dr. Thyroid, and he arranged for me to come back for a biopsy. I had never seen one done.

I returned in a week or so, and Dr. Thyroid was doing the biopsy. He prepped the area and numbed the surface. He then brought out what looked like a twelve-inch needle, which he began repeatedly jabbing into the mass. Of course, the needle wasn't that long, but when you're lying on your back and someone is jabbing you in the throat, it looks that long.

Dr. Thyroid called me and said the biopsy was "inconclusive," and that I should have the mass removed. He reassured me there was a low, one to two percent chance of it being cancer. Like most patients, I only heard the "chance of it being cancer." I wasn't a bookie and didn't gamble. All I knew was that for every scenario, someone makes up that small percentage and for them it's 100 percent positive.

I was raised with the motto "Men don't cry" and I was usually pretty unemotional. This was different. I had a wife, a nine-year-old, a seven-year-old and a two-year-old depending on me. I checked with HR at work and I had enough sick time to be off six weeks, if necessary.

I had nobody to talk to, so I called my brother. We had a cordial, but at most, twice a year relationship. He was understanding and reassuring, which was what I needed.

Dr. Thyroid was going on vacation and the first he could operate was July 5, 1985. I was so focused on getting it out, I didn't think it through. At worst, most thyroid cancer grows slowly. I could have waited a while.

All first-year residents start on July 1 and July 5 would be day four of training. They were likely in the "see one" or "do one" phase. My surgery was at 7:30 in the morning and lasted only an hour. Dolly and my mother were at the hospital. I was out-really out. I should've been in my room by noon at the latest, but I didn't get there until 7:30 P.M.! My anesthesia was dosed too high. The only thing I remembered, was waking up off and on. I apparently was vomiting as I smelled of vomit.

The nerves that serve the vocal cords run near or through the thyroid gland. Surgeons need to be extra careful to avoid them. I do remember getting awake to see a young female sticking a laryngoscopy mirror down my throat. This is an angled mirror used to see the vocal cords move. You need to have a light source, which is usually a headlamp, to shine on the mirror and make the vocal cords visible. She had no light source and was needlessly jabbing me in the throat and gagging me. Guess she was only partially attentive for the "see one" demonstration—if she saw one at all.

In addition to the vocal cord nerves, there are four parathyroid glands buried in or around the thyroid gland. They are important in calcium management, and thus they keep you overnight to monitor your calcium levels.

The next morning Dr. Thyroid came in to discharge me. I successfully pleaded to stay one more day for two reasons. First, I had a two-year-old who regularly hung around my neck. The second was the Wimbledon tennis matches going on, and I would be able to watch them in peace. Those days are long gone.

It was decided that I was to be on thyroid replacement, at high dose, to keep my own, one-half gland inactive. That was also the beginning of my never-ending summer. From then on, I would be heat intolerant.

51. "THERE, BUT FOR THE GRACE OF GOD, GO I"

In 1986, life settled into a pretty steady routine. I was much more comfortable in my new job. Dolly and the kids had their routine, which I popped in and out of, and I continued to do some "moonlighting" work at Kittanning and Union General Hospitals.

It started out to be a normal day with one discharge and a young man around nineteen scheduled for admission. He was a C7 fracture, which we knew would be a quadriplegic with pretty good arm and wrist strength, but his hands would be affected as well as his legs. I don't remember what the trauma was, but what happened after arrival was pretty clear.

Down the long hall came an ambulance crew with our patient and four adults. That was a little unusual, but was a sign of the times. The parents were divorced and each had remarried. Great! The only thing better than two parents was four! There was often a lot of communication with families about health issues, plans to be made, status updates, etc. In this case there would have to be double communications. There was no way around it. We often got older people, whose spouse would be too unreliable to receive the information. If there was one child, there would be no problem. If there were multiple children, almost invariably, there were disagreements between them, and they would want to make that our problem. Multiple people were calling to check on the patient. They would expect multiple calls, to be updated. The doctors, head nurse, and caseworker were all on the same page. One or several of us would have the same discussion and it went like this, "I'm sorry you're having family discord, but that isn't our problem. Your loved one is ill and you need to, at least temporarily, put aside your issues. We will communicate with one relative. You need to choose that person. They, in turn, will communicate with everyone else." It may have seemed harsh, but for patient care and time management, it was necessary.

The new young patient was placed in bed, and the four adults hung on our every word. I always cleared the room for the physical exam. The family was welcome to stay for the history portion. The four adults were civil to each other. That may have resulted before the accident or at the acute-care hospital. For that we were all thankful.

The patient was from out of state, which wasn't unusual, because we were one of a very few rehabilitation facilities to have a program dedicated to spinal cord injury. After the exams were done, the families were comfortable that he would be okay, and they decided to leave and find motel accommodations, nearby. Still, no cell phones in 1986. They would have to call in and leave a motel room telephone number.

The patient had arrived pretty early and one of our goals was to get them moving as soon as possible. He was placed in a wheelchair and taken to physical therapy, where he would get his initial physical therapy exam, get measured/assessed for an appropriate wheelchair and get an explanation of his schedule.

The transport wheelchair was a one-size-fits-all version with a tilt-back feature. Normally, it would have had anti-tippers on the back to prevent the chair from falling backward. One of our most seasoned physical therapists took him to therapy, where they had wheelchair- level mats to lay the patient on for therapy. The therapist decided to put his feet on the mat first, then transfer his body onto the mat. In a millisecond, the patient, who was in a halo apparatus, fell backward onto the floor when the unbalanced wheelchair tipped backward. The halo was knocked loose, the patient was screaming from fear and the therapist was in shock.

Someone called the operator and initiated a "Dr. GYAT-Pt gym" Dr. GYAT was our unique version of "code blue." It stood for "Get Your Ass There" and was used for all emergencies that required a doctor. This particular accident never happened before. We got a hard collar on him and stabilized him on a backboard. One of the doctors arranged transport to Allegheny General Hospital in Pittsburgh—our closest trauma center. He was evaluated and found unchanged by communicating with his original hospital. He was observed overnight and returned the next day.

The big problem was finding the parents. We had no idea where they were staying. Did they go somewhere to eat first? They likely went in different directions. We had to call every motel/hotel in the area. After we made contact, we had to explain the freak accident and explain where he was. You expected and received the angry reaction (times two) of the family who was just starting to develop some trust and comfort with their rehabilitation decision.

He returned and completed his rehab over about four months. My understanding was that there was some sort of settlement with the patient and family. He left a functioning quadriplegic in an electric wheelchair. He would need considerable continued help for transfers, dressing, and his bowel and bladder function. Although the day of the mishap likely did not impact the ultimate outcome, it would always be a source of concern if he could have recovered more. It was a bad day. The chair had anti-tippers devices welded on and we developed a policy that people in that situation were to be a two-person transfer.

June 1, 1986 was a tragic day—not for the patient's, but for some of the staff and our neighbors. I was at work around 4 P.M. and it started to rain. Then it began to pour, much like the Johnstown experience. Usually that intensity doesn't last long, but this just continued. Around 4:30 to 5:00 P.M. one of my male patients had chest pain, resistant to nitroglycerin. His EKG had changes consistent with an acute heart attack. We called for an ambulance, and were told all roads to us were flooded, and the helicopters were grounded. I was on duty until he could be transported. Several more hours went by. We started to get more information about what was going on. Apparently, there was a "cloudburst," where a storm stopped over top of us and dumped four inches of rain in one hour.

Saxonburg Boulevard was a windy, two-lane, downhill road that crossed every route to my home. I spent a lot of time figuring out a route that might work. Apparently, my normal route involved a tsunami of water that carried cars down Saxonburg Boulevard and deeply covered the houses along the road. There were eight people dead and ten people missing that day, including a local priest and one of his parishioners who was in his Jeep. I don't know if they were ever found. All that water emptied into the Allegheny River, eventually. The river was always in the picture.

Harmarville sat on a high plateau, which was unaffected. Where I would normally cross Saxonburg Boulevard, was some of the worst flooding. Had it not been for my patient, I could've been one of the fatalities. We eventually got my patient transferred and I crossed Saxonburg Boulevard on a high point and made it home. One of our recreational therapist's home was severely damaged. A housekeeper had some flood damage. A woman, who worked in central supply, was rescued and helped to flee up a hillside, as her home was inundated by the floodwater. Once again, God and the universe saved my life because there were so much more for me to do. The river endured.

52. DR. KELLY'S NEIGHBORHOOD

Mr. Roger's neighborhood was conceived and created in Pittsburgh for the public television station. It became a staple in American homes as a form of entertainment and education. I had my own neighborhood experience. Prior to this, we either lived in isolated areas or my long hours of school, work, and call did not allow for much socializing. Dolly was busy being a parent and a half, but she found Nancy in Punxsutawney and Annie in our Allison Park home.

We rarely had company, but one Sunday in 1986 someone was visiting. We heard an ambulance, and it was parked in front of the house across the street. We didn't know those neighbors and it might have been a minor event. It seemed like the ambulance was there a long time, and I eventually decided to go over and offer assistance. Paramedics were not a common entity at that time, but EMTs were trained to stabilize patients before transport. I entered the front door and could see several EMTs going in and out of a door where two legs were sticking out. It was a very small powder room with a man having seizures. His head and chest were wedged between the commode and the wall and the EMTs were trying not to move him. I introduced myself and didn't see any blood or obvious trauma.

I said, "We have to get him out of there to help him." I grabbed his legs and pulled him into the hallway. Now we could surround him and get him ready for transport. The EMT got a bite stick in his mouth. The ambulance had some supplies and meds, but the EMTs weren't authorized to use them. I was able to get an IV in place, and we gave him some IV Valium, and the seizures stopped. We got him on a backboard, then placed him on a litter and got him into the ambulance. His vital signs were stable, but he was unconscious. The hospital was about thirty minutes away. I really didn't want to go, because I got carsick riding in the back of a vehicle. If he needed more Valium, I would have to give it. I hopped into the back of the ambulance, knowing I would be paler than the patient when we arrived. He did need some additional Valium, but was stable on arrival. Those neighbors were never outside much, and I don't remember the exact cause, but I think it was a tumor or brain bleed. He did eventually get home.

That was my fourth ride in the back of an ambulance. One was to accompany a premature baby being transported from Punxsutawney to Dubois. Another, was to accompany an elderly person from a wedding reception where she developed chest pain while "dancing." I left another wedding reception after we moved to Allison Park. That was a sixty-year-old man who collapsed on the dance floor and had to be revived. He was going in and out of ventricular fibrillation (a life-threatening rhythm), and I was too busy giving meds to get sick. He survived and we got fruit baskets for several years. I developed a dread for wedding invitations.

About a week after the seizure incident, I was contacted by the West Deer ambulance board and asked to be a board member. They technically needed some medical input and met once a month. Ambulance services were almost always a part of the fire department. Larger communities would often have several fire departments for quicker response time. Commonly, each department was territorial about fundraising, township support, and overseeing the ambulance. When ambulance services were allowed to bill for services, the ambulance service sought autonomy. In the 1960s, Chuck and Peg Fleischer formed an independent West Deer Ambulance Service. Chuck oversaw the overall operation and Peg was the full-time dispatcher. Peg didn't seem to need sleep. She would sit next to the phone and the police monitor and quickly get a response team on the way. They both had a superior knowledge of the roads and the frequent flyers (recurrent patients). They were totally devoted to each other, their family, and the ambulance service. In the 1980s and '90s, the ambulance service was very sound, financially. The community fund drive was always successful. We had a lot of coal miners in the area and the UMW health insurance was a good payor. Even Medicare was a decent payor including, at that time, paying for dialysis transport.

We had two full-size ambulances and various other support vehicles. Early on, the EMTs were all volunteers. As they required more training and hours of in-hospital training, it became necessary for them to evolve into paid employees. Paramedics provided an advanced level of care and West Deer always seemed to be on or ahead of the curve. That was another paid employee. The ambulance service had a nice new building, which grew over the years to accommodate the vehicles and include comfortable sleeping quarters for those on call. I served from 1986 to 2001 and again from 2005 to 2007. I gave a few in-services on, for example, delivery of babies and some other things. The board was generous with the employees when we had the funds. When Medicare stopped paying for dialysis transport, the financial infrastructure began to crumble. It's always hard to go backwards, financially, and Chuck and Peg struggled with the austerity budgets. They were too emotionally involved with everyone. It was a learning experience, and an honor to serve on the board.

53. ONE OF MANY UNPAID TITLES

Sometime between 1985 and 1986, I was asked to be the medical director for the Multiple Sclerosis program. We would always have four to five MS patients on the unit at a time. My job was to monitor their care and reach out to the local neurologists to drum up business. From a medical and rehab standpoint, I will pre-apologize for anything I may say that would offend. The MS population can be difficult to manage, and it took me many years to achieve clarity. Technically, in the 1980s and before, a diagnosis of MS required the patient to have two neurological changes in different parts of the nervous system, occurring at two different times. We had no MRIs to provide evidence of neuroanatomy changes and no blood or spinal fluid test that would make the diagnosis.

From the patient's perspective, they might have numbness in a foot that quickly resolved or they might have something catastrophic like stroke symptoms, where a whole side of their body might be paralyzed for a day or months. MS caused the wires in the brain (and later, we learned, the spinal cord) to be stripped of their natural insulation-called myelin. This prevented the normal transfer of impulses through the nerve. The body had the ability to try to repair the damage, but it would often leave scarring and only partial improvement.

Many patients would go undiagnosed for years. The neurologists would often be the detective to put the story together. Because the diagnosis could be difficult to make, or take many years to make, the patients would be "labeled" psychosomatic or a malingerer. Even when the diagnosis was made, the medical community had little to offer in the form of treatment. High-dose steroids would sometimes halt the progression of disease and at those doses could provide some euphoria (a sense of well-being or happiness). For those who struggled with chronic disease, whether it's pain or symptoms related to MS, to be able to take something for relief, was like a "vacation." The patients knew the good effects of the steroids but were unconcerned about the serious potential side effects.

The physician had to assess the "cost/benefit" ratio. MS patients could be tenacious and persistent about requesting steroids. The side effects could include cataracts, glaucoma, GI ulcers, osteoporosis, high blood pressure, high blood sugar, and many more. The incidence of these side effects might be low, but would only add to the disease burden of the patient.

We had a male, minor league baseball player who had the relapsing/remitting form of MS. It literally was two steps backward, one step forward. He never fully recovered anything he lost and had relapses fairly frequently. We would only give the steroids if the neurologist approved and gave us guidance on how much and for how long the steroids were to be continued. The patient would hound us daily, and frequently he got his wish. Dr. Andy and I were both young and may have been overly concerned about the side effects.

MS patients have chronic fatigue and the steroids would give them an energy boost. It was a good fit to do the steroids while in physical therapy, to get the best improvement. MS is really an autoimmune disease like lupus or rheumatoid arthritis. The body's immune system starts to attack itself. The steroids would decrease inflammation, and that is how they worked.

When the patients couldn't get results from their doctor, they would turn to "alternative" treatment. One of the most popular was bee-sting treatments. There were "providers" who, for a fee, would subject the patients to multiple bee stings on a regular basis. They would assert that bee "venom" had some healing properties. In actuality, it was likely that the trauma of the stings resulted in an increase of the body's natural steroids, produced by the adrenal glands. Thus, they could get their steroid boost without a prescription.

Nobody knew the cause of MS, but our suspicion was that it was a glitch in the patient's immune system. We would commonly get histories of a parent or relative with MS. We had a family, who had three daughters, and they all had MS.

Last, and not least, the medical community underserved or at times shunned these patients. They would develop difficulty with walking, dressing, etc. They might need a wheelchair, and would end up choosing (on their own) equipment that was less than optimal for their needs. They had nobody to help them figure out a reasonable way to manage their setbacks, so they did their best on their own. Those were the facts that were important for the aides, nurses, and therapists to understand. I did my best to continually educate people, so that they would be more empathetic.

Those were the patients I was asked to manage. They commonly didn't like or trust doctors, had little energy for three-hours-per-day therapy and would be asked to change the way they compensated for their problems. The hallmark of MS therapy was to provide some empathy and patience, provide an environment conducive to improvement, and try to establish reasonable goals. Now that you've had the primer on MS, you can appreciate the difficulties of caring for these patients. On arrival, I would try to make time to let them tell their story, get information on their support system, assess their baseline energy (did they routinely take bed rest during the day?) and ask what their goals were. It was not uncommon for the patient to arrive with a history of being bed-confined for years or at least wheelchair-bound for years. Invariably, their goal was to walk again!

My approach and tact changed over the years. I would tell them we would assess walking as a goal, but if that looked impossible, we had to use our time wisely for working on transfers, self-care, and getting them proper equipment. They commonly didn't like that answer—add Dr. Kelly to the Dr. shit list. Learning a safe, energy conserving way to transfer was no replacement for learning to walk.

It was about this time that we admitted, probably our worst case of MS. This was a young girl, who on her honeymoon, developed quadriparesis from suspected MS. Her mother had been diagnosed with MS previously. The groom disappeared. He didn't sign up for this. One day she was sitting in the patient area, in front of the nursing station, waiting for breakfast. Dr. Andy and I were both writing our notes for the day. We both happened to look up at her and couldn't believe what we saw. She was looking in our direction, and first one eye rotated to the side, then shortly thereafter, the other eye rotated to the opposite side. She was picking off cranial nerves before our eyes! The MS was advancing at an alarming rate. She could potentially stop breathing at any time. Dr. Andy and I looked at each other and jumped into action. He called her neurologist, to send her back to the hospital while I called her mother to explain what happened. At the hospital they used chemotherapy to weaken her immune system and hopefully slow the progression of the MS. It worked, and she returned in a week or two, but her recovery was very limited and her mother took her home with some outside help.

As the title suggested, I was the unpaid "medical director" for a subset of patients that were some of the most difficult in the building.

54. "LET'S GO TO A SCHOOL BOARD MEETING AND SEE WHAT GOES ON"

Sometime in 1986, I was approached by our neighbor Doug (Annie's husband) to go to a school board meeting. This was unusual for many reasons. Although his wife, Annie, and Dolly had become close friends and our children played together, I barely knew him. We might wave as we were cutting the grass. His work in the construction industry had a lot of travel involved. I really hadn't thought anything about the school board other than we were pleased with Jason and Matthew's teachers. Sure, why not.

We took our seats in the back of the room. It was all downhill from there. Several parents were complaining about a recent incident in the school and how their children were treated. Apparently, the board had recently agreed to a discipline plan where the police would be called to manage any fights in the school. These weren't gun or knife fights, but pushing incidents in the high school. I couldn't believe my ears. Haven't these kinds of incidents gone on forever, and shouldn't the school be handling the discipline? Did the police really agree to this? The children were taken to the police station! Then the other shoe dropped. The elderly superintendent sat there and denied knowledge of the incident!

When it came time for audience input, at the end of the meeting, I was on my feet. "I can't think of a single reason why you wouldn't know that the police were called to the school." The school had a total of 2000 students—small for districts in our area. Then I asked, "Why would you have such a stupid rule to abuse the local police?" I was fuming. If they had these kinds of issues on a random day that I attended, what was going on in the other meetings? I didn't miss an open meeting for the next nine years. One of the board members, from Creighton, approached me after the meeting, asked my name and encouraged me to continue to attend.

My work life was also going to change. Harmarville decided to get involved in a diet program called Optifast. The program consisted of a liquid supplement which provided four hundred and ten calories per day. Each participant would have a psychological evaluation, physical exam, comprehensive bloodwork, and a weekly physician exam with blood work. The blood electrolytes could get out of balance, and the patient would have to stop. Harmarville had about seven in-house psychologists and additional support personnel to handle the program.

I was approached to be the medical director. I told them I would consider it, if they paid me an amount equal to my moonlighting money. That would allow me to stop the ER shifts and focus on the program. They agreed to my demands. They hired an outside person to be the program director, Joe. He was a young, organized, energetic person and we hit it off immediately.

They sent us to Minneapolis (I think) for training—business and medical. The candidates for the program had to have a BMI (Body Mass Index) of over forty. There was no shortage of participants. Each person had to attend an orientation presented by Joe and myself. We usually had over one hundred people attend, and, at its busiest, we had daytime and evening groups.

The supplement came in multiple flavors, but the best was creamsicle. Each shake was mixed with water or diet soda and you would drink five of these per day to reach four hundred and ten calories. At the time I was around 190 pounds and did the program myself. I lost 45 pounds in a short time and became a more believable presenter. If you were super morbidly obese, you had to be on the eight hundred calorie per day program, to be safe. We had our share of over 400-pound people and had to gear up with appropriate furniture. One of our patients broke a toilet and the toilets all had to be reinforced.

The hope was that adding the psychological component would help the patients keep the weight off. Sadly, though they all lost weight, they eventually regained it after the program. Obesity was very complex and continues to defy a "cure."

It took some time for all of this to get organized, so I was still moonlighting at Union Hospital. It didn't happen very often, but I was working a 7-11 shift, alone, when we got a call from labor and delivery. They needed a doctor there right away, because a patient was about to deliver, and the obstetrician was going to be late. The patient was crowning (the head was showing), and in my training, we always did an episiotomy. You cut the outside vaginal wall to make the delivery a little easier and to prevent a worse "natural tear" from occurring. I did a mediolateral cut, which normally prevented a rectal tear. You cut at about three o'clock. The afterbirth delivered right when the obstetrician walked in. The ER was uncovered, so I quickly left without sewing the episiotomy. A short time later, the obstetrician walked up to me in the ER and started yelling at me about my choice of episiotomy. She should've been thanking me for doing the delivery. It didn't happen often, but I lost it. She was my peer, not my supervisor. My reply was, "Then get off your ass and get here in time to do your own damn delivery." That was my thirty-seventh and last delivery.

55. "TAKE ME OUT TO THE BALL GAME…"

As a child, I "played" Little League, and it soon became apparent I was not an athlete. I *was* somewhat of a good-luck charm. Our team only lost one game, when I was participating in a piano recital. I would be the kid in right field, crouched like a catcher, pulling grass and pretending to be interested. I never got a hit, but I was walked several times. This rousing interest in baseball continued till death.

It was a hot July or August day, and six of the patients were to go to a Pittsburgh Pirate game with the recreation department. Only one of the recreation therapists had a class-2 license to legally drive the van. He was in a minor accident on the way to work, and the outing was to be canceled. The female recreation therapist announced that she was allowed to drive the van, but had to have a class-2 licensed person with her. "Does anyone have a class 2 license?" There, behind her, were six dejected patients, looking like they lost their best friend.

I took out my wallet to check my status, and lo and behold I had a class-2 license. The look on my face must've given me away.

I had several admissions scheduled and really couldn't take four to five hours out of my day to go to a ballgame! To say "no" would have been like drowning puppies while they looked at you. Off came the tie and into the bus we loaded six patients. All the work would be waiting for me when I got back. More to the point, how did I get a class-2 license? God's using me again.

We got to Three Rivers Stadium and were told the wheelchairs had to go to an empty press box on the top level, and the elevators weren't working! The therapist and I spent a lot of time pushing six people up all those ramps. Nobody volunteered to help.

We no sooner got them settled and I turned into a waiter. "I want tacos and a beer."

"No beer," replied Dr. Killjoy.

The next patient said, "I want a hot dog and fries." Okay, that's more reasonable, but he had to be fed, which I was glad to do. It made a dull game go fast.

The patients came out of their shells. They were joking and abusing each other and calling each other "gimps." It was therapeutic, and I was glad I had the experience. Taking them down the ramps was much easier, and I got home about 10:00 P.M. that night.

If there was a professional sport that was of some interest, it was football. Being a Steeler's fan was almost a prerequisite to be a Pittsburgher. I really did enjoy watching the game, but it was just a game. Having won four Super Bowls in the '70s, it made calling yourself a fan much easier.

It was very infrequent that Harmarville could get Steeler tickets, but we had an opportunity to catch a Sunday afternoon game. The elevators of Three Rivers Stadium were working and it was a much different experience. We had family members with us who could fetch the food and do the hands-on care. We had a sixteen-year-old, quiet young man and his father with us. He was a recent admission and was yet to come out of his shell. His father looked and was, petrified. They previously had a close relationship, but this accident and his son's quadriplegia had left them devastated. They had to establish a new normal.

Even on a good wheelchair cushion, the patients were to "weight shift" about every two hours. This could be done several ways. The objective was to redistribute the patient's weight over a different section of skin, to try to prevent pressure sores. Jeff was due for his weight shift and we used this as a teaching moment. His father said, "What do I do?" We found his father a chair and put the locked wheelchair in front of him. We tipped the chair back in his lap and he held it there for about thirty minutes. Jeff could still see the field. There was almost something intimate about this interaction. It broke the ice, and soon the two were discussing the game and smiling, much as if they had walked in and were seated next to one another. Jeff also had a very involved and caring mom. The parents took care of his needs and made life as normal as possible. He finished high school, graduated college, and eventually worked for NASA. We invited his mom back to meet with parents who were struggling to adjust to a new reality. She had a calming and reassuring way of getting through to them. Life would not be the same, but a new "normal" was possible.

56. "WOULD YOU CONSIDER RUNNING FOR SCHOOL BOARD?"

I don't remember the specifics of being asked. I was very busy with work, moonlighting, organizing the Optifast program, and trying to find time to be a father. I was attending all the school board meetings as a concerned parent. Two of the minority board members would talk to me after the meetings. I guess they decided I might be an asset if I were to run.

It must've been around February 1987. Petitions for each party would have to be circulated and submitted to the county by a certain date. One of the two women was up for reelection and we discussed that the only way to make real change, was to capture the five seats on the ballot. The four "hardline" members were running again. I wouldn't have considered it, but in meeting after meeting it became apparent that the current board had lost sight of the fact that the students and education should come first.

The current majority had dug themselves a hole and had spent down the reserve fund, underfunded student needs (like workbooks) and were facing a large tax increase, just to keep things status quo.

Dolly and I discussed my situation and decided it was better to be a part of the solution. Somehow, I could find a few hours a month. We vastly underestimated the amount of time it would take. I was very interested in education and had good organization and judgment skills. We could do this for the kids and the community.

In 1987, Deer Lakes was heavily Democratic. I was a registered Republican. To stand a chance, I would have to change my registration to Democrat. I had been keenly interested in politics since I was at least thirteen years old. I read all of the *Making of the President* books by Theodore H. White. Secretly, I had always wanted to be a U.S. Senator. That wasn't going to happen, but maybe I could do this.

Success in our local polls started by being a Democrat and cross-filing. In Pennsylvania, you could run on both sides of the ticket for school board. By this time, we had assembled five people who would run together. School board elections were won or lost in the May primary. We had to try to get the Democratic Party endorsement. Along with this, came poll workers who would hand out your cards to remind the voters who to support.

The five of us met at my house and had a strategy session. We would definitely be the underdogs, except for the current board member who had a base of support. We decided our best chance was to register new voters. There were close to 600 homes in Cedar Ridge, where I lived. We could see from the county registration list that a vast majority of those young people were not registered to vote. We created a biography sheet, giving each of our backgrounds. To that we would attach voter registration forms, which could be sent in. Finally, we paperclipped a 3 x 5 card with our five names and asked people to put it on their calendars, to remember our names for the election. There were a total of thirteen people running for five seats.

We needed a slogan. Something to make us standout. This was a relatively unique situation for local elections, having five people run together with a slogan. One of the five came up with "A New Direction." It was perfect and exactly described our goal. Better yet, the local newspaper liked it and gave us a lot of free press.

We eventually got the Democratic endorsement (the local Republican Party wasn't active) and the polling date arrived. It was a pretty heavy turnout and people had to stand in long lines to vote. We felt we had a chance when we greeted people at the polls, and they showed us the 3 x 5 card we handed out door-to-door. The results started to come in. West Deer gave our opponents a slight lead, but when the East Deer and Frazer results came in, we took over the lead.

In November, we captured four of the five seats and the fifth spot went to a newcomer with whom we could work. There was some drama due to a human error at one of the polls, but when the official count was announced, we had won. I was satisfied to just be a board member.

Behind the scenes, there was an effort to have me elected president of the board. I didn't catch wind of it until shortly before our swearing-in. That would be a different level of responsibility. I was approached by several local "dignitaries" who felt I was the right person for the job. I was flattered and naïve as to how this would play out.

On the first Monday of December, 1987, we were sworn in and we "reorganized" by electing new officers. I was elected president. We were given two small books about board responsibilities: a code of conduct and Roberts Rules of Order for conducting the meeting. We decided to conduct our meetings, differently. A copy of the agenda would be given out before the meeting and the audience would be given an opportunity to ask questions and provide input before the votes were taken. We established a nonvoting student position to give them an opportunity to give input.

A few days later I was driving past the high school (which was a beautiful campus with large grassy areas), and I was overcome with a sense of responsibility. I always put my heart and soul into my responsibilities, but this was a whole new arena. Little did we know we were about to be baptized by fire.

The school district had recently hired a new superintendent, and he considered us a hostile board. The previous board had spent considerable money for a superintendent search. They had many good candidates, who already had their PhDs and experience. The board ended up hiring the current high school vice principal, who was raised in the district and had no practical experience. He was hired for less money, but we questioned whether that was an area in which to save money. That person was basically the CEO of the school district. Our young superintendent had worked long enough to earn a six-month sabbatical, which he announced he would take to work on his PhD.

Suddenly, we had to find a substitute superintendent for six months. I was put in contact with the intermediate unit and a gentleman who would assist us. For weeks he was unsuccessful, then he found a retired superintendent from Eastern Pennsylvania who would work Monday through Wednesday each week, before going back home. He had good credentials and seemed to have a calming influence over some flammable issues. Things went well initially, but later we found out he made cosmetic solutions. The problems remained.

In January, a popular and sweet school telephone operator was viciously murdered by her ex-husband. The women in the central office had helped her leave the abusive relationship, and now he was a fugitive. The central office staff were terrified. We had to hire an armed guard for each building, because the victim's son was a student.

It might sound callous, but fortunately the murderer was found dead in his truck from a self-inflicted wound, two days later. Otherwise, he would have caused continuing terror and unrest for the school personnel and the victim's family.

We had to start negotiating a new teacher's contract around March 1988. We had an excellent negotiator who served our district for many years. He was the assistant dean of the Duquesne University Law School and was the labor negotiator for practically every police department in Allegheny county. He was a master negotiator, and it was a pleasure watching him work. He was a little earthy, and, on occasion, would let loose with a "You're full of shit, asking for something like that." We spent many hours in negotiations. The last night, we were there until 3:00 A.M. and left with the understanding we had an agreement. The teacher's union leaders would often want to continue into the wee hours of the night, because their contract said they could have the next day off.

At 6:30 A.M., I got a call from our negotiator, saying the teachers were going on strike that morning! What happened? I was furious. We agreed to meet with the board later that morning. The school had never had a strike. We were prepped, but not prepared, for what would follow. School strikes brought out the worst in everybody. The board was angry, the teachers were smug (initially), and the community was split between union and board support. Working parents had to suddenly figure out childcare. My phone was ringing off the hook.

We had a community meeting, and trying to keep control was like herding cats. One woman was sensitive to the dynamic in the room. She said, "The two sides need to put their emotions aside and get this figured out." I'm not sure how we arranged it, but the union leader and I met in a conference room at Harmarville.

The conversation started a little heated. I told him, "I don't know what this will accomplish. We've given you all the money we can afford." The mood suddenly changed, and he explained the teachers had made a mistake and shouldn't have gone on strike. The previous contract had included a provision where teachers needed to act as bathroom monitors in the high school during lunch time and at class change. For the teachers to save face, we agreed on four, $5.00/ hour bathroom monitors to be hired for the high school. I contacted the negotiator and scheduled a meeting of the board that evening. As we gathered, the business manager cautiously asked, "What did you promise them?" I explained, and he said, "That's it?" I explained that a few teachers had fueled the flame, but then they realized they had overreacted and wanted to settle.

We agreed to a short public meeting where everyone would remain silent, announce we had an agreement, and school would resume. I later called the woman who spoke out and thanked her for being the voice of reason. That whole school board journey was a learning experience. It was an honor to serve. It was far from over.

57. THEY GOT THE POWER

Back at work (yes, I'm still working), there was still drama from time to time. I was never much of an athlete, but I was in fair shape. Dolly and I liked to walk and would do so when childcare allowed. We lived relatively close to North Park—a county run park that had a 4.5-mile walking path and road system, around a small lake. There weren't a lot of physical demands in my job, but issues would occur.

When a "Dr. GYAT" was called, you responded as quickly as you could, because you were never sure how many doctors were in the building, and if they were close to the event. They called a "GYAT" on unit four one day, and I took off running from the Unit I charting desk. It was approximately one eighth of a mile distance, and time was of the essence. As I approached the main hall, I rounded the corner and forgot the seating area just outside of our unit. As I was about to tumble over a low-back chair, I made the last-minute decision to hurdle it. I did it! Why couldn't somebody have seen, or better yet recorded it? When you're not an athlete, you have some pride when you do something "athletic."

There was another occasion where I had to intervene. We had a young man who was a pretty high quadriplegic and was struggling to learn to feed himself. Even working with those patients daily, it was a struggle to understand the emotional turmoil they must have felt. Suddenly, they transitioned from being independent to not being able to feed, bathe, or dress themselves. They had no bowel or bladder control, and they were immobile. We could tell from their initial exam, what their limitations would be. It was everyone's goal to give them a victory as soon as possible. For instance, if they had biceps function, but no hand function, they could bring their hand to their face. I would ask OT to give them a utensil holder—basically a Velcro strap applied around the palm of the hand with a sleeve to hold a spoon (not a fork!!). They could practice eating on day one. Nobody made a fuss about the mess of spilled food in the bed. How could you, when you saw the joy on the patient's face, and the hope it sparked in the family.

This particular patient was soon placed in a power wheelchair. "Getting wheels" (the ability to be independently mobile) was another big event. Our building was large with multiple little libraries, a gift shop, large patios and a concrete sidewalk that encircled the entire building. The chair could be operated by a head tilt, a chin piece, or a hand device. A patient using a hand device rarely had hand function, but there were adaptation options that included a small knob, tennis ball, or a goalpost-looking device. The movement might be subtle, but forward movement would go forward, backward would be reverse, and returning to neutral would stop the chair. The patients would practice during physical therapy, and each therapist had their own definition of competence, before letting the patient take off on their own.

This young man was doing well and was typical in wanting to push up the speed adjustment. The chair speed could adjust from painfully slow to pretty fast. He was out on the patio one sunny day, and he was going in circles. I stood and watched, until I realized he wasn't fooling around. His hand had partially come off the hand device, and he lost control of the chair. I had to try to intervene.

The motors on these chairs were fairly powerful, because they had to be able to propel the patient up a steep hill. When out of control, they could be dangerous. I thought, "This is like jump rope. I have to time this so I don't get hit and swat his hand off the control to stop the chair." Fortunately, my timing was good and the chair stopped. The patient was upset. I don't know how long he had been in this predicament. The easiest action would be to use the control and steer the chair myself. I gave him time to compose himself, put his hand back on the control, and told him to drive back to his room. I channeled my grandpa Kelly and made him drive again before this became a phobia. I also turned the speed down, with no patient complaint.

Power chairs provided infrequent drama over the years. We had a thirteen-year-old female who was doing pretty well when her hand slipped, and she put one foot through the wall. After getting her out (she hit between the studs), we x-rayed the foot and leg and found no fractures. The only injury was to her ego, which quickly repaired with the comic remarks of her fellow patients, the staff, and her doctor. The hole was a tourist attraction before it got fixed. It was known as "Sharon's demolition."

Not all outcomes were that fortunate. We had an elderly female admitted with long-term rheumatoid arthritis, and a common side effect of a C1-2 fracture. Her bones were very brittle and she had surgery to stabilize the bones, which basically held the head on the neck. She was in a halo apparatus and had enough weakness that she couldn't walk. When a C1-2 fracture was on the admission list, we knew before seeing the patient that their problem would be weakness. That was otherwise known as a "hangman's fracture," so you either died or just had weakness. Shirley was traveling down the main hall when she lost control and wrecked into the wall, without going through it. We x-rayed her foot and leg and found multiple fractures, which required intervention in case she regained the ability to walk.

Every once in a while, a foot would come off the footplate and they would run over their foot. To prevent more harm, the chair would have to be lifted off the foot. The chair weighed around 500 pounds.

58. THE GUARDIAN ANGEL

The ER work was coming to an end, but there were several memorable events. I was at Union Hospital, when we got a call that they were bringing in a lawn mower accident. The ambulance was close and didn't give much of a report. Was there a laceration? Was a foot or hand cut off? My mind was racing and the adrenaline was pumping.

The ambulance arrived and the crew seemed to be taking their good old time unloading the patient. They finally came through the door, and the patient (Mr. Bad Luck) was lying on his stomach, propped up on his elbows, smiling at us. The adrenaline started to drop. Apparently, Mr. Bad Luck, about fifty-five, was cutting his lawn and had stopped to do something else, letting the mower run. At that time, there was no emergency bar on the handle and you could let go and the mower would keep running. He lost his balance and sat right on top of the mower. Most mowers had a screened, open top to allow ventilation. You could see the top of the motor was turning, which meant the blade was also turning.

The force of his fall broke the protective covering, and the spinning motor drilled into his buttocks. Upon arrival, the patient's embarrassment was overriding (no pun intended) his pain. In the exam room, the patient said, "I sat on the mower, and it literally chewed my ass out!" He had us all in stitches (again, no pun intended). The wound was large, deep, and dirty. This was going to need surgery. I called the on-call surgeon who was typically unhappy about getting a call, particularly if he had to come in. The injury was difficult to explain to the surgeon, and he finally agreed to come in. The surgeon evaluated the wound and agreed to take the patient for surgery. The wound wasn't bleeding much and could be handled by a pressure dressing. They had to call in an anesthesiologist and an OR crew. He stayed with us until the OR was ready. We did an EKG and preop blood work, which looked okay. They finally called for the patient. On leaving, he said, "I hope the surgery isn't all it's cracked up to be." He could've been a comedian.

About an hour later, we got a call he had passed away. We were in shock. There was no obvious reason other than he might've had some unknown cardiac disease which manifested itself under anesthesia. That is why elective surgeries require a preop clearance to try to prevent these events. We were devastated, but had to finish out our shift. I certainly wasn't *his* "guardian angel," but I supposedly was for another patient.

There was a bad motorcycle accident with the driver dead at the scene. The twenty-year-old female passenger was in route with back pain. This was considered a high velocity injury since she was thrown from the motorcycle. The X-ray of her back showed multiple fractures of the thoracic vertebrae with some dislocation of the bone fragments. She was paralyzed from the abdomen down. This was an exam I was used to, but never in the acute phase. This was a trauma center case. With the on-call surgeon's approval, we put "Motorcycle Mama" in an ambulance and sent her to Allegheny General Hospital in Pittsburgh.

About two or three weeks later, I saw her name on our admission list for spinal cord rehab. Having recovered, the smiling, incessantly talking female was very glad to see me. Her mother was in attendance and gave me a hug for saving her life. The patient was a mother of several children and, though paralyzed, was happy to be alive. Her story with me would continue later on. Her mother always called me her "guardian angel."

59. "IT WAS WORSE THAN I THOUGHT!"

During the teacher strike we had to do the budget preparation for the next year. Most of us had never dealt with a budget other than our own. Even in a small school, it added up to millions of dollars. Most of the work fell on the business manager, and school administrators. They had to anticipate the unknown. How many students would there be? How many teachers would retire? How much would the utilities go up? What unexpected problems would occur?

I had attended most of the "open" budget meetings in the previous year, but only knew the topics discussed. Little did I know there were topics that weren't discussed, because the previous board would not entertain them. With a new board, the administrators felt they could resurrect the old issues.

The previous board refused to buy workbooks and told the teachers to copy the old workbooks. This certainly saved money, but it violated copyright laws. Thus, it was not discussed in public. There was no plan to update the current lesson books, and through wear-and-tear and time, they were becoming outdated and unrepairable. The previous board was committed to not raising taxes and they made a colossal mess.

In addition to those horror stories, we were told the floors of the buses were being repaired yearly. They were safe, but barely passed inspection. We had our own buses and mechanics who did a great job. They went over and above to keep the fleet running. That was really true of most of the staff, teachers, cafeteria workers, custodians and administrators. We developed an appreciation for the employees. They were using buses that were thirty years old. Something had to be done.

We pledged to replace a bus every year and considered doing more on an emergency basis. The transportation manager was thrilled. It was a "good faith" effort they hadn't seen. We had an education administrator who came to us with a plan to replace textbooks every five years, starting with those in the worst shape. The price was frightening, but wasn't the education of students our mandate? The business manager said he would find the funds. We were naïve, but we were well aware a tax increase would be necessary.

People had a choice to send their children to public, private, or parochial schools. The decision to use private or parochial schools was based on personal finances, beliefs, and a lack of faith in public schools. Those parents still had to pay real estate school taxes. Before our tenure on the board, the state had decided that the public schools would be responsible to bus private and parochial students to their school, if it was within the district or within 15 miles of the perimeter of the district. Deer Lakes was a huge geographical district, so we were responsible to bus to practically every school in the greater Pittsburgh area, at a cost of $100,000 plus per year. That was worth three and one-half mills of tax, then. Consortiums were formed with other districts to accomplish this feat and save some money. Literally, every issue was an eye- and wallet-opener.

It was my job to try to explain these and other issues to the public. They had a right to know how their tax dollars were being spent. At times I felt like I was thrown to the wolves. The most outspoken tax haters were the elderly, who had no children in school. That scenario had gone on for decades. The obnoxious ones were often seen getting into their brand-new Cadillacs at the end of the meeting. On one occasion I lost it during a particular tongue-lashing we were given. I remember saying something like, "There was a time when grandparents and the elderly taxpayers took pride in the fact that the children of the community were getting an education." A calm came over the crowd, but it was short-lived.

In addition to education. We had other issues to attend. A developer bought 300+ acres in Frazer Township, next to Route 28, to build a huge mall and additional land for stores like Walmart. It would be a major asset for real estate taxes and would bolster our budget. That 300+ acres of land, at that time generated about $1700 per year. With this project, we could receive millions of dollars. For the project to move forward, they had to build a cloverleaf (flyover) on Route 28 to handle traffic into the mall. The money for it would come from a partial abatement of real estate taxes from Frazer Township, Allegheny County, and the Deer Lakes School District. It seemed like a "no-brainer," but there was staunch opposition from the Frazer community, who valued their rural lifestyle. There were negotiations going on all the time. The East Deer and West Deer supervisors weren't directly involved, but they had a lot to say.

This went on year after year, in the background. At one point, I had to take a vacation day to appear at a hearing of the Allegheny County commissioners, to present an impact statement for the school district. This gets into the history of my graft and corruption, of which we were all suspected. The developer took us to lunch, and I had a $10 meal. That completes the summary of my graft, corruption and kickbacks!

The abatement program was very complex and I spent hours describing the school's position. Frazer people were always present and vehement in their opposition. They were well organized and used every excuse from traffic and crime control, to protection of wetlands. The non-Frazer crowd was supportive, but not organized. The mall was built long after I went off the board in 1995. The school's take was far less than what we had negotiated.

Everything was going on simultaneously. I honestly don't know where I found the time, but I did. The family time was always compromised, and Dolly always shouldered the load. She was torn between pride in "our" civic duty and her desire to have more help with the children. They turned out to be good people in spite of (or maybe because of) my minor input.

60. IT ONLY TAKES A SECOND

With the exception of spinal tumors and metastatic lesions, the majority of the spinal cord patients transitioned from "normal" to "abnormal" in a second. In some cases, they could blame themselves or others who caused an accident. Then there were cases where it was an act of God (I hope not!). Any of those life-changing accidents were hard to accept, but having nobody to blame, made them a "Why me, Lord?" kind of moment.

We had a young female college student who was attending a southern university. It was a normal day of classes, but a storm was blowing in. She was walking quickly as she didn't bring an umbrella. Suddenly everything went black.

When she woke up, she was in an emergency room with nurses scurrying around and a doctor sitting on a stool doing something to her head. They saw she was awake, and they told her she was at University Hospital. She was found on the ground with a brick lying next to her. She had a gash on her head and at the very least a concussion. They couldn't find an ID on her (remember—no cell phones yet). She was Jane Doe.

"What's your name sweetheart?" a pleasant older nurse asked. She immediately said, "Linda."

"Who can we call to let them know you're here?"

"Call my parents, they live in Pennsylvania. Their phone number is…. I'm a little foggy; give me a minute."

The minute was actually an hour. The accident was about three hours prior. Nobody knew she was hurt. She finally came up with a number and nobody was home. They had to leave a message. Linda was alone, terrified, and still pretty foggy. They wanted to get skull X-rays to make sure there was no fracture. If she needed a CT scan, she would have to be transferred to a different facility.

The pleasant nurse said, "We want to change these bloody sheets. Grab ahold of the side rail and we will turn you." Linda tried to do what she was told but couldn't.

"I can't move my arms!!" she cried. "I can't feel my body! Are my legs moving?"

On arrival, she was unconscious with a scalp laceration and normal vital signs. Nobody considered a neck injury. "Doctor, I need you over here," the nurse said forcefully. They began talking over her as if she wasn't awake. "She could have a spinal injury. Get a Philadelphia collar on her and send her for C-spine films, stat!"

Linda was petrified. What does that mean? Do these people know what they're doing? She wanted her parents. Had they called back? They are nine hours away!

That situation was not uncommon. That was the beginning of a nightmare that seemed to never end. Her parents called back, while she was in x-ray. They wanted to leave immediately, so they didn't speak to her.

A brick had blown off the roof of a building and hit her on the head in such a way that her neck flexed forward she had a C4-5 fracture. The bones were poorly aligned, and she would need surgery to relieve the pressure on the cord.

There was no time to wait on her parents. The neurosurgeon reviewed her films and talked to her. She heard the words "surgery" and "permanently paralyzed" and she needed to give permission. She wasn't prepared to answer. She was in shock. She eventually said, "yes" and they prepped her for the OR.

Mom and Dad were probably still in Pennsylvania, and there was no way to call them. Some guy in a mask said, "Count backwards from ten and take a deep breath."

When she awakened, the room was spinning, and she was nauseated. "Where am I? What's going on?" She could see nurses moving from bed to bed.

"About time you got awake," said a nearby nurse. "Your parents are here and want to see you. Let me get you something for nausea, first."

She must've fallen asleep again, then she got awake and saw her mom holding her hand and crying. Her dad looked worried and frozen. They told her where she was, what apparently happened, and the surgeon said the surgery went well. The spinal cord was damaged, but was intact. There was a chance of recovery!

In the following days her parents did some research, and Harmarville Rehabilitation Center in Pittsburgh had a spinal cord unit. As soon as she could travel, she would go there. As with most patients, she had her setbacks. First, she got sick with a urinary tract infection, which had to be treated. She wasn't getting out of bed and developed pneumonia, which required IV antibiotics and breathing treatments. She was coughing up mucus and thank God her mom was there so she could help her spit into a tissue.

Mom stayed with her day and night. Dad came every day from the nearby motel. Four weeks had gone by. She could finally make the trip to Pittsburgh, by ambulance. A thoughtful nurse gave her pain and nausea medicine before she left. She slept much of the way, with her mother by her side.

"Welcome to Harmarville," said the head nurse. She took a thorough history, vital signs, and checked her from head to toe. "The doctor is busy with another patient. We're going to give you a shower." The patient was ecstatic. Mom was scared.

"How can you do that? She hasn't been out of bed?"

"We have a large shower and we will do it on a cart, after we cover her collar with plastic to keep it dry," said the nurse. "You can come with us, if it's okay with Linda."

Finally, someone recognized her as a person and gave her an option. "Will you wash my hair? It hasn't been washed for a month!"

"We will shower you from head to toe. The hospital doesn't have our equipment," said the nurse.

After the shower, the patient was smiling and her mom was crying tears of joy. "We picked the right place. These people know what they're doing." My partner and I came in and did thorough physicals. We explained that only time would tell the outcome, and the progress would be slow. Her age and good health were in her favor.

Next came the therapist from PT. "We want to get you up in a chair and take you to therapy. We know this is your first time. You may get dizzy, but this chair will tilt back and we will be laying you on the mat for our evaluation."

Instead of feeling fear, Linda felt excitement. "More good things have happened in a day, here, than in a month at the hospital." All the employees exuded confidence, and the patient and her parents began to breathe easier.

It only took a second.

61. IT ONLY TAKES A SECOND—PART 2

Brad was a sixteen-year-old, popular student. He had just gotten his driver's license and with the help of a friend of a friend, had a part-time job at the Allegheny County Airport. It was a small airport and Brad assisted one of the mechanics. It was a sunny day and a dual engine plane had landed because of an engine not sounding right. The pilot kept the engine running, so the mechanic could hear the problem. "Go get the other tool chest," said the mechanic, and Brad, forgetting where he was, backed up and turned into the path of the propeller. In a second, it chewed him up and spit him out onto the pavement. There was blood everywhere with severed limbs and exposed organs, but amazingly, he was breathing.

Life flight was called and a paramedic from the local ambulance was quickly on the scene-trying to stabilize the situation. Soon the doctor and nurse from the helicopter were helping and calling the hospital to get their blood supplies to the emergency room. He lost a lot of blood. The helicopter ride was about ten minutes.

At Allegheny General, the bed was surrounded by staff. They started several more IVs, in places they normally didn't have to use. Blood, platelets and plasma were replenishing his supply, but he was still losing blood. He had to be moved to the operating room, where a team of surgeons were repairing his abdominal injuries, and did amputations of unsalvageable limbs. They had never seen anything like it, but as in any area of medicine, you prioritize the problems and take care of them as best you can.

In two days, he received 150 different blood products. He began to stabilize. He had at least ten more surgeries planned (many of them skin grafts), but he had to stabilize first. He was in the acute care hospital for two months. There were only four cases in the literature of people surviving propeller incidents. He had a loving family who had their own horror story about the day of the accident.

We were warned about the patient, but had few facts about how he was overall and what he would need. The admission committee decided he would be best cared-for on the spinal cord unit. The patients tended to be younger, and the staff had more experience with wound care. The physicians had experience with prostheses (artificial limbs) and could consult other physicians in the building for anything beyond their expertise.

The first thing we saw was a ten-inch-high pile of records to review. The hospital rarely sent a discharge summary, because there wasn't time to do one.

Dr. Andy and I organized the pile into sections of essential and nonessential reading. The day-to-day nursing and therapy notes usually did not give us the information we needed. We wanted to formulate a problem list, from which we could navigate his needs.

After several hours of reading, we decided to go see him together. We walked into the room expecting the worst. There he was, sitting up in bed, wearing a grin from ear to ear. The rest of what was left of him was wrapped in gauze. We examined and photographed all the wounds. They were so extensive, but the smile was and would be a fixture.

Everybody loved this guy. He blended right in. The twenty-plus year-olds took him under wing, and he inherited a whole flock of "grandparents." His parents were very happy with his care. The nurses pampered him and I'm sure I did too. I had trouble with the young patients who could've been my children. "There, but for the grace of God go they…." It wasn't distracting. If anything, it made me more empathetic. In retrospect, I treated all my patients like family. I would only refer them to doctors I would see myself. That sounds like patting myself on the back, but I had no allegiance to anyone or any hospital system. The patients always came first.

Brad was with us for probably four months. He had three prostheses and was frequently in outpatient for adjustments. He was still growing and was very active. He graduated high school and was accepted at Duquesne University in Pittsburgh.

It was a cold snowy day in January of his freshman year, when we got a call from his mother. He was in a car accident on an icy road, and he didn't survive. I think she called us from the ER, and before she contacted her family. She was so grateful for the last two years of quality life. She attributed that to us, but it was all

Brad and his attitude. Everyone was crying. We walked around like zombies. We couldn't quickly put that aside. We were all too emotionally involved.

Again, it only took a second. He was dead at the scene. Every second was precious. I was tearing up while I was writing this.

62. NOTHING IS SIMPLE

The ambulance board and the Optifast program were relatively stable. I was comfortable at Harmarville, but every day had manageable problems. The school board was another issue. I was elected Board President four times. The superintendent and I were both learning our responsibilities. On several occasions, he wanted to share information with me and not the board. I refused, because my office of president was to conduct meetings and keep things under control. We both knew we had a board member who was leaking information to the newspaper, but all board members had the right to information. We caught and confronted the "leaker" eventually. All in all, we had an excellent, thoughtful board.

We had a small, empty school building in Russellton that had been closed for years. The building was salvageable and in a good location. We were offered $50,000 for the building. To get it off our hands and on the tax rolls would be fantastic! Finally, something positive was happening.

Our solicitor had to research the deed. It went back to the 1920s. At our next meeting, he dropped the bomb. The land was donated by the local mine and there was a stipulation that if the land was not being used by the school, it reverted back to the mine.

It took some time to find out which mine was the donor. It no longer existed and had been sold several times. It ultimately became part of LTV Steel. Ling-Timko-Vaught was a large conglomerate whose steel division was in bankruptcy court! You had to be kidding?! For months, we had the buyer breathing down our neck and threatening to withdraw his offer. The solicitor spent a lot of time researching the situation. The next thing we knew, we were before the Superior Court of New York petitioning for a separation of a relatively useless piece of property. It took a while, but the petition was granted. The sale went through and we netted whatever was left after the lawyer bills. It probably wasn't much. I don't remember the number.

Simultaneously, we had an elementary building in Creighton that we needed to close for multiple reasons. It was the grade school I had attended. Creighton was gradually declining, and fewer students were attending that school. Some teachers had only ten to twelve students in a class. We couldn't afford or justify those ratios, when the West Deer elementary schools had twenty or more students in a class.

In addition, the school had asbestos-coated pipes and asbestos in the basement floor tiles. In Pennsylvania, the state will provide funds for realistic renovation, but prefer to put their money into new construction. There were no renovation funds, and we couldn't afford the needed abatement program. Geographically, we were a large district. The middle school, high school and the other grade schools were located close together and were almost dead center of the district, geographically. Our plan was to close the school and absorb the affected students into the other buildings. It would have been easier to rob Fort Knox. The meetings were filled with emotional pleas to keep JFK (renamed for President Kennedy in 1967) open. It was portrayed as the last vestige of social life in Creighton.

I offered to attend and answer questions at a PTA meeting in Creighton. I had an organized presentation, including the fact that we could not promise that their students were safe in the building. The basement was cordoned off, but that wasn't a permanent solution. The elderly citizens were more sentimental than the young parents, but they were all upset. It baffled me that they didn't understand that I, too, was emotional, but forced to be rational. I was getting used to being pummeled in public. It never felt good. The building was closed and the students were bused the same distance (or less) as my children. Twenty-five years later, I was still known as the Dr. Kelly who closed JFK!

63. "TO BE OR NOT TO BE…"

Making time for school board and work was often challenging. There were a few cases where the two crossed paths. Janet was a sixteen-year-old, popular student in school. She was a better than average student and involved in extracurricular activities. It was a normal day at Deer Lakes, when she developed an unusual feeling. She asked the teacher for a hall pass to go to the restroom.

She left the classroom and collapsed on the floor in the hall. She was fully awake and called for help. There was no feeling in her legs and they wouldn't move. I'm sure there were bystanders who thought she was faking it.

The ambulance was called and she went to a local hospital. They were unable to find a cause and sent her to a Pittsburgh hospital that had better imaging equipment. Since her findings were limited to the lower extremities, it was felt this was a low thoracic spine problem. Her exam showed a line at the level of her bellybutton, below which she had no feeling. The MRI scan showed some swelling in the cord at T10–11.

The spinal tap was unremarkable and a presumed diagnosis of transverse myelitis was made. The rest of the picture fit. She had cold symptoms about two weeks earlier. Transverse myelitis is an inflammation of a section of the spinal cord, which became swollen and blocked normal function below that level. The cause was not specifically known, but was thought to be a virus that settled in that area of the spine and was attacked by her immune system. This caused the spinal cord damage. Sometimes people will develop back pain and sometimes not. The prevailing thought was that a DNA glitch in her immune system caused it to overreact. We never saw multiple family members with this disease, so there was something specifically different in that patient. After about a week in the hospital, she was transferred to Harmarville, which was close to home. She was scared but unemotional about the situation. Our exam showed a T10 paraplegia—probably "complete."

This was a term we did not discuss on admission, but was a useful medical description, depicting a situation where there were no physical findings of nerve activity below T10. She had no sensation for simple touch or pinprick. None of the leg muscles were seen to work. She had an absence of bowel and bladder function. Someone in the hospital told her she was a complete injury.

The acute care personnel needed to tone down the "complete" injury rhetoric. With it went the presumption that there would be no return of function. Conversely, an "incomplete" injury left the door open for improvement. Being young, "incomplete" and in good health had a much better prognosis. We had seen our share of "complete" injuries become "incomplete" over time. Unfortunately for Janet, the spinal cord damage was complete, and she would remain wheelchair-bound. She completed high school, did some technical or college training, got married and had children. Paralyzed females are able to bear children and we always made sure they knew their fertility was not compromised.

My family practice specialty allowed Harmarville to take patients below the age of eighteen. My medical partners were all internal medicine boarded, which allowed them to do adult medicine, but not pediatric.

We admitted a thirteen-year-old boy who was walking with some friends when, through horseplay, he was pushed into a pond headfirst. He had an instant C5–6 fracture. Fortunately, his friends prevented him from drowning. He was from out of state, but sent to Pittsburgh for acute care, then referred to us for rehab. His injury looked "complete" and the decision was made to stabilize his spine and not worry about the cord compression scenario. He was placed in a halo apparatus, after surgery, and eventually sent to us.

He was a quiet kid, and scared, as they all were. He could feed himself, with help, but he was dependent for all other care. We soon got him "wheels" and he began to open up. He had, at that time, a typical four-month rehabilitation. Halos were almost always on for three months. It was a special challenge for the nurses to keep them clean and comfortable during that time. We sent him to the neurosurgeon for halo removal at three months. He was in the final phase of acute rehab when one morning he could consciously move his right great toe. At that moment he became "incomplete." There was some urgency in his situation, because there was continued cord compression that the neurosurgeon hadn't addressed. We sent him back to the hospital for corrective surgery. When he returned, even more muscles were working. That was like starting at the beginning.

He was with us for three more months, but they were much happier months. He continued to improve and had a goal to walk out of the building. Fortunately, he achieved his goal. It was life-affirming to see his fellow patients be so supportive and joyful for his accomplishments, even though the same was not happening for them.

Thus, you can see why we didn't like to use the term "complete." You just never knew what would happen. Normally, we would give the patient some guidelines. If big changes were to happen, it would usually happen in the first nine months. We had seen patients get changes up to two years post injury. That gave them a framework to use for hope and reality.

64. "I WON'T INVESTIGATE AN ELECTED OFFICIAL"

We, obviously, faced many challenges with the school board, but the biggest was yet to come.

In small townships, it was common for there to be one tax collector for the municipal and school taxes. East Deer and Frazer had long-serving tax collectors who did an excellent job. It was not unusual for people to be reelected to that position. West Deer had a lady who collected taxes for years. She was a bit unorthodox in her bookkeeping. She used shoeboxes and collected a lot of cash. In those days, there were a lot of old coal miners who paid everything in cash. She began to become forgetful and didn't run again. A man I will call Mr. Bad, decided to run for the position during the same year we were elected to the board. He was no sooner in office, when he began heckling the board to raise his compensation. We were powerless to do so. Pennsylvania law stipulated that the compensation had to be amended before the election and would be put in place after the candidate was sworn in. The previous board had not done that. We were stuck with the current plan. He apparently approached West Deer Township, also, and they gave him an increase. In fairness, he handled many more accounts than the other two tax collectors, but he was paid the same. We tried to even the playing field by setting the salary based on a specific number of accounts, and then paying extra for accounts over and above that number. He didn't like the compromise. The school district worked on a fiscal year, July 1 to June 30, and the township budget was on a calendar year. That gave the taxpayers a break between payments, but was an ill-conceived plan.

The first month, after the tax bills went out, was the biggest influx of money. It decreased in subsequent months. We were at the mercy of the tax collector to deposit the funds. Mr. Bad decided he would make small deposits to interfere with our cash flow.

I'm not sure how we found out he was embezzling—I think he was bragging about how he was "giving it" to the board. He had to submit a monthly report about collections, and it was way out of line. We were suspicious he was stealing money. He had the ability to move funds back and forth between the township and the school accounts. Since the township met his demands, we were likely on the short end. He was out of town a lot, and people were complaining they couldn't pay their taxes.

The solicitor contacted the Allegheny County Sheriff and was told the following, "I won't investigate. He's an elected official." The solicitor relayed the message, and we were flabbergasted! We asked the solicitor what we could do. He told us the tax ledgers were technically ours, and the business manager had a key to the tax office. We deputized him to take a police officer with him and confiscate the tax books and put them in our safe.

We found out Mr. Bad was in Atlantic City, New Jersey, and the solicitor contacted the FBI. We hired a forensic accountant to go over the books and confirm our suspicions. The FBI found his car, but couldn't find him.

He eventually showed up in Las Vegas, and after he blew all the money, he committed suicide. He was bonded for $500,000 and that was the amount taken. We spent another approximately $60,000 on accountants and lawyers. That was the amount we lost.

This was close to the 1991 election, and you repeatedly heard from the older people, "He really stuck it to you guys."

My response was, "No, he stuck it to you. It was your money."

65. WHAT'S THE ODDS?

In early 1988, I was approached by Dr. Gil to get involved with a new spasticity control program. Medtronic, who made the abdominal pump that I already talked about, made a new, computerized pump and was starting FDA trials. A neurosurgeon, at Presbyterian Hospital in Pittsburgh, was interested in participating in the implant portion, but not the maintenance part of the program. Since I had previous pump experience, I was a logical choice. The physician who did the original investigation was Dr. Penn in Chicago. He discovered that Baclofen, our first-line oral spasm medicine, could be delivered directly to the spinal fluid (in liquid form) with this pump. It was one of the first treatments where the medicine could be delivered directly to the area where it was needed. When you gave oral medicine, only part of it was absorbed. Once it was in the blood, it had to cross the "blood-brain barrier" (which protects the brain from infection and unwanted materials), to get into the spinal fluid, which circulates around the brain and spinal cord. The pump would deliver the medicine right to the spinal fluid where it was needed.

The spasticity that developed with spinal cord, head injury, multiple sclerosis, cerebral palsy, and stroke patients was what we called upper motor neuron spasticity. The muscles talk, through the spinal cord, to the brain all the time. The slightest movement could cause a message that would split and go to the spine and brain. In normal function, the brain would send a quick message back saying, "Don't react." When the spinal cord, or that specific part of the brain was damaged, the "control" was lost. The spine would send a message to the muscle to react. The "uncontrolled" movement was a spasm. They could be so severe they would interfere with dressing, transfers, sleep, and walking (in "incomplete" patients).

Practically all of our patients developed spasticity. Spasms weren't all bad. They flexed that particular muscle, even though it was uncontrolled, and prevented atrophy (wasting) of that muscle. When spasms interfered with function, we started treatment. The first medicine was called Baclofen (Lioresal was the brand name). We would push the dose to a total of 80–120 mg per day. If that didn't work, we would add dantrolene (Dantrium), which worked a little differently and had a lot of potential GI and acne side effects. If those two meds didn't work, we would add diazepam (Valium), which was a cousin of Baclofen. Sometimes it worked, sometimes not. Dr. Gil always said, "Don't give more than twenty mg of Valium per day. They may still have spasms, but they don't give a damn." That was sage advice. Also, we had a lot of "entrepreneurs" who figured out the Valium was selling for five dollars a tablet on the street. That's one of the reasons Valium became a controlled substance (treated like a narcotic).

To get a good orientation, Medtronic was having a conference in New York City. One of the senior neurosurgeons from Presbyterian Hospital was also going for a technical conference on implantation of the pump. I had met him once, and knew his wife had recently died. Dolly came with me for a weekend getaway. We wanted to see a Broadway show and could only get tickets for one show. We ran into the neurosurgeon, and asked if he would like to join us for dinner and the show. He agreed and we were able to get another ticket. The show was *Blythe Spirit* by Noel Coward. Remember, no cell phones or Google, so we blindly were going to a show about which we knew nothing. We got to the theater and soon discovered the show was about a widower's deceased wife who comes back to haunt him and his new wife. What's the odds?! Dolly and I were mortified and wanted to slither away. He was very gracious about it, and we apologized profusely. Talk about throwing salt into a wound!!

Back to the pump. Dr. Gil had a perfect patient to get the first Pittsburgh Baclofen pump. Lou was a young man who was injured in a motorcycle accident. He was an incomplete injury and would be able to walk, except his spasms (on all three medicines) would throw him off balance. He was essentially wheelchair-bound.

He had a pump put in sometime in 1989, then came to Harmarville. At the beginning, I had a very cumbersome computer with a phone (old-style) looking wand. To take a reading from the pump you would use the wand, and you also used it to send a message back by radio waves. Before the pump was implanted, Lou had a test that he had to pass. He was brought into the hospital and had a spinal tap, through which he received a 50µg dose of liquid Baclofen. He was monitored every hour, and the spasticity was tested. At about hour two, his spasms were gone, and he could walk with a cane. Unfortunately, the effects lasted about eight hours, and the spasms came back. He was eager to proceed.

Surgery went well, and he came to Harmarville for me to titrate the right dose. The pump could be set to run at different rates at different times of the day. For instance, if the spasms were worse in the morning, you could set the night dose to increase about two hours before he awakened. It had to be stressed that the pump worked off the clock. Your schedule needed to be consistent to get the best results. Lou did well and rarely used the wheelchair. He had a gnarly, wooden, homemade cane that became his trademark.

The second implant patient was Susan, an MS patient. She was wheelchair-bound, but her spasms interfered with her care. She couldn't tolerate most of the oral meds because they made her sleepy. She was given a one-half test dose and did well. MS patients, in general, were more sensitive to medications. By putting the medicine right in the spine, she didn't get the sedation side effects. The major rule for any MS patient, with any medicine, was "go slow and go low."

Susan often came into the office with her two adorable granddaughters, who were very well behaved. I would let one hold the wand when we took a reading, and the other would do it when we were sending the message back to the pump. They were thrilled!

The refill procedure required you to do a surgical prep over top of the pump, then insert a needle into the pump, remove the leftover medicine and then instill the new medicine. If the patient was thin you could easily feel and mark the edges. The refill kit had a plastic overlay with a fourth-of-an-inch opening, in the center, to guide where the needle needed to go.

If the patient was heavy or the pump was implanted deep, the above task became much more difficult. Some of the patients gained a lot of weight after the implant, and I had to use the entire length of the needle, after having to stick them multiple times. If I could figure out their particular anatomy, I would draw a "map" on the chart for future use.

Poor Lou hated needles, and I had to work out a system where he closed his eyes, took a deep breath in and while blowing it out, I would quickly stab the needle into place. His abdomen had zero fat and his abs were quite strong. If you weren't quick enough, his abs would flex and throw the needle off course.

Over a relatively short time, I had twenty-two pump patients enrolled in the FDA study. Each patient visit had a special form, where you estimated the tone (or stiffness) in the legs and then filled in their dose, etc. This went on for three years. In the twenty-eight years I worked with the pumps, there were no infections. I was proud of that, and the fact that I was the guru for adult pumps in Pittsburgh. Children's Hospital used a lot of pumps for cerebral palsy, but their rules didn't apply to adults.

There was one peculiarity about the pumps that caused some friction between the neurosurgeons and myself. When the catheter was threaded into the spinal fluid, it was to go toward the head. It was a blind procedure for the neurosurgeon, who assumed that as long as the catheter was in the spinal fluid, it would do its job. I x-rayed all the patients on admission, to see how high the catheter went. Over time, it became apparent that if the catheter went down instead of up—it didn't work well. I would call the neurosurgeons and ask them to reposition the catheter. We commonly would argue the issue, but eventually they gave in and the pump would work better. They began to do the procedure with x-ray guidance, to be sure the catheter was correctly positioned.

Years later, I was invited to attend a Medtronic conference in Minneapolis, Minnesota. There was a panel of young "experts" on the stage who presented, then had an open forum. Someone asked if the pump had been used in pregnant patients. One of the "experts" said there were two cases recorded, but he didn't know much about it. I raised my hand and said I managed one of the cases, and related that it didn't interfere with the pregnancy or delivery.

Another person asked, "Can this be used in familial spastic paraparesis?" The "expert" said, "We haven't had any experience with that." I raised my hand again and explained I managed three cases with the disease and described their outcome. After another question was unanswered, and I gave them some information, the expert said," You should really be up here."

I replied, "I wasn't invited."

At the peak of my pump practice, I had over one hundred patients and on some clinic days, filled, and reset ten to twelve pumps in two hours.

66. KICKING A MAN WHEN HE'S DOWN

We had a young man admitted, from a motor vehicle accident, with quadriplegia. He, unfortunately, was a "complete" injury. He had some upper arm function but no hand function. He was a pleasant patient and did well. He was dependent for all aspects of his care except for feeding and some face washing. Even with eating, the food had to be cut up and a plate guard attached to give him the ability to push the food onto a spoon or fork. He also had to have the Velcro strap, which held the utensil, placed on his hand. With so little potential, the ability to pick which food you ate and how fast you ate it, was a significant win for the patient.

During his four-month stay, it became obvious he had little to no family support. I don't remember what the issue was. In any event, he was estranged from his family, and the fact that he had such a catastrophic injury had no bearing on the situation. His discharge planning was very difficult because he needed a place to live and 24-hour care.

Fred had a desire to get a college education. Edinboro University (in Edinboro, PA) was the only school set up to accommodate his needs. Pennsylvania had an agency called the Bureau of Vocational Rehabilitation, who would provide significant funding to help people training for a new vocation and return them to the tax rolls. I believe they helped Edinboro to provide special housing and aides for their disabled students. We got good feedback about that program.

I don't remember what Fred was studying, but he was only about two years into his training when he noted he was feeling weaker and having trouble feeding himself.

Fred called and made an appointment to see Dr. Andy. It was decided that we might need a team approach to figure it out. He was admitted for a thorough eval. The nurses and everyone were glad to see him and catch up on his accomplishments. We, essentially, were his family, and he was glad to be "home."

I was the first doctor to see him. Even though he had a thorough physical two years previous, I repeated my usual physical, looking for any abnormality. Was this a nutritional or chemical problem? Could he be anemic or have electrolyte problems? After updating his history, I started my exam.

He opened his mouth so I could check his mouth and throat. It was proceeding normally until I looked at his tongue. The surface of the tongue was moving as if there were 100 ants running around just under the surface. That was called "fasciculations." It indicated that the muscle fibers were contracting individually and not as a controlled unit. This could be seen in any muscle in the body, where the muscle had lost its nerve input. I stared at it for a while. I wanted to be sure I had the finding right. This could not be explained by his original injury, and it was an ominous finding.

Dr. Andy saw him next, and he, too, saw the abnormality. We discussed the finding and shared our fear that this was amyotrophic lateral sclerosis or Lou Gehrig's disease. In that disease, the motor nerves are diseased and stop working, causing weakness, balance issues, etc. The fact that he had so few muscles working, likely delayed the diagnosis. There was no treatment for that. It was ominous that the cranial nerves were affected, as witnessed in the tongue findings. We wanted to be sure we were right, and the neurologist confirmed we were correct. We preferred to tell him ourselves. This was a terrible situation.

Dr. Andy and I set aside some time to meet with the patient and explain. He, to this point, didn't understand the gravity of the problem. We explained what was happening, neurologically. In the 1990s, the life expectancy, after diagnosis, was usually no more than six months. Over the years I developed a belief that there were multiple forms of ALS, because we had people who lived for years after their diagnosis.

We had no idea how long Fred would have had symptoms, but the tongue findings were very serious as they were located close to the brainstem, which controlled breathing. He had to know that he likely would develop a breathing complication, and if he was placed on a ventilator, he wouldn't come off. Since there was no treatment, he should probably refuse ventilator support and choose hospice. At the appropriate time, he would have to be heavily sedated until his breathing stopped.

I'm sure our voices were breaking, because our hearts were. When you go into medicine, you don't realize how you might be put in this situation. How can one person be so unlucky? He wanted to be discharged to a nursing home near his home. He only lived a month or two.

Much like a "100 year" flood, the river devastated this individual, presenting a situation from which he could not recover.

67. ON THE LIGHTER SIDE

We had a thirty-year-old, stocky, white male admitted as a quadriplegic after a motor vehicle accident. He had been on a ventilator and had a tracheostomy tube. We could normally take them out after a few weeks. Getting out of bed and breathing deeper during therapy would help them become more stable.

This particular patient was very unstable. We had to send him back to the hospital for deterioration of his respiratory situation. He returned in about a week and wasn't a lot better. We had trouble managing his respiratory secretions. He also had several urinary tract infections and was not "turning the corner." In addition to those problems, he had terrible spasms, and his feet would continually fly off the wheelchair foot pedals. We had to get pedals with loops to keep his feet on the chair.

One day, sitting in front of the nurse's station, he had such severe leg spasms the whole wheelchair flipped over backwards. Since his feet were bound to the chair, the whole unit flipped back and he hit his head. We had carpet on the floor and he wasn't knocked out or had any apparent injury.

From that day on, all of his medical problems started to resolve. His respiratory situation became more stable. We were working toward removing his trach. The fevers were gone. He seemed more alert and was improving in therapy. He had "turned the corner," a phrase I commonly used to provide hope for those patients who were stubborn to stabilize. "There will be a day, and I don't know when, that these medical problems will resolve and you will 'turn the corner.'"

It was our joke that I told him, "If I had known that would work, I would have dropped you on your head a month ago!" Unfortunately, his spasms were still an issue, but we found relief with medications. His injury was too recent to entertain a Baclofen pump.

We had a woman in her late twenties who was quadriplegic from a motor vehicle accident. She was scared and pretty withdrawn. Sally was going through her initial depression, and we had to give her some time and space.

One day, around noon, I was seeing another patient and heard someone repeatedly screaming, "Nurse! Help me! Nurse!" I was trotting around the semicircular hall of the unit to find who was screaming. The culprit was in room 104. The nurse and I got there about the same time.

I asked Sally, "What is wrong?" Sally had no meaningful movement in her arms and a housefly got into her room. She panicked and started to scream. Unfortunately, the fly flew down her throat, her worst nightmare.

She tearfully asked, "What are you going to do about this?"

I seriously turned to the nurse and said, "Go get the can of Raid." The patient's eyes got very big, and she stopped crying. I said, "What can I do about this?" There was a moment of awkward silence, and all three of us began to laugh. She told everybody that story, and how I was going to spray her throat with Raid. The moral of the story was, "Put on your call light and keep your mouth shut!"

It seemed like I was always in a hurry, not with the patients, but to get to my next destination. We had three admissions, and I needed to evaluate all three. My office was right next to the nurse's station, and I had just finished reviewing the records of the first patient. With my medical bag in hand, I exited my office quickly, not knowing the tile floor was being mopped. In a split second, I remember seeing my feet in front of my face, and thud, I was flat on my back.

Several patients witnessed the spectacle, and were concerned I was injured. I was a little sore, but my pride took the beating. Lesson learned—slow down.

68. FALLING FROM GRACE

The school board work continued to take a lot of time and attention. I was completing my first four-year term and had been president for all four years. We were getting things done, and I was willing to continue that role at the pleasure of the board.

We had a resignation from the board that needed to be filled. The proper advertisements were completed, and we had several applicants to interview. They all seemed genuinely interested to serve and be team players. There was one candidate who interviewed particularly well and worked in drug counseling. I felt she would be a great asset to the board. We had, at that time, only a few instances of drug problems. This person's insight would be invaluable. I had to convince the board to accept this candidate, and they eventually did.

The November election was upon us. The current board was reelected. One of the board members didn't feel I was aggressive enough, particularly concerning the mall project. He secretly put together a five-member majority to take over as president. I was surprised, but not devastated. It might actually be nice to sit on the side and have someone else do all the talking. I was disappointed that the newly appointed board member voted against me. In all fairness, they didn't know how I campaigned for them behind the scene.

I took a seat on the side, but continued to contribute to the discussions. The work had calmed down some and our biggest time challenge was repeatedly hiring assistant high school principals. It seemed like that position was vacant about every three or four months. The position was to assist the principal with teacher evaluations, but primarily was to handle student discipline.

That was a real challenge, as our configuration was seventh through twelfth grades in the same building, that had one principal and his assistant. Junior and senior high were more challenging, and they had roughly one thousand students in that building.

The most frustrating part of that hiring frenzy was that neighboring districts would "cherry pick" our new hires. It seemed like we were continuously grooming people for other districts. We hit a period where there was a shortage of good candidates. We had one applicant, that had two years of teaching a more minor subject, and felt he had accomplished his role as teacher. He was ready to move to administration. We did not agree. During interviews, I liked to present a scenario and ask them to explain how they would resolve the issue. Their answers would demonstrate their logic and critical thinking skills under pressure.

Unfortunately, we had a second teacher strike, and I wasn't in charge. The teachers certainly had their right to strike, but it brought the ugliness out of everyone. The strike was finally resolved and things calmed again.

We had building issues that needed to be addressed. The majority of the board was in favor of reducing the number of buildings to three. The total number of students was fairly stable, but we had some housing developments underway. There was no way to estimate future needs.

We planned to do some renovation to the Junior/Senior high school, and a major addition to what would become the middle school. We wanted K-5 in one building, 6-9 in the building being expanded and 10-12 in the existing high school. We felt that grouping made more sense, and I was a roof counter.

Every roof needed replaced every ten years or so and the fewer the better. Each roof required a nurse, librarian, and an administrator. I had no problem with any of those vocations, but in the school system, they are probably less productive than the teachers and the cost is considerable. Fewer roofs means less duplication of services and less replacement costs. One problem was that the construction included no provisions for air-conditioning. We kept hearing there was a push for year-round school, at the state level. I insisted the plans be redone with at least ductwork for air-conditioning to be added.

We had to have open meetings and explain the project. It was very unpopular because we would close another building about two miles away. People developed an unhealthy fondness for their local school. Everyone enjoyed a shorter commute, but the economics were bad, especially when the tax base was limited.

We got as far as securing funding for the program, but the antagonists were growing in number. It became clear I could not be reelected, and I decided to leave at the end of my second term.

When you were so devoted to a job, you always had concerns about things not yet done. I had to make peace with the fact that I was expendable. Fortunately, the people running were the newer generation, not the old guard. Leaving the board freed up a tremendous amount of time. It was almost like an early retirement, but my work was soon to change. Optifast had run its course and was being phased out.

69. "ALCOHOLIC DOCTORS—WE DRINK AND DRIVE"

In 1989, Medicare made some drastic changes, which apparently would impact Harmarville negatively. Up to that time, all of the physicians were contractual employees. The CEO met with the physicians and said we had to form our own group and bill for our services.

Normally, a medical group started with maybe a couple of physicians who got to choose future partners. Our group would consist of a very diverse cast of characters. Knowing we had no experience in such an endeavor, Harmarville suggested we form a not-for-profit group under the Harmarville umbrella. It was to be called HRC outreach. Our work would stay the same except we had to keep track of our visits and generate bills for each patient. Harmarville selected a neurologist, from out of the area, to form the group. They also hired an office manager to organize the billing and schedules. It was a painful process. The medical director, who knew nothing about our operation, was "negotiating" for us and not getting our input.

He later met with us and told us what he had given away! He "negotiated" to give away all our sick time. I went berserk. I was pounding on the table and screaming at him, "Who authorized you to negotiate for me. I had a private contract and never gave you permission to give away my vacation and sick time!" I was particularly sensitive about the sick time after my previous thyroid scare. Hardly anyone else was speaking. The medical director and the office manager sat there in disbelief. I realized we would have to make concessions, but those issues needed to be phased out over several years. His negotiation was unacceptable. He finally got permission to phase out those benefits over two years.

What we didn't realize was that, as a nonprofit group, at the end of the year any excess money would have to be donated to another nonprofit organization. We did this for many years and "donated" well over $1 million. As we became more autonomous, we decided to form a "for profit" group. The medical director was phased out. We formed an executive committee of which I was the vice president. The business manager was handling the transaction and grooming us for the coming changes. She met with the physicians to present options for an off-site office, staff, and a name for the new group. Our physicians tended to be quiet and passive, but we took a turn for the worse. We were providing serious options for a group name. The manager suggested we might want a name that started with an "A" to alphabetically appear near the top of a group list. Things started to fall apart. "How about, Acceptable Physicians—We're Just Okay." Someone else suggested, "Alcoholic Physicians—We Drink and Drive." It went on and on. We were tired and laughing so hard we were crying. The manager was amused, but angry. That was the most animated the group had ever been.

I think the manager decided we would be ChoiceCare Physicians. It sounded more like a dog food, but we relented. We had eleven physiatrists, four medicine doctors, and one industrial medicine physician. The inpatient doctors were continuously busy and had to carry the outpatient doctors who were variably busy. As we were now "for-profit," the drain on the profit was always the same people. It wasn't their fault. They had to hustle and market their program, and the inpatient doctors had a continuous source of patients. After many years of the same scenario, our patience was getting thin.

Our business manager had her hands full, trying to keep the group together and at peace. There was a real mix of productivity. The internists (and the family practitioner) carried the load, and the other inpatient doctors were less productive. You would think that peer pressure and pressure from the governing board would improve their performance, but it didn't. The group was made up of thirty-year-olds, so energy should not have been an issue. Everyone received a base salary and some were satisfied with just that. When we had a board meeting, the personnel discussions were always about the same people.

I felt like the historian for the group. If we had a vacancy to fill, we would sometimes interview previous residents. Most of the residents were good, and we did hire a few. There were other residents who were party animals and made less than a good impression. There were some basic ethical and behavioral expectations that were a minimum. We usually had six or more months of experience with each resident. On multiple occasions, I had to remind the board of previous infractions. We certainly believed people could mature, but some leopards don't change their spots. Nobody had time to babysit new hires. I was given credit for helping us dodge a bullet on multiple occasions.

Our very seasoned office manager and I became close. I had respect for her experience, and she respected my sincerity and devotion to the group and the facility. I totally gave Leila credit for developing my ability to step back and see both sides of an issue. It was painful at times, but was always the right thing to do.

Leila, also had good intuition about new hires and she had a big heart. She hired Danna, fresh out of training, who she knew would step up and be an organizer. There was one problem. This employee had to depend on public transit to get to work, and we were far enough from the city, that it would require several transfers. The employee's goal was to buy a car, but getting credit approval was an issue. Without blinking an eye, Leila cosigned on her loan and she got a car. What came first, the chicken or the egg? Did Leila see something inherently special in this applicant or was the hire so grateful for the opportunity that she became one of our best employees.

Another employee, who was hired as a secretary for the physicians and as a receptionist, was very reliable and pleasant. She had one major flaw. When she answered the phone, she demonstrated poor self-esteem. It was totally unwarranted because she was excellent at her job and everyone respected her. I often had to call the office and she would answer by identifying the practice, then drop her voice and sound like Eeyore, when she gave her name, Linda. After a while, I couldn't stand it any longer. I called in and she answered as usual. I said, "Linda, you are one of our best employees. You have no reason to have low self-esteem." I made her practice answering the phone with confidence. She just needed a pep talk. It shouldn't have, but it might've carried a little more weight coming from a doctor.

We hired a few bad apples—everyone does. Overall, the staff turnover was minimal. Leila could be a rough task master and was "Sybil" (multiple personalities) at times. She treated the staff rougher than she treated the doctors. We called her on the carpet several times, and she would settle down, for a while. Leila was ahead of her time and wanted us to computerize, long before it was "perfected." We had many meetings about the sizable price tag. It was decided to be put to a vote. We were evenly split, and the deciding vote was cast by the oldest member in the group and the doctor least capable of adapting. He voted in favor of the computers.

It was obvious the software did not address our type of practice and many hours were spent trying to make it usable. In the end, the written office notes were scanned into the electronic patient charts. We were eternal skeptics, and the worst happened.

Leila arranged for a professional company to back up our system, off-site. She made all the right arrangements, but the company she picked, turned out to be incompetent. I don't know what they backed up, but it wasn't the appointment schedule or the accounts receivable (the billings yet to be paid). Of course, our system crashed, and we expected our backup systems to be intact. We discovered we had useless backup. We hired a computer specialist to try to retrieve our information, but it was money wasted.

We spent the next six months not knowing who would show up to be seen on any given day. In addition, we lost about

$400,000 in billings that we were unable to reconstruct. Of course, our backup company declared bankruptcy, and we had nobody to go after.

Shortly thereafter, Leila was diagnosed with metastatic cancer that had spread to the brain. We worried about the business decisions she made, because we had no expertise. Fortunately, our financial officer, Tara, was able to pick up the slack and eventually became the new office manager.

The physicians were poorly prepared to help and were grateful Tara had been so attentive. Lesson learned—always have a Plan B.

70. DEVELOPING A HOBBY

With school board done, Optifast done, and only one job, I had some free time. I accumulated some tools and bought myself a Sears table saw and router. Wood was my new hobby. I subscribed to a woodworking magazine, which taught me a lot over the years.

I always bought hardback books with the desire to have a library. There was always a book next to the bed. My preference was nonfiction, because there was just so much to learn about our history. I also bought a set of Encyclopedia Britannica, but we didn't have a good place to display them. I decided to build two bookcases and a corner desk to go in our family room. I got furniture grade plywood and made my own plans. The shelves were supported in the back so they wouldn't sag under the weight of the books. We had a lot of audiotapes and there was a cabinet on the bottom of each bookcase. I installed three pullout shelves with dovetail joints. This was serious business. I built the corner desk and installed a laminate top to protect it. That was our computer desk for many years.

To assemble the desk, I had to stand it upright in our garage. When it was all finished, I needed to be able to get it horizontal to get it out of the garage door. Well, it was so tall we couldn't tip it on its side. Yep, I had to cut a hole in the plasterboard ceiling to get it on its side! It was a minor and fixable solution. The family room ceiling was higher, so it fit well.

The family was getting to the preteen era. Dolly and I discussed buying another house. The kids all had their own rooms in our current house, and that was no problem. I wanted to have a game room, so they would be home more, and we could monitor their behavior. We had room to build onto the house. With the help of a home-equity loan and a good contractor, we built a three-car garage off the back of the house. The contractor put a flat roof over the garage and framed the base of a deck. I wanted to complete the two tier, three-car-garage-sized deck myself. My magazine had an example of a sunburst wood railing, which I made and installed. The deck boards formed a diamond shape above each garage section. I had a fair amount of wood waste, but it was "a thing of beauty." I made two flower planters that doubled as extra seating.

Empowered by that accomplishment, I had the contractor install a sliding glass door and a wall with two windows where the original garage doors had been. Now I had a two-car-garage-size family room, unfinished. The garage had a center drain, so I had to construct a level floor over a sloped cement floor. Luckily for me, they had a nail gun to shoot nails into the cement floor. It was far from perfect but leveled out pretty well and the project was underway. After laying the plywood floor and screwing it down, I got started on building and insulating walls. The labor was all done alone, and I loved it. The bottom of the walls would be paneling. The top was wallboard covered with wallpaper. Those kids were dirt producers and wallpaper wiped off easily. I had carpet laid in the TV section, and I was installing expensive linoleum blocks on the other half, where the pool table would go. Everything was going well, until Dolly decided to put down her own row of tile—not next to mine. Now I had to install a row between two rows, which were sticking very well. They would have cracked if I had tried to remove them. She had been one 32nd off, and that's what I had to trim off about six squares of tile. We made an understanding that it was a solo project.

I wired the room for lights and outlets and hired someone to wire it into the fuse box. Just like medicine, you needed to know your limits. I learned to make sure each corner had two surfaces on which to screw the wallboard. I also learned that a live wire will make a hole in your medical school ring, if touched!

In 1993-94, we decided to build a three-season room on the closest part of the expansive deck. My contractor came back and formed a 12 x 20 room and I wired it and used tongue and groove pine on the walls and ceiling. It was a great addition. Of course, we ordered some expensive rattan furniture for it. We also had room for an octagonal picnic table with eight benches that I had made when we lived in Punxsutawney.

There were chores I wouldn't address, like cleaning gutters on the back of the house, which were thirty feet off the ground. I hired a neighbor to do that. My parents happened to visit at the time, and my father chided me for not doing it myself.

I told him, "It's your fault that I'm afraid of heights. That's why I became a doctor, so I could pay someone else to do it!" At the age of ten or eleven, my father had the bright idea to make me hold a ladder, while he cleared out the second floor gutter. He had one foot of the ladder on the roof and the other hanging over the side of the porch. I was petrified I would lose my grip and watch him plummet two stories between our house and the neighbors'—which was two feet away. Thus, my fear of heights.

My dad was in his late '70s when my mother remembered to tell me he was up on the roof with the ladder. He could barely walk straight. My father, for all his faults, didn't curse, but I bet he thought of a few words when I put his ladder in my car and drove off with it. Score one for the "meatloaf" kid.

I only did two or three oil paintings after we left Punxsutawney. Wood was now my thing!

71. REHAB CHAMPIONS

Almost everyone, who goes through rehab, is a champion. When you're ill or have post-op pain, going to therapy three hours per day (or more) is a challenge. Each unit would pick a patient who stood out, either because of their accomplishments, their attitude, or both. I always worried about those who had a good attitude the whole stay. Did they grieve before they came to us, or would they crash after discharge? My preference was that they did it at Harmarville, because their peers and staff (including psychology) would make sure they could cope with the demands of their situation.

Starting around 2009, we began to have a luncheon banquet to honor the champions who were nominated by each unit. There were many champions who preceded the formal recognition. In fact, the honorees were called The Rex Newton Rehab Champions. As referred to previously, Rex Newton was one of the first physiatrists (rehab doctors) and a patient himself. He went through life with a painful club foot deformity. In his later years, he decided he would be better off having it amputated. He would use a prosthetic foot. Whether he was hobbling on his clubfoot or taking off his prosthetic foot to demonstrate its ease of wear, the patients responded to a doctor who could "walk the walk." His courage and tenacity were an example for all who knew him.

One afternoon, we admitted a young man in his twenties. He greeted us with a huge smile. He was a bodybuilder who had entered some competitions. With his blond hair, blue eyes, and handsome face, he would be formidable. He immediately hung a picture from his portfolio, which showed a very muscular, darkly tanned male with about 1 percent body fat.

He was hunting and was up in a tree stand. He related he was in a crouched position for a long time. He went to stand up and everything went black, until he awakened on the ground. He couldn't move anything, and it was quite a while before someone found him. He was taken to the local hospital, then transferred to Pittsburgh with a cervical (neck) fracture causing quadriplegia. His injury was so high, he had no muscle movement and developed respiratory compromise, requiring a trach. He was in the acute care hospital for months.

On exam, it became very apparent that the body in the picture was quite different from the body in the bed. Without developing his normal "pump," the muscles would be smaller. With no nerve input, he underwent a tremendous amount of wasting (deflation of the muscles), and his extremities were literally bone covered with skin. Without his rigorous workouts and everyday movements, the muscles vanished. Bodybuilders spend a lot of time in front of mirrors, not just for vanity, but to know what to emphasize to achieve the aesthetic balance they wanted.

It was traumatic for any young person to see the changes their untrained body would undergo. We could only imagine the emotional devastation of a bodybuilder. He was proud of the body he sculpted. Now he would work as hard to try to feed himself. He was a long way from that goal. He never regained any leg movement.

After three to four months, he could drive a power chair and feed himself. He was totally dependent for bathing, dressing and transfers. He had a love of the outdoors and was determined to resume some type of activity. He wanted to go fishing and with the help of friends, developed a fishing rod that could attach to the chair and be operated by the patient. Dr. Andy got to see the final project and said it was quite impressive. He made his fishing pole available to others in his situation. Scott was a perfect example of a rehab champion.

Another male patient was admitted after his car got stuck on the railroad tracks, literally feet from his home. The train crushed the car and he, too, was quadriplegic. He had some respiratory problems, but his injury was a little different. His spine damage was lower in the neck area. He eventually developed the ability to raise his arms and extend his wrists. The biceps and deltoids worked well and his triceps were pretty good. He, too, had a pleasant demeanor, but it hid a storm of concern.

His father was an abusive alcoholic, but Ken had been able to protect his mother, physically. After his injury, he had constant worry about what was going on in his absence. He would no longer be able to intervene physically, but figured out how to control the situation, vocally. His goal was to return home and be the peacekeeper.

Ken was exceptional in his recovery. He could do a lot of his own dressing. He fed himself with set up. Ken was considered a C6 quad because he had good strength in wrist extension (bending the wrist back). He accomplished one feat we never saw duplicated. Without the use of his fingers, he could get his hands inside his support stockings, extend his wrists and spread the stocking open to put it over his foot and pull it up. It was truly amazing! Most able-bodied people found that hard to accomplish, but Ken did it with a smile!

"Motorcycle mama" (the woman I saw in the ER and in rehab) had a love for horses. She wasn't going to let her paraplegia prevent her from riding. She developed and sold an adapted saddle for paraplegics. I never saw it, but by her account, it was quite successful. Her drive and her personality would have made her a rehab champion.

Tom was a thirty-year-old male who was injured in a work-related accident. He was paralyzed from the waist down. He had a long history as an outdoorsman. He always wanted to be a taxidermist, but the training was expensive and time-consuming. He had to have an income. His accident put his life on hold. The vocation department worked with him and BVR (Bureau of Vocational Rehabilitation) to schedule a taxidermy course after he had a little more time to recuperate.

He completed the course and he wanted to donate his first (and award-winning) project to Harmarville. The first I knew of his gift was when I saw maintenance pushing a huge glass cylinder down the hall. It would sit on a base, which had a forest floor depicted. Enclosed would be a huge brown bear, standing on his hind legs showing his 6-inch claws. The wall behind the chamber had a forest and sky painted on it. The bear was huge and was displayed in the main hall outside of the spinal cord unit.

The "bear" was a continuous reminder that wheelchair-bound patients could be productive contributors to society. It was also a source of fascination for children and adults. To complete such a huge project from a wheelchair was mind-blowing. The patient added a finishing touch. A plaque at the bear's feet read, "no need to stand." This was a reminder that anyone in a chair could set and achieve reasonable goals.

That was a small list of the "champions" I had the honor to serve.

72. THE DARKEST HOUR

I've struggled with the decision to include this chapter in the book. One of my attributes/faults was and is that anyone dealing with me knows I am honest—brutally honest. The information to follow is purely my recollection of the events. I will exercise my right of "free speech" to give a front-line opinion of HealthSouth.

Harmarville had been a nonprofit rehabilitation hospital. It was surely one of the first in the US and had national and international recognition. In the early 1990s, the CEO, who had set the rehab course and had the vision to build the new building, retired. He was replaced by a seasoned, outside administrator of the board's choosing. It was a new and uncertain time because "managed care" was on the horizon, and the thought was that we had to reposition our facility to remain solvent.

A new rehabilitation facility was built in the Monroeville area, which Harmarville fought, based on duplication of services. The new facility enticed some of Harmarville's employees to jump ship. It wasn't HealthSouth but a different for-profit chain.

One of the "ship jumpers" was evaluating potential spinal cord patients in the acute care hospitals and lying to the patients and families about Harmarville. He told them we didn't have TVs or phones in the rooms—that was true. Then he went on to tell them we gave "mass" showers—meaning multiple people at a time. That was totally false. We had large showers that could accommodate carts for those who couldn't sit. We did have bedrooms that accommodated four patients and a few semiprivate rooms. That would sound intrusive and barbarous, without any further explanation. For those who did not explore Harmarville as an option, and chose Monroeville, they would receive a lesser rehab experience. Their doctors weren't certified to do spinal cord rehab, and the therapy staff didn't have our depth of experience. The families who came to tour our facility were immediately impressed by the structure alone. Our tour was conducted by staff from admissions or social service. I decided to become a part of the tour. I would sit down with the family, get some history about the patient and explain our peculiarities. The families, to that point, didn't understand how therapeutic a four-bed room could be. Their loved ones needed support and good examples—not privacy. I explained how much more productive the nurses could be in a four-bed room. Most of the respiratory patients were in semi-private rooms. If we got to meet and talk with the families, our "capture" success was well above 90 percent. Doing those meetings with the families took time. I was disgusted that it was necessary to counteract the lies.

Eventually, that facility was bought by HealthSouth, whose scruples were no better and probably worse. We knew we wanted nothing to do with HealthSouth.

Our new CEO was convinced that Harmarville needed to be a part of a larger business to compete in the managed-care arena. There was an outfit called Advantage Health, out of New England, who owned a chain of rehab facilities. The CEO was negotiating with them to buy Harmarville. Not knowing how important that could be, the physicians continued to be busy with patient care and were not involved. I happened to be the medical staff president during this time. I was not a part of the board and didn't have any info. We had met with administrators and a physician from Advantage Health, and we were resolved that things would be different.

I knew there was a board meeting going on while I was on my way to Unit V to cover an issue. Something told me I should crash the meeting and beg them to stay independent. I didn't do it. They were intelligent people, who had much more economic info and exposure to corporate mechanics. What did I know?

The deal was to be finalized on a Friday. On Saturday or Sunday of that very weekend, HealthSouth bought Advantage Health! Either Advantage Health kept that info from Harmarville or our CEO negotiated a position for himself and sold us "down the river." The physicians were called into an emergency meeting on Monday, to be told what happened.

My worst fear came true. I was struggling to find any positives in the situation. Obviously, HealthSouth was willing to wait to capture the crown jewel, Harmarville, in the deal. Surely, they would highlight our programs and make us a center of excellence. We had no computerization other than in billing. Hopefully, they would bring us into the twentieth century with more computerization. In the next couple days, Mr. Scrushy (the CEO) and his entourage flew in for a "pep rally." We began to hear things like, HealthSouth wanted to adopt our computer system, because it was better than theirs!? The story only got worse.

They changed all the road signs to have a large HealthSouth and a tiny reference to Harmarville. We were known nationally. Every time we identified that we were calling from HealthSouth Harmarville, the call recipient would say, "Where?" Your next statement was, "Harmarville" and the response would be "Oh, okay." HealthSouth's lack of insight that name recognition was important in a competitive market, was the first sign of their stupidity. That evaluation of them only ever got worse.

HealthSouth now had two facilities in the Pittsburgh area. I would've thought they would organize care so that the more complex cases would come to Harmarville, and the easier cases would go to the other facility, which lacked experience and depth in the medical, therapy, and nursing departments. HealthSouth proceeded by having their two facilities fight over the same patients. It was akin to a "cockfight," with which I was sure they had experience.

Their administrative approach was to treat every facility with the same cookie-cutter reasoning. What worked in a 40-bed hospital-based rehab would work in a 200-bed tertiary care rehab hospital. They made no investment in our facility for years. Many outside physicians were reluctant to refer to a "for-profit" rehab. They had never had to deal with "for-profits" before. The staff at Harmarville was in mourning for the facility we had been. Many people asked me how I put up with it. My answer would always be, "I put my head down, do the best work I can, and pretend they're not here." I think most of our seasoned employees did the same. My never-answered prayer was that one of the large Pittsburgh hospitals would buy us and take over. That was never going to happen, because we were a "cash cow" for HealthSouth.

Not only did they not invest any money or marketing strategy to help us, they continually took things away. We had our own CT scan, which allowed us to manage more complicated cases. When the CT needed repair, they just dismantled it. Why should Harmarville have a CT when their other 40 bed units didn't? They were never interested in quality—only quantity. They wanted a facility in every state, regardless of their size or reputation.

Staff members would bring in articles about HealthSouth corporate and in particular the CEO, Richard Scrushy. "Our hearts would swell with pride" to read about him owning something like nine airplanes/jets, multiple helicopters, and he had nine full-time pilots. The CEO of Exxon probably didn't have that kind of fleet. Later, he would be convicted of fraud and a list of other activities. What a surprise that was! The stock was overvalued at pennies a share. I'm proud to say I never, knowingly, owned any stock in that company.

On one occasion, I had to chair the pharmacy and therapeutics committee for that day. The pharmacy manager timidly gave us a new pharmacy policy from corporate, in Alabama, that blatantly would be illegal in Pennsylvania. I can't remember the specific issue, but I do remember my response, "Tell them, that like cock fight's, this policy would be illegal in Pennsylvania and we have no intention of adopting it." One of our building admin-

istrators always attended the meeting, and like the other attendees, saw the humor in that response. Just when you thought they
couldn't be less intelligent—they were.

73. COMMITTING THE ULTIMATE SIN

Now that Dolly and I lived in the "enlightened" age, we saw how very many mistakes we made. We raised our kids on skim milk! We sweetened their cereal with honey! We paddled them when they deserved it. When they were older, I was known to give out some pretty hefty punishment when the kids were starting down the wrong path. Maybe someday they will write their memoirs, and you will see what an ogre I was. This is my story (and Dolly's) and I'll stick to that script.

Diana, the youngest, graduated from high school in June 2001. All the magazines and talk shows warned us not to convert her room to an exercise room, and we didn't. We sold the house. In 1998 we made a trip to Deep Creek, Maryland. Dr. Andy had a lakefront home down there and sang its praises. It was less than two hours away. We arranged to have a realtor show us around to look at property.

Deep Creek was a man-made lake located in the Appalachian Mountains of western Maryland. It was originally built to be a source of electricity for the steel mills in Johnstown, Pennsylvania. It is in the center of a small triangle surrounded by West Virginia. In 1998, it was still a well-kept secret. It had a ski area called Wisp. The lake had many coves and covered 3900 acres with 65 miles of shoreline. Homes were subtlety tucked into the mix of deciduous and coniferous trees. The lake was bustling with motorboats in the North and sailboats in the South.

We just wanted a piece of land to build on in the future. He took us to a development in the middle of the lake to see a "lakeview" lot. Every piece of property was sold with or without dock privileges. Our budget was modest, and I had no desire to own a boat. Even in 1998, a dock "privilege" (no dock or boat) was worth an extra $36,000. The lot he showed us was below the main drive and had a plateau on which to build. I was very skittish about drilling for water and using septic systems. The lot already had a water well on it, and the development had access to city sewage. The purchase price was reasonable. We put money down on it that very day.

We had always dreamed of having a log home. That was probably stimulated by our Cook Forest experience. We tried to find a cabin to buy in Cook Forest, but we were unsuccessful. I was not willing to start building until I had saved a year's worth of salary. The mortgage rates were plummeting, and work was good. By the year 2000, we were ready to find a builder. There were a lot of log homes down there, but the vast majority were D-shaped logs cut from local wood. We were encouraged by the realtor to check out Yellowstone Log Homes.

Two young gentlemen were building homes out of 11-inch logs from Yellowstone National Park. Each log had a section milled out called a Swedish cope. It was part of the shape of an 11-inch log, so they stacked perfectly. Each layer of log was secured with 16-inch screws which ended in the heart of the log below it. The interior walls were rounded log, just like the outside. They were cut down and shipped from Yellowstone National Park. The end of each row overlapped the end of the perpendicular wall, just like Lincoln logs. The logs were standing deadwood, with about 15 percent moisture compared to local logs, which had a much higher moisture content and had to be kiln dried. Because they fit perfectly, there was no chinking (grout) between the logs.

We started creating a grandiose floor plan, that we couldn't afford. The guys at Yellowstone told us to tour a bunch of rental homes and pick a layout we liked.

Railey Realty sold land and homes, but they were also a rental realty. We went to visit on a weekday, and they graciously gave us the keys to about six homes. We made our rounds and found a house we really liked. Yellowstone assured us they could get the architectural plans and give us an estimate to build. Things began to move quickly, and we secured a construction loan. That was the best of all worlds, because we controlled the funds. The contractors had to meet certain goals and have the inspector's blessing, before they could collect the next payment.

The contractors started the foundation and we hit a snag. They ran into solid rock in one corner. That required a piece of equipment from Pennsylvania and with permits and rental would cost an extra $5,000. We were committed and absorbed the extra cost. The logs arrived and went up in a few days. Soon it was under roof. We snuck into the house on Friday evenings and camped out on an air mattress. We took a potty chair and stayed till Sunday, as often as we could. We used that time to familiarize ourselves with the area and do some preliminary furniture shopping. It was technically illegal to stay there, but Deep Creek was pretty laid-back. We were very psyched to build our dream house. The original plan did not have a garage. Most of the houses in the plan were bigger and had garages. The plan was to make a final move after our parents were gone. I wanted to work down there and then retire in that home.

The house was finished in 2001. We sold our Pennsylvania house for full price in three days. It was a big move with our large dining room set and a Yamaha baby grand piano, bought with a home equity loan. Dolly did most of the packing. We got rid of a lot of furniture that was too formal for a log home.

We drove the Yellowstone guys a little crazy. Up till then, they only stacked logs one story high. Anything above that was framed with wood siding. Dolly wouldn't take "no" for an answer. She wanted logs stacked to the peak of the roof on both ends. We were building a one-story house with a loft.

They would have used a quarter of a roughhewn log for the mantel of our stone fireplace. We had seen pictures and examples of a half log being used as a mantel. I don't remember the dimensions, but the fireplace was a central focal point in the great room and was 8–10 feet wide. A 13-inch log cut in half would be a significant weight. The builders thought it would be too heavy for the stone supports until the stonemason assured them that it would be okay.

We got to choose a decorative log to help support the loft. We had many from which to choose. Our eyes immediately went to a log that twisted during growth, and it was definitely a conversation piece.

We were very impressed by the builders. You had to preplan every outlet and pipe placement so you could drill vertical holes before the next row of logs were placed. They had a unique plumbing approach. They used three-quarter inch mainlines then one-half inch supply lines. All the hot water lines fed off a rectangle of pipe, which kept the wait for hot water very short. Every section of the house had its own shut off valve.

I had done some research and found a gas fireplace (which worked with a thermostat) for the basement. If the power went out to the propane furnace, the fireplace would light and keep the pipes from freezing. The great room fireplace was wood-burning.

We had them install rough plumbing for two full baths in the basement. To start, we only had the master bath and the powder room on the first floor. When the initial house was completed, the interest rates continued to fall. I refinanced twice in three years. Each time I borrowed more money to complete the project. The next part was to build a two-car garage and a room to connect the garage to the house. The builders convinced us to use log siding (one half of an eleven-inch log), which would be indistinguishable from the outside and would save a lot of money. The builders, and the two of us, sat on our huge rock (that we had paid to have removed from the foundation), and sketched it out. It was constructed in a flash.

The contractors built a "suicide" driveway from the road straight into the garage. It was much too steep for an area that got 100 inches of snow a winter. We had the ability to have the driveway start in front of the house and curve down to the garage. They felt it would require a retaining wall, which would be costly. They began to move earth and called to say the curved driveway worked well. A retaining wall was unnecessary. We were all learning from the process.

The next project was to finish the basement. Diana had decided to switch from Westminster to the University of Maryland. She was on her summer break. I took some vacation, and Diana, Dolly and I started framing the large basement. I taught them how to plumb the walls and we framed, insulated and wired the basement. We created three bedrooms, two full baths, and a large game room. I let Dolly and Diana wire one of the bedrooms while I did something else. They put an outlet box about every three feet. I didn't have the heart to correct it. I hired people to do the drywall, plumbing and carpeting.

The house was almost done. The main floor had a 12 x 40 deck, and we needed to build a second deck below it. I took a week of vacation, and Dolly and I feverishly worked to get it done. The joists were resting on dirt in some sections, and Dolly had to dig out spaces for the joists while I continued framing. It was backbreaking work.

We were ready to have the pool table set up and refurbished. The job was completed. Jason was living near Philadelphia, and Matt was at Fort Bliss in El Paso Texas. They probably only got to see the house once or twice. The river was reaching its widest point and calmly flowing around another bend.

74. HAPPY BIRTHDAY TO ME!

My mother had a sister who always lived fairly far away. As a youngster, Bernice was known as a tomboy and a ruffian. As an adult, she married a local man who became a Free Methodist minister. That religion was pretty strict. They didn't believe in jewelry, alcohol, and dancing. My uncle Dave was a very sober person, who I met maybe five times for about three minutes each. On the rare occasion, when they came to visit, he would immediately leave to visit his sister and her family. Dave and Bernice had two children. Richard was the oldest, who died around twelve years old from an undiagnosed, ruptured appendix. The second child was a daughter, Ruthie, named in honor of my mother.

Ruthie was very intelligent and upbeat. She got her personality from her mother. She was one of the family's four high school salutatorians. She was really the first in our generation to complete college and got a Master's degree in school psychology. She was the driving force for her parents moving farther away. Her father didn't make much money as a Free Methodist minister, and they never invested in a home. They were moved to different churches very often. Ruthie would buy them things they couldn't afford—like cars and eventually a house to be near her in Rockford, Illinois. I don't know if she ever dated, but her life revolved around her parents.

On one of their rare visits, Ruthie and Aunt Bernice came to our house for dinner. We always enjoyed their visits. After dinner, Ruthie asked if I would be willing to be their medical power of attorney. It sounded like a harmless request, and at that time, they were all in good health. My aunt Bernice later developed Parkinson's disease and had a prolonged, rough course. She became very immobile and later developed psychosis (hearing and seeing things that weren't there). She died in 2002. Ruthie assumed the task of caring for her father in his home.

On my 54th birthday, we had a dinner and cake to celebrate. I think it was only Dolly, Diana, and myself. The phone rang and I answered. At the other end a female said, "I'm Ruthie's friend. What do you want us to do with your uncle Dave? We put him in a nursing home. Ruthie died yesterday." I'm sure there was a pregnant pause. You would've thought she could have led with the death information. "What happened to Ruthie?" I asked. "She didn't show up for work, and she didn't answer her phone. I went to her house and saw her lying across her bed—not moving. I called 911 and found a key to let the police and emergency services in. She was dead. We don't know the reason."

I got her friend's number and the number for the nursing home. It hadn't all sunk in, but I said I would go to Rockford in a few days. After composing myself, I called the other cousins to let them know. My cousin Jack was "retired" and unencumbered.

He offered to drive out with me. I had traveled a good bit, but had never driven farther west than Ohio.

I was glad to have Jack's company. He was about seven years older and lived a life, about which I knew little. He was currently living in the one-room house where Dolly and I started our married life. Jack was a Mensa member (very high IQ). In high school he scored fourth in the nation on his SATs and had a full scholarship to Princeton. He dropped out during his first semester. My understanding was he just didn't fit in, socially.

To pass the time during the drive, I encouraged him to fill in the blanks of his life, and I did the same. I wasn't sure I would enjoy his company, because I just didn't know him. I can't remember all the details. He did work for a local steel company in their lab. They had recently bought an electron microscope. Nobody could figure out how to use it. He was a voracious reader. With the huge manual, he was able to solve the mystery of electron microscopy.

He moved from the area and eventually ended up in Boston. He had a myriad of jobs, which all seemed to last a short period of time. He met, married, and divorced a girl who was very smart, but socially out of his league. She died young from some type of blood disease.

Jack eventually completed a correspondence degree from a New Hampshire college and an MBA from Boston University. His last job was as a bank vice president?! Apparently, his father-in-law was in the business. Jack remained an enigma, but less so. I thoroughly enjoyed our trip. We arrived in Rockford late in the evening and found the house key for Ruthie's place. We entered and did some preliminary searching for business papers and the key to her safety deposit box. The following day we went to the nursing home to take our uncle Dave to the bank, walker and all. He was a cosigner on her accounts and her safety deposit box. We had found a will in her desk, but he said she had a more recent one. We expected to find it in the lockbox. We opened the box only to find some coins she had collected. Although uncle Dave was in his nineties, he was very sharp for his age. He spent a lifetime looking down his nose at the jewelry ridden, alcohol imbibing in-laws, but was touched that we made the trip to help. We tried to get as much of Ruthie's financial information as we could.

We returned to Ruthie's house to resume our quest to find her will. It was a little creepy to be staying in her house and going through her things. We were about to give up when I decided to go through the closet in her office. Finally, there it was, in a shoebox! Along the journey through her papers, we discovered that she taught at a local college, part-time. She was a member of a stock club and seemed to have multiple investments. She had prepaid all her funeral expenses, right down to transporting her body back to Pittsburgh, where she had a short viewing. She had a burial plot next to her mother and brother.

We found out from the coroner that she had a ruptured bowel and died of sepsis (infection in the blood). It was a wonder she didn't call 911 due to the pain. I contacted the school where she worked and had them send the papers for her retirement funds. Next, I called the college where she taught part-time. People were trying to be helpful, but there were confidentiality issues. I asked if she had a retirement fund. The employee relations person nicely told me she couldn't answer that. I tried a different approach.

"If we got all the appropriate papers together and submitted them to you, would we be wasting our time?"

She answered, "No."

Jack and I attended a memorial service for her, which was arranged by her friends and colleagues. They asked me to say a few words. On behalf of the family, I thanked them and had just a couple personal comments. I had to get back to work, but Jack and uncle Dave worked on a plan that Jack would stay to get her affairs in order. When all was said and done, she had a nice estate that paid for her father's stay in the nursing home and more. He died shortly thereafter.

75. TAKING OVER THE REINS

In 2005, Dr. Gil was having problems with administration not responding to his requests. He got so disenchanted that he began to look elsewhere for a job. He was offered a position at one of the large Pittsburgh hospitals. He gave notice that he was leaving.

Dr. Gil had a possessive feeling concerning the spinal cord program, which he did create. He, unfortunately, tried to recruit staff to go with him. The staff were employees of HealthSouth, and the administration heard about it. The CEO decided his departure would have to be immediate. He left on December 11, 2005.

I was in a meeting when I saw someone crouch down next to my chair. They leaned in and said, "Dr. Gil is no longer working here. Will you be the interim medical director for the spinal cord unit?" I was dumbfounded and needed some questions answered. We left the room and the CEO explained this was very sudden, and she didn't want the team to be without a captain.

It had only been the two of us on the unit for years, and I was the best equipped to take over. I went back to the unit and found several therapists and nurses in a tizzy that the program would dissolve. I assured them I would not let that happen, as I was just asked to be the interim director. They felt better about that, and things began to settle.

Dr. Tom was Harmarville's medical director and specialized in brain injury. He was well-rounded enough to cover the rehab side of the admissions. I took on more responsibility, but his help was much appreciated. After a while, we got a little out of balance. Families would come in with questions that were difficult to answer if you weren't a part of the staff conference. The conference occurred every Monday at 8:00 A.M. All of the therapists and nursing gave a report on the accomplishments and goals of each patient. It gave you the ability to see the whole picture at once.

It didn't make sense for two doctors to attend. The tradition was for the rehab doctor to conduct the meeting. Dr. Tom and I discussed it, and it made sense for me to do the staffing's because I had the bigger presence on the unit. I could organize the information for the patients and their families. Almost simultaneously, he was trying to get another physiatrist to take over the spinal cord unit.

Dr. Laura and her physician's assistant Susan were brought on to help. This occurred around the end of 2006. It was a good fit. Although they had less experience with spinal cord patients, they had a good general rehab background. Over the years we had less and less traumatic spinal cords and had to accept general rehab patients of all kinds. Laura was very soft-spoken, empathetic, and thorough (with the help of Susan). We hit it off right away. They still had responsibilities in Monroeville, but were there daily, during the week, to see the patients. It was like the old days when Dr. Andy and I shared info to make sure we had a thorough and accurate history and a problem list. They, like Andy, were the Yin to my Yang. Together, we were whole, and better than we were individually.

With Dr. Gil leaving before Christmas 2005, there was a hole left in the holiday experience. For as long as I could remember, he had arranged for a bagpiper to come in and a quartet from the Mendelssohn Choir of Pittsburgh. I didn't have those connections, and that event stopped when he left. I did have the ability (and desire) to continue the spinal cord award program.

Every year, each therapist, nurse, or doctor (who worked on the unit for three consecutive years) would be recognized. We valued experience and wanted to encourage good people to stay. They would get a plaque or engraving to celebrate the three-year accomplishment. In addition, there would be a special award for a team member who distinguished themselves during the previous year. It was an opportunity to thank and give recognition to those who went the extra mile in patient care, teaching their peers, or organizing discharge planning when the resources kept dwindling. I spent a lot of time evaluating what we had done in the past, and how we could improve it.

When Dr. Gil was in charge, the recognition ceremony was at Harmarville. That evening, there would be a banquet at a fancy restaurant, which would cost forty to fifty dollars a head. Most of the staff could not afford that, and it came off as being exclusive. I wanted to preserve the recognition and make the celebration more inclusive. If I was going to organize it, I wanted to make it fit my personality and goals.

The original motto for the unit was "Whatever It Takes." We lived that every day. I wanted the motto to be more specific to what we did. After much thought I came up with, "In their darkest hour, we bring the light of hope." Perhaps it was a little wordy, but it depicted our role. We always wanted to leave room for hope. Time and nature would supply the ultimate answer. We did serve the patients in their darkest hour, and I was very proud of the job we did.

We wanted a banquet, off-site, that was affordable and fun. Our condominium had a clubhouse that was the perfect size and very intimate. We either had a caterer or we got Olive Garden take-out. I contacted our very generous vendors, who would provide Pirate baseball tickets, Steeler tickets, or gift baskets. The local businesses donated zoo, science center, and history center tickets. These would be used as door prizes for the employees. It was like a bonus, and everyone was grateful. The cost was ten dollars apiece, which I felt was affordable for everyone.

That first year, the therapy staff were unsure if my usual calm demeanor hid a beast inside. To add to their insecurity, I dressed as Hannibal Lector, complete with prison mask, and arrived on a dolly in a straitjacket. They were used to my candor, but the playful side was new and popular. I usually wrote an epic poem and would dress as Caesar, Vanna White, a hula dancer, etc. Caesar was extra special because we made a chariot out of a shower chair which was pulled by two male nurses in pretty short tunics.

Each banquet had food, prizes and games. The games were assigned to the therapists. Michelle, from OT, was our program director. She and Christie would make up programs and Christie put together a slideshow of the honorees and the special honoree. Dolly would do the decorating. It was a group effort and enjoyed by all.

The staff conference was hallowed ground to me. I was too busy with medical issues to get to the therapies and observe the patients. I had a form that I filled out and would serve as the note for the day. The patients were all seen and examined before the staff conference. The therapists gave their reports, and I would provide them info about medical issues and how aggressive we could be. HealthSouth was always looking for a way to shorten staffing. They wanted us to only discuss barriers to discharge. That didn't serve my needs, so I chose to ignore it. One of the therapists wanted to introduce Venn diagrams. I was not opposed to progress, but that concept didn't enhance my knowledge of what was going on.

We had a tradition of doing a patient/family meeting about three weeks after admission. It wasn't needed for the general rehab patients, but the spinal cord patients had many issues they didn't understand. I would start the meeting by reviewing their history. Then I used models and diagrams to explain the neuro-anatomy injury. That was followed by an explanation of issues particular to their case. Neurogenic bowel and bladder were explained as was spasticity and dysreflexia (if they had those issues). We reviewed labs and gave an explanation of all their medicines. Then I answered their questions as honestly as I could. They were told that if they were to recover, it would probably start to show up in the first nine months. We had seen changes up to two years after injury. That gave them a reasonable time frame for recovery. Every day without change enhanced their insight that it might not happen for them. One of my worst pet peeves was any movie that portrayed miracle recoveries in those who truly wanted to get better. It was a disservice to our patients. I never met a spinal cord patient who was lackadaisical about their desire to get better. The severity of the cord injury decided the outcome. We had no microscopic way to evaluate the damage. Thus, time and nature provided the answer.

Many would ask about stem cell injections. They weren't available in the US, but other countries allowed it. My answer would be that they held a lot of promise for the future, but we had a long way to go to make sure they ended up in the spinal cord and their growth was controlled and accurate. We had many people raise funds to travel for those treatments, but I never saw results that couldn't have an alternate explanation.

There were few cases where the MRI of the spine showed transection (complete cutting) of the cord. People commonly thought the cord was severed in most spinal cord injuries. On the contrary, it was a very uncommon occurrence. Between 2005 and my retirement, I saw three such cases. When we did their family meeting, I would advise them that recovery was unlikely. It wasn't fair to string them along. We did have a case where the MRI report was "transection." He started to get leg movement before our meeting. I contacted the neurosurgeon, thinking somebody mixed up the films on our patient. He assured me it was the correct MRI, but the reading didn't match what we were seeing. Someone was misreading the MRI. A repeat MRI wouldn't change the aggressive therapy he received on the basis of his obvious recovery.

76. GOD IS SENDING ME MESSAGES

We admitted patients with spinal cord damage from accidents of every kind. We also admitted many people with nontraumatic spinal cord injuries. There were many vascular spine injuries, particularly aortic aneurysm repair problems. The vasculature to the spine is very small and fragile. In the best of hands, events occurred during surgery with dramatic effects. The vascular injuries were less likely to repair because there was no direct insult to the cord and little swelling to resolve. Sometimes the body can shunt blood from another artery. The older the patient, the less likely their situation would improve.

The other major cause of nontraumatic disease was cancer. It could be primary malignant tumors like chordomas, or primary "benign" tumors like meningiomas. They were benign in that they wouldn't spread and could be removed by surgery. Metastatic tumors, by definition, had already spread from prostate, breast, bladder, and a host of other cancers. They could sometimes be removed or debulked to relieve pressure on the cord. Many tumors were radiation sensitive, and the symptoms might improve with radiation. Commonly, those patients would arrive in bad shape. Often, they couldn't eat because they had radiation burns of the esophagus. They would arrive with no treatment prescribed other than some temporary topical anesthetic that they would have to swallow. It wasn't very successful.

I racked my brain to come up with a better treatment. We commonly used medicines for reasons other than those for which they were officially approved. One of the first non-antacid medicines approved to treat stomach ulcers was a medicine called sucralfate or Carafate. Carafate was a medicine that was meant to coat ulcers and protect them from acids, enzymes and bile salts. We knew from endoscopy reports that radiation caused ulcers in the esophagus. The reason that happened so frequently was because the esophagus traveled in front of the spine bones and would take collateral damage.

I started treating those patients with oral local anesthetic before meals and a liquid Carafate cocktail after meals. The nurses had to grind up the Carafate tablet, which was huge, and mix it with water to make a "slurry" to coat the ulcer tissue when it traversed the esophagus. Once the protective film was in place, the ulcers seemed to heal faster. Within a few days the patients would have less symptoms and could concentrate on their therapy. That was always the goal! I gave God the credit for steering me in the right direction, and having my brain retain the mechanism of action to use in a different situation. I shared this "empiric" success (not proven by clinical trials) as often as I could. The company eventually made the medicine in a slurry form. I also used it to treat skin burns in ostomy patients. If the bowel content or the ostomy paste was irritating the skin, I would have the nurses coat it with Carafate when changing the bag. It seemed to work well there too.

I was not a deeply religious person, but I always prayed and felt that God (and Grandma Lord) was watching over me. We admitted a man in his fifties who had spinal damage from metastatic thyroid cancer. He was pretty sick on arrival, but almost everyone was. He gave it his best, but pain and fatigue limited his participation. He had a doting wife who would cheer him on in therapy. He wasn't getting better and looked worse after about ten days. I learned that insight was better when the patients experienced it.

One morning, on rounds, I privately asked the patient to assess his progress. "I'm losing the battle, Doc. My wife is so sure rehab is the answer. I can't let her down."

I asked him, "Have you two had a serious discussion about this?" He told me they avoided that discussion. I asked him, "What do *you* want to do?"

Without hesitation he said, "I want to spend my last days at home with my family." I told him he had to have that discussion with his wife. I would help.

While writing my daily notes, I could see who was arriving. His wife arrived and I took her aside. I told her that her husband didn't want to disappoint her, but he felt he was slipping away. First, she was shocked and then tearfully admitted she was of the same opinion. That was a recurring theme. The patient didn't want to upset the family and the family didn't want to "give up" on the patient. Nature was going to win, regardless of their posturing. I told her that the world needed to revolve around him. Her feelings were important, but his had to take precedence. After she composed herself, we went back to the room. I made sure he relayed his honest feelings. Then I left them to discuss the situation. I had the nurses stay out of the room.

About twenty minutes later his wife came to the front desk and announced she wanted to take him home that day. Since he was going home, we needed two days to order and deliver equipment, and train her (and anybody who could help her) in his care. We would order hospice, and they would be well supported. She thanked me for facilitating the discussion. A few weeks later she called to tell me he died, and they were so grateful to have that precious time at home.

That was a pretty emotional case for me. My PCP palpated my thyroid yearly, but I made an appointment and suggested maybe we should do an ultrasound. I had it done and sure enough, I had another lump. My original surgeon retired, and a young female surgeon took his place. She wanted a biopsy.

Once again, I'm lying on a table with two female fellows standing over me with huge needles. They stabbed away, but again the results were inconclusive. The surgeon wanted to remove the remainder of the gland, and we scheduled a date. I would be in the hospital one night. That was one night too many. The mattress was very soft, and I limped out of the hospital with tremendous back pain and spasm. I finally got the back pain under control and returned to work.

I got a call from the surgeon's office that the tumor had one small section in the center that was malignant. My surgical recovery was different from the first surgery. My voice was weak and got raspy about mid-day. I was a car "singer" and noticed I couldn't sing—at all. There is a nerve called the recurrent laryngeal that runs through or near the thyroid and controls vocal cord function.

I went back to see the surgeon for an afternoon appointment. My voice was raspy, and I was essentially whispering. The surgeon heard this and angrily got in my face and yelled, "Why are you whispering?"

I was shocked and replied, "This is the voice you gave me!" She began to protest that she did not damage the nerve. She wanted an ENT consult.

At that time, we had an ENT doctor who came to Harmarville about every two weeks. I asked if she could see me there, to evaluate my vocal cords. She did, and indeed one of my vocal cords was partially paralyzed. She suggested I see her in three months. I did, and the paralysis was some better but still there.

The thyroid surgeon wanted to see me again, and I refused to go back to that a*****e. I thought about filing a malpractice suit to teach her a lesson. I decided against it, but I had no tolerance for surgeons who refused to believe they made a mistake. After a year, I could sing again, but I aspirated liquids more easily and ran out of breath before the end of a sentence. That was a deficit that never cleared. I could forgive the mistake, but not that performance in her office. Talking was a major part of my practice, and the voice weakness made life more complicated.

On the positive side, the tumor was caught before it grew and spread. God sent me a patient who needed me, and through him, warned me to reevaluate my own thyroid. He had a lot more work for me to do.

77. "WAS IT BLACKMAIL, PURE AND COMPLEX?"

In 2007, Allegheny General Hospital (by then a part of the West Penn Allegheny Health System or WPAHS) apparently had an external evaluation done to evaluate their patient care. One of the conclusions was that they needed a more extensive continuum of care. Someone decided that rehabilitation was a logical addition. We would never have guessed that we would be the pawns in a very complicated set of events.

ChoiceCare physicians had been trying for years, to form a rehabilitation department at Allegheny General Hospital. Rehabilitation services came under the control of the orthopedic department. The department chairman continuously blocked that request.

Harmarville was very dependent on the West Penn Allegheny Health System hospitals for patients. Thus, HealthSouth Harmarville was always trying to keep WPAHS happy.

Somebody at Allegheny General Hospital decided that if they acquired the four medical doctors at HealthSouth Harmarville, they would have a mechanism to ensure that WPAHS patients stayed in the system after transferred to HealthSouth Harmarville. Little did they know that all four of us always tried to send patients back to the referring hospital, for medical or surgical emergencies. Our "acquisition," would satisfy the aforementioned study's conclusion and provide a better continuum of care.

A lot of discussions about the four of us were taking place, and we were clueless. Some person or persons at WPAHS had two important discussions. They contacted ChoiceCare's president and said they would get the Allegheny General Hospital contract, if the four medicine doctors agreed to be "acquired." The other contact was with HealthSouth Harmarville. They were allegedly told that the patient referrals to Harmarville would drastically decrease if the four medicine doctors refused "acquisition."

Suddenly, the four of us were a hot commodity. Two of us, including myself, were officers of ChoiceCare physicians. Around the middle of September, 2007 ChoiceCare's president asked to meet with the four medicine doctors. He made us aware of all the negotiations taking place. Harmarville contacted him and said that if the four of us didn't cooperate, they would severely curtail the number of cases ChoiceCare had at Harmarville.

Since this was the first any of us heard about this, we were in shock. In a second, we went from being partners in our own group to being pawns in a much larger game. We had until the end of September 2007 to decide. Decide what? We were totally dependent on Harmarville for patients. Without them, we could not make a living.

ChoiceCare had just completed an internal negotiation to try to improve the senior partner's pensions. Financially, we had a history of being in the wrong place at the wrong time. We were the oldest partners and had some catching-up to do. Suddenly, everyone had amnesia about those negotiations.

It seemed to be a done deal. No one else was advocating for us. We had a WPAHS contact person who was to negotiate our contracts. We got a small increase in our base salary. We negotiated a good bonus system. We were all the same age within six months of each other. We were fifty-six or fifty-seven years old. We got them to agree to a nine-year contract. That was incredible. We had heard about short, sweetheart contracts, that turned into bad deals on renegotiation. Nine years would get us to sixty-six years old. That was the year we would become Social Security eligible.

Making this kind of change is a very complicated situation. ChoiceCare had to buy each of us a malpractice "tail" policy, to cover us for an additional three years. We each owned a share of stock, which had to be purchased by ChoiceCare. Each of us had to get a new provider number for every insurance company we billed. There were a lot. Medicare was the worst. You could only apply for a new provider number after you stopped using your current number. Medicare told us we would wait three months for our new numbers after we applied.

Trying to get everything in place by January 1, 2008 was hectic, but it happened. The transition had to be explained to all of our patients. In January 2008 we were assigned a young female practice manager. She met with us and explained that WPAHS expected the group to lose $50,000 the first year. We would not be penalized. They vastly underestimated our abilities. We made a small profit even though we gave Medicare patients free care for the first three months of 2008. That would've been a considerable amount of money.

After the first fiscal year, we got a financial update. In total, we were in the black. They proceeded to inform us that my Baclofen pump program lost $50,000. My partners were scowling at me. The pump refill program always made a profit. It was complicated billing, and each bill might have had two or three payors. ChoiceCare had offered to train one of the WPAHS billers, but their offer was ignored. I was livid.

I got a copy of the previous year's billing from ChoiceCare and a copy of the 2008 billing from WPAHS. There were mistakes on practically every patient's billing. I found the $50,000 plus a small excess. They called a meeting at Allegheny General Hospital, and I presented my information to about ten billers. They rebilled what they could, but some of the bills were too old. I spent a lot of time reconstructing all the issues, and I gave them a bill for my time, which they paid.

As you can see, a doctor's life isn't only seeing patients. There are often non-medical issues that consume time and patience. Overall, our acquisition provided more pay for our services, but everyday issues would go into a black hole. You commonly had to make multiple calls to get them resolved.

There was a lot of turbulence in this section of the river. Was it blackmail? I'll let you decide.

78. "DON'T GO TO YOUR LOCAL HOSPITAL"

Our unit took care of another disease process, that didn't involve the spinal cord. There was a disease called Guillain Barre. It could affect people of all ages. The symptoms were somewhat insidious but consistently the same. Patients would develop numbness and weakness in the lower extremities, which over time would ascend. In some, it happened slowly and in others it could be quite rapid. We had no idea why it presented that way. It was an uncommon disease, but because we were a more tertiary rehab, we saw about eight cases a year.

Interestingly, this disease affected the peripheral nervous system (nerves after they exit the spinal cord). Like MS, the nerves were stripped of their insulation and would be unable to conduct the "electricity" to trigger the muscle. One of the hallmarks of the disease was a lack of reflexes, which was the opposite of MS. They would have a flaccid (no spasms or increased tone) paralysis. It might be limited to the lower extremities or it might affect the arms and the nerves that control breathing.

One of our physical therapists called me at home in the evening. That was a truly rare experience. My after-hours calls were

99 percent from the nurses. Chris was an exceptional physical therapist and liked by all. He was calling me about his father. Chris knew the answer before he called, but it was his dad, and he needed to know how to proceed. He related that about two weeks prior, his dad had cold symptoms. The day before this call, his dad (who was in his fifties) complained of numbness and weakness in his ankles. The dad called Chris about his symptoms. Over the next twenty-four hours, they progressed. Chris thought it could be Guillain Barre.

After hearing the story, I agreed. I told him, "Take him to the emergency room. Don't go to your local hospital! They probably won't know what it is and will send him home. Go to the large Pittsburgh hospital of your choice and tell them your concern." This was a good idea for three reasons. First, the doctors in the larger hospital were more likely to know of and maybe had seen a previous case. The larger hospital would have more neurologists and may be a neurology residency, increasing the odds of making the diagnosis. Third, sharing his concern, that it was Guillain Barre, would make them think more about ruling it in or out. He needed to be hospitalized and quickly evaluated for intravenous therapy.

There is no cure for Guillain Barre, but it's progression can be affected by giving IVIG (pooled antibodies from thousands of people) or plasmapheresis (an attempt to decrease the number of self-destructive white blood cells by filtering them from the patient's blood).

They made a preliminary diagnosis of Guillain Barre, which was confirmed with EMG (electromyography—a test of the electrical activity in the affected muscles) and nerve conduction tests (recording how fast and effective electricity is conducted through a nerve). He was given IVIG and the progression stopped. He still had leg weakness and couldn't walk. Once stabilized, he came to Harmarville and slowly began to get return of function, and walked.

Guillain Barre is considered an autoimmune disease, because again, the body's immune system sees the nerves as foreign material and try to destroy it. The unfortunate patient probably had a glitch in their immune system that allowed this to happen. If, indeed, it was stimulated by a virus or bacteria, we would have seen household members get it, also. Fortunately, we never saw that, which supported the theory that the affected individual probably had a genetic mutation in their immune system.

The general rule of thumb still applied. Young, healthy patients tended to have a better outcome. We admitted a man in his sixties who was the worst case, ever. He had been a relatively healthy individual, until he developed Guillain Barre. His version was so severe it affected his respiratory system. He was on a ventilator for a year! At that time there were no nursing homes or extended care facilities that did ventilator care. He came to us with a tracheostomy tube, which you hardly noticed because of his huge smile. He couldn't talk effectively, but he tried constantly. After we got him up to program, his respiratory situation improved, and we were able to get rid of the tracheostomy tube. He had a whole year of unexpressed words in there, and they poured out, constantly. He spent six months with us, then went home in a wheelchair. About three months later he had some improved function and came in for another three months. He was able to feed and dress himself and did limited walking with a walker. That case occurred while Dr. Gil was still there.

We had a special case admitted after Dr. Gil left. That gentleman was in his sixties. He had a doting wife who was trying to eat very healthy. She found a farm that sold non-pasteurized milk. She had no idea that it could contain bacteria called Campylobacter, which was a known stimulus for Guillain Barre. Her husband contracted a severe form of Guillain Barre and was paralyzed from the neck down. He didn't develop respiratory problems. The admissions department sought my counsel before admitting him. We had an in-house skilled nursing unit at that time, and he was placed on that unit. I was assigned to care for him because he was so complicated. Our skilled unit had exceptional therapy, but his situation wasn't improving. He had a Blue Cross insurance policy. The case manager and I decided to request one week of acute rehab care to order equipment, and train the family in his care. The therapists on the skilled unit had good previous experience but were less equipped and too busy to do that work. The insurance company finally agreed, and he came to Unit I for exactly one week and was discharged.

I saw him in outpatient about three months later, and he had little change. He was dependent for eating, bathing, and dressing. His wife was managing most of his care. I scheduled to see him in three months. I walked into the exam room and his arms were flailing around, and he could pick his legs up off the bed. After completing his exam, I told him I wanted to admit him to acute rehab with the goal for him to feed himself and try walking. He was ecstatic. Admissions contacted his insurance and they said, "No."

I called the insurance and reminded them we had only used one week of rehab days. The answer was "No." I called and demanded to talk to a rehab doctor. Most of their regular reviewers were family practice or retired surgeons. Again, I couldn't get them to understand that we had done everything right. We didn't use rehab days, because he wouldn't have improved. The issue was different now, because self-care and walking were reasonable goals.

The fourth level of appeal was an "independent" company contracted to evaluate cases. They, too, couldn't see the rationale for admission. I became very angry and demanded another appeal. This would occur with a judge, and testimony could be given over the phone. I wrote a detailed summary of the care he had received, and how we judiciously did not use his rehab days until he showed more improvement. Blue Cross's lawyer wrote a report, but did not attend the hearing.

On the appointed day, I was sworn in and read my testimony into the record. The judge asked me some very thoughtful questions, and thanked me for my concise report. He was audibly angry that the case went through five levels of appeal.

The judge asked, "Dr. Kelly, how much time would you need?"

I replied, "We will need a month of intense inpatient therapy." He explained he needed to review the insurance company submission and then render a verdict. He was the last level of appeal. He then totally surprised me when he announced, "I'm going off the record." That meant the court stenographer was dismissed, and what he was about to say would not be recorded.

He told me he was sick and tired of the insurance companies collecting their fees each month and not providing the needed care when warranted. We would be hearing from him.

A few weeks later, the patient called and excitedly read the court letter. In summary, the judge sternly told Blue Cross they would pay for twenty-eight days of acute rehab. That was very gratifying, but was extra special because if Blue Cross had agreed to our first request, they could've given us just two weeks and that would have satisfied their responsibility. I could hardly stop smiling. On several future occasions, when I was speaking to their reviewers, I reminded them they lost a fifth-level appeal for twice the cost. I mischievously added, "I think the judge likes me."

The patient completed twenty-eight days of rehab. He could feed himself, and partially dress and bathe himself. As predicted, he was able to walk with a walker for household distances. As always, the outcome was very satisfying for both of us. It was a highlight of my career.

79. "I'M SENDING HIM TO THE ER, WHETHER YOU LIKE IT OR NOT!"

Just like with AIDS, every once in a while, something new came along and suddenly you were in "uncharted waters." In 2005, we had a delightful young teacher sent to us with a diagnosis of transverse myelitis. She came from one of the larger teaching hospitals. We never got much information before the patient arrived. On admission, I was going through her records and was dumbfounded by her MRI report. I knew she was a quadriplegic, so I expected to see a report that the MRI showed some changes in the cervical region. I was horrified to see the MRI showed changes from the cervical through the lumbar area. That was unheard of. Transverse myelitis usually affected a small section of the cord, like C-3 to C-5.

I examined the patient, then spoke to her and her very supportive family, which included her husband and her parents. There were no follow-up instructions, so I asked them when she was to be seen by the neurologist. They replied she was to be seen in six months. After I left her room, I called the neurologist to verify. The neurologist nonchalantly repeated the six-month follow-up. I questioned if that was appropriate in a case where the cord was so extensively involved. I was giving her an opportunity to rethink her decision. She was standing her ground.

I didn't agree with her cavalier approach. That was a very unusual presentation. I wasn't comfortable with that timeframe. If that was an active process, it could go higher in the cord and brainstem and kill her. I went back to see the patient and family and explained the presentation on MRI was very unusual. I recommended a second opinion with an aggressive neurologist at Allegheny General Hospital. They were shocked but agreed to get the second opinion.

I called my contact, described the MRI findings, and my concern that she could be in danger. He agreed to see her the next day.

After assessing the patient, he called me and said he, too, was uncomfortable with the situation. He felt she needed some chemotherapy to weaken her immune response. I wouldn't normally challenge a specialist, but her original physician was way too complacent about a highly unusual case.

She completed her rehab and did not get worse. She had little independence, but between her husband, parents, and unusually good friends, she returned home. With the help of a teacher's aide, she returned to work and resumed her duties as a mom. She, too, was a true rehab champion.

About a year later we had a male admitted with transverse myelitis. His exam indicated he was a T4 injury. His motor and sensory deficits were from the nipple line down. I reviewed his MRI report and it showed destruction of the cord from the thoracic area to the end of the cord. There was a reasonable follow-up plan for him. I asked OT to evaluate his grip strength on a daily basis, to warn us if he was getting worse. Things went well for a week or two, then on a Friday, the OT came to me and said his grip strength was weaker.

I immediately called his referring physician, but he was unavailable. I asked to speak to whoever was on call for the weekend. I explained the case and the abnormally aggressive transverse myelitis. The physician I talked to was not grasping the seriousness of the situation. He wanted us to "watch" the patient over the weekend. I mentioned the previous case, and how chemo was used to slow or stop the disease process. He wouldn't budge. I told him, "I will not watch this paraplegic turn into a quadriplegic over the weekend. I'm sending him to the ER whether you like it or not. I'm making it a discharge so you can't send him back." That ended the conversation. I couldn't understand how the doctor could defend his complacency.

The patient was admitted but had no treatment until the original referring physician saw him on the following Monday. By that time, he had significant weakness not only in his hands, but upper arm muscles as well. He was given chemo, but it was too little, too late. He returned to us as a quadriplegic. I didn't know for sure that the progression was reversible. I couldn't defend the inaction over the weekend. The arm weakness did not improve with therapy and his new prognosis was much worse.

I saw him once after discharge; then he never returned. I felt as though he blamed the situation on me. I wasn't qualified to prescribe chemo, and I did my best to get him the proper care.

We didn't see any more of those cases before I retired. After I retired, I saw an article about the CDC collecting data on unusual transverse myelitis cases. I contacted my female patient and got permission to report her case to the CDC. The second patient had moved and we had no idea where he was.

80. MY MIDLIFE CRISIS.

If medicine had taught me anything, there were some undeniable truths: 1. Every family is dysfunctional—some more than others; 2. Humans are sexual beings, regardless of their convictions; 3. Death is inevitable. We need to respect it, plan for it, and embrace it so we can give it the dignity it deserves; 4. People will have a midlife crisis. They need healthy ways to express it.

My daughter's birthday was in midwinter in 2002. We took her to her favorite restaurant. On the drive home we passed a used-car dealership that sold more specialized cars. I wasn't in the market for a car, and rarely bought a used car. There sat a 2001, yellow BMW Z3 (two-seater convertible) with a black top. I couldn't take my eyes off it. I didn't say a word. The next day was Sunday and I took a trip to "visit" it.

I never had a convertible and didn't think I wanted one, but this was love at first sight. Of course, it was a stick shift and I always enjoyed that. I never was a vain person. I wasn't into brand-name shoes or clothes. When I had hair, I wanted it to be neat—not stylish. The "luster" of polishing shoes was gone very early, because polishing shoes was a Saturday evening chore before attending church—in a suit. (Remember, I had 676 consecutive Sundays without a miss). I liked new cars, but it was for the smell, gadgets, and ease of care.

I went home and told Dolly, "I'm going to buy that car."

She said, "No you're not. You've never done anything that selfish." I probably should've reacted to the "selfish" term, but she didn't mean it in a negative fashion. We would buy cars for kids, cars for transporting the elderly parents, etc. I never bought a car for me. We wouldn't have had the money for a new one, but I was truly excited, which didn't happen often. She supported my decision. I jokingly told people, "I said to Dolly, 'It's that car or an affair!'" I bought the car in February, and yearned for a 40° day, so I could put the top down. The plastic rear glass would fracture at lower temperatures. The day finally came and with a ski cap, winter coat, windows up and the heater on—we went for our maiden voyage. The car was quite the attraction, because automobile and personality-wise, the doctors were a pretty dull bunch.

One of the nurses, with great concern, asked me if I had cancer. That was an odd reaction until you took into account that I was a pretty open book, and that car was way out of my league. She thought it might be my last wish! She asked with such concern, but I couldn't stifle my laugh. "Nope. I just did it for me."

We were living with Dolly's mom at the time since our home was in Deep Creek and our work was at Harmarville. The neighbor's reaction was even better. You would have thought I bought a diamond the size of a car. She was very concerned with its safety.

The area was low on crime, but the car was parked close to a very busy road and could have been a casualty of a careless driver. I fear she stayed up all night to watch the car. It was precious, but not that precious!

Soon, the weather was more conducive to drive a convertible. We were making our weekly trips to Deep Creek. Part of the trip was on the Pennsylvania Turnpike, which was under construction, as usual. We would be stopped in traffic, and a trucker or a passerby would give a thumbs-up, while thinking, "What a waste of a good car on a middle-aged guy." I had a stylish ball cap. Dolly had a straw hat with a colorful scarf to keep the hat from blowing away.

The trip to Deep Creek and the trip back-and-forth to our next home were a dream. There were lots of curves and passing sections on the way to Deep Creek. I knew where they all were and with one push on the accelerator, it took off like a jet.

We took the "Bimmer" to a medical conference in South Carolina. On the way home, we took a detour to Norfolk, Virginia to see an elderly great aunt. We were about five miles from her home. There was an accident on the other side of the road. People were rubbernecking. We were stopped in traffic with two fresh cups of coffee. It was too hot to have the top down. I looked in the rearview mirror, and saw a young lady coming at us too fast to stop. I started to say, "We're going to get hit!" and the impact lifted the back of my car and jammed us under the car in front, which hit the car in front of it. It was a benign accident, because nobody was injured. It was Friday afternoon. We were covered in coffee.

We were in a less than great part of Norfolk. Dolly was calming the young teacher (and baby) who hit us, and I was trying to find a rental car to drive home. We discovered that a certain rental car company won't "pick you up" in an undesirable section. The police were there until my car (the only one undrivable) was towed. The policeman went to get in his car and leave. I stopped him and said, "Are you just going to leave us here? We're from Pennsylvania. We have nobody to come get us." There was a car rental place about a mile away. I asked him to give us a ride. It was 90-plus degrees out, we had luggage, and it seemed as though he could help us out. My aunt was in her nineties, and I wasn't going to call her. The minor pain in my back was getting worse. I wanted to get home.

Finally, he begrudgingly agreed to give us a ride. We got to the car rental place, and I had to browbeat the salesman to let us rent a car to drive home. They would charge me a $500, one way, drop-off fee. I'm covered in coffee, my back hurts, people were being pugnacious, and I probably just lost my pride and joy car. It was a great day!

We got home, and the next week I got a call that the insurance totaled my car. They offered me what I considered a low settlement. I called my Philadelphia lawyer, Alan, and he wrote them a letter. He pointed out that I had just had an $800 maintenance on the car, bought two new tires and in Allegheny County, we paid a 7 percent sales tax when we bought the car. I got an additional $3300.

I needed a car and went to a local Chrysler dealership and bought a Sebring convertible. I didn't have time to research or car shop. It was okay, but it wasn't a Z3. I grieved the loss of that car for a long time. Dolly finally said, "You need to get another car and get it out of your system." I went back to the original dealer, and told him I wanted a medium blue Z4 with a blacktop. He would look for one at auction.

A few weeks later, he called and said he couldn't find a black top, but they had a low mileage, blue Z4 with a beige top and beige interior. He bought it to sell, but I wasn't obliged to buy it. After seeing it, I rationalized the beige interior would be better in the summer, and I bought it. They had made a few improvements, the nicest of which was that you could remotely put the top and windows down, which was nice in the summer.

Unfortunately, that was about the time my knees started to get bad. I resolved that when it looked pathetic entering or exiting the car, I would trade it in. That occurred in less than two years. We entered the SUV age. That was the beginning of "Ol' Man River."

81. NO GOOD DEED LEFT UNPUNISHED.

There are a lot of good deeds that aren't punished, but that doesn't make for a good read. Most of our patients were far from clergy. We did have two rather memorable cases which had similarities. A Protestant minister and a priest go up on a roof....

We admitted a fifty-six-year-old male, Protestant minister who was trying to save the church some money. The older church needed the roof tarred, and he enlisted the help of a young parishioner. They were both working to coat the roof. The minister stepped back onto a section his helper had tarred and slid off the roof. He didn't have a spinal cord injury, but he broke many bones, including some in the spine. He was in the hospital for more than six weeks and was ready to start mobilizing his joints. Everything hurt, and the rehab was grueling.

In spite of it all, he had a pretty sunny disposition and spent much time tending to his rehab "flock." He had an aggressive OT who was ruthless in her attempt to get his hands and wrists mobilized once more. He refused the pre-therapy pain meds I offered. He would get through it. He said to me one day, "My

OT is a woman that I hate to love." I had to think about that, but he made his point. That person pushed him to the max, but he knew her tenacity would make him better. In the end, he walked with a limp but overall did very well. It had been about a thirty-foot fall.

A priest in his late forties was working to repair the roof of the rectory where he lived. He lost his footing and had a shorter fall, but a more permanent injury. He had a back fracture and was paralyzed from the waist down. His hospital stay was short, and he knew all too well what was going to happen.

Over twenty years previously, his younger brother had an accident and was a quadriplegic. He had helped with his care. It must've been easier to win the lottery than have two siblings become spinal cord injuries in unrelated accidents. He was familiar with all the care his brother needed. He was probably surprised by how much of his own care he would be doing. On arrival, I would assess the patient's immediate potential and get them involved in their care. His arms and hands were normal. He needed to be catheterized four times a day and would start learning on day one. No man wants to do, what looks like torture, to himself, but it was necessary. Over the years, the insurance would demand we shorten rehab stays, and every day needed to be used to the max.

Father X had a way of blending in and making people feel at ease. He was a good-looking fellow and dressed in his civilian clothes. We had a female frequent-flier (recurrent patient) who latched on to him. She always wanted him to pray with her, probably to be forgiven for her unholy thoughts about him.

Father X and I became very close and had continuous co-medic banter. I was in the nurse's station one day when he rolled up with another young priest in tow. He announced, "We're here to 'exorcise' you."

My answer was "It's been tried before—unsuccessfully." We all had a good laugh.

I used Father as a source of information. We had a large Roman Catholic population in western Pennsylvania. I noticed that the Catholics seemed more resistant to signing a DNR. I wondered if the Catholic Church viewed DNR (do not resuscitate) as a form of suicide. He reassured me that was not the case. It helped me to approach the topic in some cases.

A Protestant minister, a Catholic priest (and his groupie) go up on a roof…. Sounds like the start of a good joke, but it wasn't.

82. REFLECTIONS OF A VETERAN DOCTOR

My practice of medicine spanned thirty-eight years. To maintain my license, I had to have fifty hours of CME (continuing medical education) each year. Some of those hours include classroom study or journal articles with quizzes associated. Most physicians in fact do more hours, looking up current treatments, etc. All of the effort was and is on prolonging life. We need to be setting guidelines for how we approach longevity.

Many complex issues come to mind and because of their complexity, we aren't addressing them. In the past, a lot of hypertension was undiscovered, leading to heart attacks, strokes, and renal failure—all of which can cause death. With the myriad of medicines we have (and more in the pipeline), our ability to treat hypertension is better than ever and people survive longer. The same is true of hyperlipidemia and heart disease. What was once a natural "thinning of the herd" wasn't taking place.

Unfortunately, our ability to treat or stave off the onset of dementia has not kept pace with our advances in cardiac care. The result is that we are overtaxing our ability to provide meaningful long-term care. In fact, that is the conundrum of this whole situation. We have a multitude of disciplines striving for a singular goal—longevity, and nobody is stepping back and looking at the big picture.

My comments may give you the opinion that I am opposed to longevity, but I'm not. I'm opposed to the situation where longevity trumps quality of life. My grandmother Lord lived probably ten years after her dementia became bad. It broke my heart to watch that twinkle in her eyes fade into a dull, meaningless expression. She was a bright, charismatic person who had a positive impact on so many lives. She would've been mortified to know she lived so long in the meaningless fog of dementia.

My mother suffered the same fate. As her primary caretakers, Dolly and I repeatedly made painful decisions about her care. My mother made the decision to move to the personal care facility located in the building where I attended high school. Mentally, things went downhill pretty rapidly after that. She begged us to let her come live with us and we did for several months. She was losing the deepest memories—who we were and our names. She had no concept of time, and she would get up and want to wander at night. I had to work. We still had kids at home. We couldn't watch her twenty-four hours per day. We decided to use a toddler's gate on the door of her bedroom. For a short period of time it worked and gave us some peace. Then she learned how to take it down. I distinctly remember my reaction when I stood at the bottom of our stairs and she was at the top, holding the gate in front of her.

It was a combination of anger and frustration when I said, "You are so going back to the personal care home!" She showed no understanding of what I said, but it was cathartic for me.

She did go back to the previous personal care home, but it quickly became apparent she needed an intensity of care beyond their means. We made the decision to move her to a different facility. That facility gave me a tour of their groundbreaking dementia program. All I could see was a sea of lifeless faces—some staring aimlessly, some tending to their baby dolls. It was more than I could digest. My mother wasn't there, yet. The facility wisely gave into my choice to try their personal care section. I was there every evening, trying to orient her to her new surroundings. Dolly was there almost every day. It wasn't working. After about ten to fourteen days, I got a call from the administrator, who very tenderly convinced me that it was time to move her. They would take care of everything, and assured me she would be safer and much happier. It was the best decision, and I was eternally grateful for their wisdom, allowing me to reach that decision on my own terms.

She was more content. She could wander around the facility unrestrained. They would feed her regular meals and at other times, when she asked. They had a secure, fenced-in exterior where she could walk outside, light and weather permitting. My mother was a "greeter." That was a resident who stood vigil near the front door (with her purse in hand), and greeted all the visitors as they entered. That was a role she had played most of her life.

Mom displayed a new persona that we had never seen before. She gravitated toward all the men and could be seen walking hand-in-hand with every new guy admitted. I don't doubt she craved affection, which was provided on a very limited basis by my father. We would go to visit, and I would separate the couple and gently guide her "fellow" back into the hall, before I closed her door. It became such a routine that I lovingly referred to her as the "trollop" of Woodside Place. She would've been mortified to know she was even capable of such a performance.

After about three or four years of more deterioration, she did not know our names. All she knew was that, frequently, smiling people would come see her and separate her from her paramour du jour. My mother had been hypertensive for years. I contacted the facility and asked them to stop her blood pressure meds. At this point, I viewed the meds as life-prolonging and she wouldn't want that. If she had adverse effects, I would have reversed that request. Her attending physician had a geriatric fellow working with him. That person accused me of attempting euthanasia and asked the ethics committee to evaluate the situation.

You would've thought I was holding a gun to her head. I was livid that I had to defend my request. I fired her physician and chose another. The ethics committee found my request reasonable. After a week or so of turmoil, the meds were stopped, and her blood pressure didn't change.

My mother was very meticulous about her fine, sparse hair. She had a style that never changed. It was impossible for the facility to maintain that, but someone made the decision to chop her hair really short. Unfortunately, this happened close to the end of her life. It was the only issue we had with her care. She had a wig, but never wore it because it was so not her, and it had too much hair.

One day I got a call that she had a stroke, and they needed to move her to their skilled nursing facility. She had a dense hemiplegia (paralysis on one side) and lost her ability to swallow. We refused a feeding tube and felt the end was near. It wasn't. We were there every day and so was her lifelong friend, Gertie. All through this experience, Gertie would come to visit—taking her for walks, getting her to sing hymns with her (they were both in the church choir), and she had one-sided conversations, feeling that her old friend was in there and appreciating the attention on some level. It was a part of Gertie's grieving process. She was losing her best friend.

I was there the last day Gertie visited. We had a good conversation, and she felt Dolly and I were handling everything well. When leaving, she kissed my mom and said, "Save me a seat in the choir. I'll be there soon." We didn't know how prophetic those words were. About a month later, Gertie was instantly killed in a car crash. I could see the two of them joyfully reuniting and singing in the choir.

Mom lived for two weeks with no food or water. I told Dolly we should donate her body to the Army for an autopsy. How could she live that long with no intake? We would moisten her mouth and she seemed comfortable. One day I walked in and was horrified. There she was, looking at me with a clarity in her eyes, which I hadn't seen for years. She couldn't speak, but her level of alertness was enhanced. I sat there thinking, "She can't be clearing up!" It lasted for a few hours and was gone. She died the next day.

My brother was in the Army reserves and had been deployed, as a surgeon, to Afghanistan. We were trying to get him home after the stroke, but it was a difficult process. I called the funeral director and asked how long he could keep the body presentable for a viewing. I was told about a month. She survived until my brother got home, and she died a day or so later. I'm sure it was coincidence. She had no idea he was deployed.

When she finally passed, I had a very limited reaction. I had been grieving her loss, slowly, for many years. There was little emotion left. I felt a little guilty, but finally had clarity for my version of that process.

In 2003, while we were living with her, Dolly's mom passed. She had a cardiac history and for months had repeatedly gone into heart failure. She decided she was never going back to the hospital so her care was my responsibility. I would manipulate her meds, and she would recover. She developed a pattern of going into failure when we left to go to Deep Creek. I asked her if being left alone made her anxious. Uncharacteristically, she admitted it did. Dolly had many siblings in the area, and they rotated staying with her when we left for the weekend.

One day she developed heart failure during the night, which involved more of her lungs than usual. She knew it was different. I told Dolly this might be the end. I had to go to work and tie up a few loose ends. Dolly called me several hours later, and said she was gone. It was the end of an era. We had been there for all the parents, and Dolly was at their side when they died.

We went through a period of time when we were totally empty-nesters and didn't have medical responsibilities. A couple of Dolly's brothers died. They lived in Tennessee and Florida and we weren't involved in their care.

About 2012 my brother developed some precancerous cells in his bladder, which were treated with very painful instillations of chemotherapy into his bladder. The cells would disappear then recur. He eventually developed overt cancer and his bladder was removed. Throughout all that, and his hip replacement, he continued to work. He was in his late sixties and could have retired. I encouraged him, but he told me he still enjoyed the work and teaching new residents. He had a small hiatus from treatment, then the cancer was back with a vengeance and it had spread.

He was tolerating the chemo, but lost a good bit of weight. We, as adults, usually saw each other about once or twice a year. I saw him more frequently and tried to be supportive. In 2016, he got much worse and had a prolonged hospital stay. It was obvious things were not going well. The oncologist continued to be aggressive, long after he should've stopped (in my opinion). Bob's kidneys were affected and he began to swell tremendously, to the extent that it took three nurses to turn him and provide his care. At that point, taking him home wasn't an option.

His wife, Tina, was an RN, and on some level knew the end was coming. Bob's two children were adults, but this was probably their first experience losing someone that close. Tina had the hardest time adjusting and was holding out for a cure.

I was at work when I got a call from Bob. I couldn't understand a word of what he said, but he sounded awful, and I immediately left for the hospital. It seemed like they were doing CT scans or treatments every time I was there. I felt like they were torturing him. That morning he had an excellent nurse who encouraged him to sign for palliative (comfort) care, which he did. When I got there, Tina and his children were there. He was basically unconscious. After seeing him, I felt he had called for my help.

I took the family out in the hall and gave them my opinion that he was being tortured with all the procedures. One might think the attention was because he was a physician, but it was a pattern I had seen too often. Tina reluctantly agreed to transfer him to hospice near their home.

We made the request and within hours he was on his way. The hospice care was extraordinary, and we all felt calmer. He lived for about a day and a half and slipped away peacefully.

Bob had served as a well-respected, well-liked surgeon in three area hospitals. Tina couldn't handle the thought of a massive number of people coming to his funeral. I told her, "This is your call. You can't make a wrong decision." It was decided the funeral would be for immediate family and close friends. The obituary would wait until after his burial. He had a military funeral, and it was moving and intimate. He had become a colonel. I asked if I could write his eulogy. The words flowed from my pen, like water from a spring. It was more like a roast with some tender moments. It mirrored our life as siblings. He would have approved.

As you can see, we had our share of experience with prolonged and, at times, meaningless life. It is a drain on finances, emotions, and society. I'm not suggesting we have geriatric death squads. I am suggesting we evaluate our current unorganized care. Doctors should have mandatory end-of-life courses to help them facilitate a dignified end-of-life. Perhaps people over eighty, or anyone diagnosed with dementia, should stop taking statins and let nature take its course. The money saved from that could go into a Medicare home-care fund, available to those who need help caring for their loved ones at home. I truly don't have all the answers, but I know we're not even asking the right questions, at this time

83. TIME TO RETIRE

November 15, 2016 was the day I chose to end this storied adventure. My contract concluded on December 31, 2016. I had a miserable Thanksgiving and Christmas in 2015, so I decided to retire before the holidays. On Christmas morning 2015, I was doing three admissions from the night before. Poopsie, one of my office nurses, texted me a Merry Christmas message. I was busy and didn't notice the message was sent to thirty other people—mostly her relatives. I let loose with an expletive enhanced tirade about my situation. Dolly was one of the recipients and frantically called me to stop. It was my worst, ever, faux pas.

The rehab hospital, which was my second home, sponsored a rather lavish retirement party the previous Friday, and I was shocked by the number of well-wishers. Or were they celebrating my leaving? The current staff stopped in, but there were many previous staff and former patients who took the time to attend. In addition to the elaborate spread of hors d'oeuvres and desserts, there was a pillow to autograph made from one of the monogramed lab coats I refused to wear. It wasn't my style and it was too hot. My thyroid medication made me hot all the time, and the lab coat would be intolerable.

A previous patient came quite a distance to be a part of the festivities. Many of the attendees triggered memories of events from the past. This young man was a quadriplegic from a motor vehicle accident where he was a backseat passenger, and the only occupant seriously injured. He was with us, as an inpatient, for a good while, and he learned to feed himself and drive a power wheelchair with a chin drive. Annoyingly, he also mastered using an iPhone for gaming. The phone was attached to the wheelchair, and he typed with a pencil attached to the other hand. He appeared to be quite agile with this setup and like many people had to be reminded to stop the gaming during our outpatient visits. He would see me for spinal cord follow-up and maintenance of his Baclofen pump.

His particular spasticity issues were rather remarkable. He likely was always slender and was even more so now. After his inpatient discharge, I saw him in follow-up and his spasticity became unusually violent. It took three people to bathe and dress his lower extremities. We normally don't put a pump in cases less than a year post injury, but he didn't come under control with oral meds. His mom and grandmother were exhausted from the extra demands caused by his spasticity. During my exam his knees clamped together, and it took tremendous force to separate them. He was very resistant to the idea of a pump, but after several visits, I convinced him to have the trial injection, which was part of the normal protocol for pump consideration. I ordered the higher dose for the test, because I knew I had one chance to prove its worth. The injection was completed, and after several hours his spasticity almost totally disappeared. Now he and the family couldn't wait to have a pump implanted. He did well with the pump and was taking no oral medication. He attended the Community College of Beaver County, hilariously referred to as "Cacabaca." Between that, and my ruthless complaints about the long hair (that constantly fell over his face) we formed a special almost father-son bond. He was an extra special guy, and I really miss him.

Lisa, the wife of a deceased patient, attended, and her recounting of the special bond between the three of us was heartwarming. There were hundreds of cases where I perceived a special bond, but I was unsure of the patients' perceptions. Seeing these patients daily as they came to grips with their situation, and the medical setbacks that followed, was unique in the medical profession. In an office practice you diagnose a problem, prescribe a medication or treatment, and if you're right, they don't return. That poses the conundrum of feeling elation because you were successful, and insecurity that they didn't return because they went elsewhere. Just another hurdle to overcome on the uphill journey of becoming a physician. In my rehab practice, I had the luxury of observing, over months, if my diagnosis and treatment worked or if it needed fine-tuning. Bob and his wife Lisa had a very difficult journey. They were in the prime of their life with good jobs, a nice home, two kids, and a strong relationship. In a millisecond, Bob made a tragic mistake. He was demonstrating his acrobatic skills in their four-foot pool, when the inertia of his massive body caused him to hit his head on the bottom of the pool. He fractured his neck and became motionless.

It's not unusual for people to drown in this scenario. Bob was always clowning around, and it took several minutes for the other attendees to realize he wasn't feigning distress. The panic of being unable to move, and about to drown, must have been tremendous. His 260-pound body was flipped over, and Lisa had great difficulty extracting him from the pool. His trauma center experience was anything but smooth, and he received inadequate skin care. Most hospitals are not equipped to manage someone his size, who doesn't move. Also, it would require more people to turn and position him, and thus it wasn't done. When he came to us, he had huge bed sores that would not improve with good nursing care, extra special beds, and even plastic surgery repair. This severely compromised his care and health for the several additional years of his life.

His injury was so high, he never developed arm movement adequate to feed or help himself. Upon discharge, we tried to secure every avenue of community and medical care available to assist Lisa at home. She was a trooper but physically she just couldn't manage. Dolly and I made several house calls to assess how things were going, and it became obvious that he needed a skilled facility. I suggested he be admitted to Harmar Village where I had privileges. His case would need careful oversight so he would not get worse, but he did. The medical problems only ever became more complex. It's a wonder the facility admitted him when my name was attached. I, inadvertently, only sent them the worst, fragile, costly cases. The administration never complained, even when the insurance ran out and the monthly cost of the specialty bed was more than their total monthly reimbursement. Their nursing department, staffed for a much lower level of care, would respond to the extraordinary demands of the meticulous, type A doctor. I long ago learned that courtesy, praise and explanation of the complex orders, go a long way to secure better care for your patients.

Bob was such a gregarious young guy that people gravitated to him, in spite of his extraordinary needs. His male occupational therapist took him under wing, and became a special angel involved in his care, over and above the norm. Unfortunately, Bob continued to develop new problems. His massive bed sores would continuously weep tremendous amounts of protein which caused a special problem called "anasarca." This disease causes the fluids in the blood stream to leak into the tissues all over the body, because the protein in his blood was too low to prevent this from happening. He developed terrible edema, which made his skin even more fragile and increased his weight to probably over 300 lbs., which is a nursing nightmare.

Over time he developed kidney and other issues, which would cause his demise. Often the nursing facility would feel he required hospital care, and he would go back to the hospital, where he usually got worse. The three of us had to have "the talk." Every patient has the right to refuse treatment if they decide they've had enough. At this point Bob had spent years completely dependent on others for every aspect of his care, including feeding. His health continued to decline, and there was really no hope of changing that. I rarely counseled someone to refuse care, but I did summarize the problems, gave my honest assessment of the prognosis, and made sure that they were aware they "could" refuse treatment. The decision had to be theirs. For those, like Bob, who were of the Catholic faith, I worried this would be tantamount to suicide. I was advised by several priests that the church does NOT see it that way.

Bob and Lisa finally decided to opt for no hospital transfer, no CPR, and comfort measures only. It was a slower process than I expected, but he eventually succumbed. I got there right after it happened, but we had said our goodbyes a few days earlier. I was so touched when I saw every available person, including the CEO, gather in the hall and hold a silent vigil for Bob and his family.

Lisa wanted me to know that Bob, from years ago, had great affection and respect for me as a friend and physician. It was the ultimate compliment and the high point of my career.

The river had reached its mouth. It made its contribution and now happily became indistinguishable from the rest of the sea.

CPSIA information can be obtained
at www.ICGtesting.com
Printed in the USA
BVHW040447020322
630385BV00002B/10